Mad Cow U.S.A.

Could the Nightmare Happen Here?

Sheldon Rampton

AND

John Stauber

Common Courage Press

MONROE, MAINE

First edition

Copyright ©1997 by the Center for Media & Democracy

Common Courage Press
Box 702
Monroe, Maine 04951
Phone: (207) 525-0900
Fax: (207) 525-3068

Typeset by Strong Silent Type, Madison, Wisconsin
Cover by Matt Wuerker
Printed on chlorine-free paper

Library of Congress Cataloging-In-Publication Data

Rampton, Sheldon M., 1957–
    Mad cow U.S.A.: Could the nightmare happen here? / by Sheldon Rampton and John Stauber
        p.   cm.
    Includes index.
    ISBN 1-56751-111-2. (cloth)
    1. Creutzfeldt-Jakob Disease—United States. 2. Bovine spongiform encephalopathy—United States. 3. Beef industry—United States.
I. Stauber, John C. (John Clyde), 1953–   II. Title.
RA644.C74R35 1997
616.8'3—dc21   97–22500
                                                          CIP

Contents

This book is dedicated with gratitude
to Richard F. Marsh
(1939–1997),
a scientist who understood
the precautionary principle.

Acknowledgments

Thank you to the staffs and boards of the following nonprofit foundations: CS Fund, Foundation for Deep Ecology, Rockwood Fund, Florence and John Schumann Foundation, Roy and Niuta Titus Foundation.

Thanks also to the following individuals for their support, ideas, encouragement, criticism and inspiration: Grant Abert, Greg Bates, Laura Berger, Peter Cox, Linda Crawford, Ronnie Cummins, Carol Bernstein Ferry, Carleton Gajdusek, Clarence J. Gibbs, Wade Greene, Michael Greger, Christine Grimando, Michael Hansen, Linda Jameson, Liz Keith, Howard Lyman, Joe Mendelson, David Merritt, Alida Messinger, Doris Olander, Tom Pringle, Renee Rampton, Scott Robbe, Debra Schwarze, Flic Shooter, Louis Slesin, Gar Smith, John H. Stauber, Courtlandt Thomas VanVechten, Nancy Ward, Virginia Waddick, and Walda Wood.

Foreword

"The good news is that people may not be contracting Alzheimer's as often as we think," anchorman Peter Jennings told his TV audience on the May 12, 1997 edition of *ABC World News Tonight*. "The bad news is that they may be getting something worse instead. We agree that's pretty harsh language to describe a situation that has not been getting much public attention, but it is fairly accurate," Jennings continued. "This is about something called Creutzfeldt-Jakob Disease. It is fatal. It destroys your brain, and what is worse, it is infectious."

Creutzfeldt-Jakob Disease (CJD) may not yet have gotten much public attention in the United States, but in England this obscure but terrifying illness has become a household word because of its association with that country's epidemic of mad cow disease. On March 20, 1996, the news that ten young people had contracted CJD from eating infected beef shook England and all of Europe. Now ABC was reporting that undiagnosed cases of CJD could already be much more widespread in the United States than anyone had previously realized.

"Health officials have maintained there are only about 250 new cases of CJD in this country each year, but several autopsy studies suggest this disease has been under-diagnosed," explained ABC's John McKenzie. "The studies show that when pathologists actually did autopsies and examined brain tissue from patients with Alzheimer's and other brain disorders, they uncovered hidden cases of CJD, anywhere from about 1% to 13%. These preliminary findings suggest a public health problem is being overlooked. If larger autopsy studies at more hospitals in this country confirmed that even 1% of Alzheimer's patients had CJD, that would mean 40,000 cases, and each undetected case is significant because, unlike Alzheimer's, CJD is infectious."

The math is obvious, and the potential ramifications are disturbing. If the true number of CJD cases in the United States turns out to be 40,000 instead of 250, the implications for human health would be severe. It could mean that a deadly infectious dementia akin to Britain's problem has already entered the U.S. population. And since CJD has an invisible latency period of up to 40 years in humans, 40,000 cases could be just the beginning of something much larger. Mad cow disease and CJD are related "transmissible spongiform encephalopathies" or TSEs. (The technical name for mad cow disease is "bovine spongiform encephalopathy" or BSE.) Of all the scary "emerging diseases" that have been spotlighted in the past few years, TSEs may be the most bizarre and least understood. They are sometimes called "cannibal diseases." Although difficult to transmit naturally, they can be spread through unnatural feeding practices such as cannibalism, or through 20th-century medical innovations that a Nobel-winning TSE researcher describes as "high-tech cannibalism" because they transplant tissues from one person's body into the body of another. If a TSE has established a beachhead within the human population, it could spread not only through the food supply but through organ transplants, contaminated medical instruments, the blood supply, or pharmaceuticals made from animal products.

As disturbing as these facts may be, the ABC report was also carefully edited with the interests of the U.S. food industry in mind. Michael Hansen, one of the scientists interviewed by ABC's news crew, has been warning for years about the danger that a BSE-like disease could be silently spreading in U.S. livestock, with potentially disastrous consequences for both animal and human health. But the ABC report downplayed Hansen's warnings about potential dangers in the U.S. food supply. "Interestingly, no mention was made of BSE or the British problem," commented industry consultant Robert LaBudde with some satisfaction. Even so, he worried that "the honeymoon is over in the U.S. Look for recurring and increasingly provocative news shorts on these subjects."[1]

The "honeymoon" is ending because dangers that were once dismissed as miniscule and unimportant are now looming larger. "Bovine spongiform encephalopathy"—the scientific name for the epidemic of mad cow disease which has been killing British cattle since 1986—began generating garish headlines in London tabloids in the late 1980s. Some British doctors and scientists warned early on that the strange deadly epidemic claiming British bovines could pass into humans eating meat from infected animals. After nearly a decade of denial, the British government itself admitted that this possibility—once dismissed as "ridiculous" and "far-fetched"—was indeed "the most likely explanation" for the emergence of what scientists have labeled "new variant Creutzfeldt-Jakob Disease" or nvCJD. The number of deaths so far is small, and it is certainly possible that it may *stay* small, but it is by no means certain. Creutzfeldt-Jakob Disease, BSE and the other transmissible spongiform encephalopathies often take years, even decades to incubate, during which time there is no practical way of testing to determine if a person has become infected. Existing evidence cannot predict the future course of such a disease, and some scientists worry that the handful of deaths to date may be only the tip of an epidemic iceberg that could eventually claim hundreds of thousands of British beef eaters.

Most Americans first heard of mad cow disease on March 20, 1996, when the British government reluctantly announced that the disease appeared to be passing into humans. Amid the unbelievable spectacle of the collapse of the British beef market and the pending extermination of millions of British cattle, an opinion survey showed that while people in the United States were concerned about the issue, most believed that the U.S. government and the meat industry had taken measures to prevent such a disaster from happening here. Unfortunately, as this book demonstrates, the necessary precautions have *not* all been taken.

We were initially drawn to this story as writers who specialize in investigating the propaganda techniques used by governments and major industries to protect vested interests. We edit a quarterly newsletter, *PR Watch,* which focuses on manipulative and misleading practices of the public relations industry. Shortly before the British mad cow news made world headlines, we published our first book together, an occasionally humorous exposé of the PR industry titled *Toxic Sludge Is Good For You.* We had already been following the evolution of the mad cow crisis, fascinated by the British government's efforts at what the PR industry calls "crisis management," and equally fascinated as we watched those efforts unravel. *Toxic Sludge* even made a brief passing reference to mad cow disease, in a section discussing the Monsanto Company's PR campaign for recombinant bovine growth hormone (rBGH), a controversial, genetically-engineered drug which forces dairy cows to produce more milk. We noted that some scientists had suggested a possible link between the drug and mad cow-related safety concerns:

> Cows treated with rBGH need to consume more protein, often in the form of "rendered animal protein" derived from the carcasses of cows and other dead animals. Cows consuming animal byproducts are susceptible to bovine spongiform encephalopathy, also known as "mad cow disease." This disease has plagued England for a decade, and some doctors worry that it could migrate from cows to humans as a fatal dementia called CJD.[2]

The more we looked into the mad cow crisis, the more fascinating it became. We knew that the issue was being monitored and managed by anxious officials of the U.S. Department of Agriculture (USDA), the Food and Drug Administration (FDA) and the meat industry. Through a Freedom of Information Act investigation, we had obtained copies of risk assessments and a PR plan written by the USDA—plans which left us concerned that our own government was glossing over the dangers to U.S. consumers of a possible BSE outbreak here. We watched amazed as the federal government and the beef industry successfully launched an orchestrated PR campaign aimed at misleading the public into believing that U.S. cattle producers had voluntarily abandoned the practice of "animal cannibalism"—feeding cows with "rendered animal protein" derived from other cows. Although scientists today disagree over many aspects of the mad cow outbreak in England, there is widespread consensus that the use of rendered animal feed was what enabled the disease to grow into an epidemic. In England, this feeding practice was banned in 1988, but we knew that it was continuing in the United States and was in fact more widespread here than in any other country in the world.

Since 1993, some consumer groups had been pressing for the U.S. government to follow Britain's example and ban the offending feeding practice, but their appeals had gone unanswered—a response which is dismaying but hardly surprising to people who have followed the long history of collusion between government and the agriculture industry.

The consumer movement exists because Americans want safe foods raised in old-fashioned and environmentally sound ways by caring family farmers. Consumers want to base their food-buying habits on plentiful information about how it was raised and what chemical additives or unnatural processes might have occurred during its journey from the farm field to their plate.

Unfortunately, what the public wants and what it gets are often two quite different things. The food industry has been operating for the past decade in "crisis management" mode, spending hundreds of millions of dollars each year to quell and turn aside the public's concerns about pesticide-contaminated vegetables, milk laced with antibiotic residues, chickens and pigs from factory farms, genetically-engineered growth hormones injected into cows, human genes spliced into pigs and fish to increase growth, fake fats that can cause loose bowels, and fake sweeteners that may be linked to brain cancers. We saw this book as an opportunity to examine the players and planners involved in what has become an all-out war for the hearts and minds of American consumers. The food industry's enemies in this war have included critics of high-fat diets, consumer organizations, animal-rights activists, scientists who fail to "get with the program," and journalists who report on the downside of industrial agriculture. Its weapons have included hired scientific experts who tout the safety of questionable practices, lobbyists and politicians who rewrite U.S. laws to weaken First Amendment protections for food-safety activists, and smear attacks that label industry critics as extremist, irrational "food terrorists."

As we began to study more deeply in preparation for this book, however, we realized that we were looking at an even more complex story than we had originally imagined. Our research took us into unexpected territory, inhabited by strange people with even stranger passions—from eccentric scientists in gleaming laboratories to cannibal tribes in the South Pacific, still relying on technology from the Stone Age. Among other things, the story of mad cow disease is a scientific detective story whose scope and intricacy exceed the best mystery novels, and which may contribute eventually to understanding and treatment of Alzheimer's Disease.

We also came to appreciate better some of the dilemmas facing government regulators and industry insiders. They were indeed doing their level best to calm the public, offering reassurances that were often misleading. At the same time, we realized that government and cattle industry officials were as worried as we were—perhaps even *more* worried—about the potential consequences if even a single case of mad cow disease should be detected in the United States.

What regulators and industry fear most deeply is "consumer panic." The issues surrounding mad cow disease are difficult even for scientific specialists to grasp, and policymakers fear that any airing of these issues will trigger misunderstandings, media sensationalism, and consumer boycotts of beef, milk and other products. But boycotts are probably inadequate to protect consumers from the dangers of mad cow and its related diseases. Animal products with possible infectivity are used in everything from garden fertilizers to cosmetics, and it is simply impossible for anyone to avoid them all.

Instead of individual dietary choices, these issues can only be dealt with at the level of systems, policies and regulations. The irony of the mad cow crisis is that notwithstanding its many complexities, the main regulation needed to minimize human risks is quite simple. *We must ban the practice of feeding animals with the remains of their own species.* Even in the absence of science, simple common sense tells most people that this practice of animal cannibalism is a bad idea, and yet it continues, a perverse and bloody ritualistic tribute to the power of the modern "agribusiness" lobby.

As this book neared completion, the regulatory action that consumer groups had been advocating for years moved closer to becoming reality. On June 5, 1997, the FDA announced regulations that ban the practice of feeding rendered sheep and cattle back to ruminant animals. "There is a growing body of data and information that affirmatively raises public health concerns," stated the agency in explaining the basis for its action. "The data and information raise concern that BSE could occur in cattle in the United States; and that if BSE does appear in this country, the causative agent could be transmitted and amplified through the feeding of processed ruminant protein to cattle, and could result in an epidemic. The agency believes that the high cost, in animal and human lives and economics, that could result if this scenario should occur, justifies the preventive measure reflected by the proposed regulation."

The regulations come almost a decade late and are still inadequate because, among other shortcomings, they allow continued cannibalistic feeding practices in *non*ruminant animals which are consumed by humans. Pigs and chickens, for example, are routinely nourished with feed supplements derived from the bones, brains, meat scraps, feathers and even feces of their own species. The FDA rules do nothing to change these practices. Even with these shortcomings, however, the new regulations mark a step in the right direction—a step which even the meat industry today feels obliged to support.

What remains, of course, is an obvious question: Why have government and industry waited this long to begin taking action, in the face of a "growing body of data and information that affirmatively raises public health concerns"?

This book attempts to answer that question. It is not a biology textbook or a dietary guide. It is a book about politics and how it operates in the real world. It explains why and how government officials have placed concerns for the food industry over human health and welfare. In addition to telling the story of an exotic, mysterious and frightening disease, we have written this book to report on equally dangerous legal and political trends which threaten not only our physical health, but also our fundamental democratic rights to discuss and debate concerns about the food we eat, and to choose in the marketplace as informed, educated consumers.

THE BURDEN
OF PROOF

The Girl Who
Wouldn't Go Away

Blonde, blue-eyed, freckle-faced and full of life, fifteen-year-old Victoria Rimmer was just at the age where she was starting to show an interest in boys and makeup, but her main loves in life were still dogs and horses. She loved swimming, dancing and ballet, and she went horseback riding every chance she got. She owned an English springer spaniel named Sophie, and worked evenings and weekends at a kennel near her grandmother's home in North Wales.

Vicky had always lived with her grandmother. She had been born when her own mother, Helen, was just a teenager herself. After four months spent nursing her, Helen went off to work at a summer camp. Vicky stayed with the grandparents, Beryl and Robert, who continued to raise her even after Helen married and moved away permanently to start a family of her own. The grandparents were impossibly fond of Vicky and spoiled her terribly. "She was the sunshine of my life," Beryl said.

In May of 1993, Vicky disappeared one day for several hours, and afterward couldn't remember where she had been. She began showing signs of clumsiness and poor eyesight, fatigue, and rapid weight loss. She would come home exhausted from school and collapse immediately into bed. In June, she wrote a note on her calendar that said, "I want my life back." By early August, her condition deteriorated to the point that she had to be hospitalized, and by the end of the month she was blind, unable to walk, talk, swallow or move.

A specialist told Beryl Rimmer that he suspected Vicky was suffering from a condition known as Creutzfeldt-Jakob Disease (pronounced *Croyts*feld-*Yaw*kob). CJD occurred worldwide but was so rare that normally it was only seen in about one person per million per year. Vicky's diagnosis was remarkable, because CJD was known as an old person's disease that almost never struck young people. "Onset is usually in the sixth or seventh decade of life, although patients as young as age 20 and as old as 79 years have been reported," stated a 1983 medical textbook.[1] At age fifteen, Vicky was the youngest person in England ever to contract the disease.

Her age was not the only factor that made her case remarkable. For all its rarity, Creutzfeldt-Jakob Disease was almost as notorious in England as the troubled love lives of the royal family. CJD was the most common human form of a class of diseases called "transmissible spongiform encephalopathies" or TSEs—fatal dementias that destroyed the brains of their victims by filling them with microscopic, spongelike holes. In sheep, the disease was called "scrapie" and was first discovered more than two centuries ago. A TSE called "chronic wasting disease" had been seen in U.S. deer and elk, and mink ranchers occasionally saw outbreaks of "transmissible mink encephalopathy." In 1986, a British zoo saw the first known case of a TSE in a captive African antelope, and later that year veterinarians confirmed the existence of a hitherto unknown spongy brain disease in British cattle. Scientists and government officials preferred to call the cattle disease "bovine spongiform encephalopathy" or BSE, and were irritated when journalists and the general public began calling it "mad cow disease," referring to the unusual behavior of affected animals—staggering, drooling, signs of fear, grinding of teeth, aggression toward other animals.

Seven years had passed between the time that BSE was first identified and 1993 when Vicky Rimmer fell ill. During that period, the British public had seen mad cow disease grow from an obscure veterinary curiosity into a disease affecting more than 120,000 animals—and those were just the *known* cases. Like the other transmissible spongiform encephalopathies, BSE was known for its exceptionally long incubation period of up to eight years in cattle, and no one had been able to come up with a test capable of detecting the disease in live animals. It stood to reason, therefore, that many infected but undiagnosed animals had gone to slaughter. The government and cattle industry were especially dismayed as consumers in greater and greater numbers began to worry about the fact that they were eating meat from animals infected with a mysterious new killer disease. The beef market had fallen off dramatically, falling further with each new allegation that mad cow disease might jump from cows to humans.

Many scientists believed the risk was remote, but there were a few renegade biologists who insisted on making statements that the others considered alarmist and irresponsible. One professor in particular, Richard Lacey of Leeds University, had gone so far as to warn that England "could lose a whole generation of people" unless Her Majesty's government took the extreme measure of destroying the country's entire beef herd. Journalists, moreover, had helped spread the alarm by printing stories speculating that contaminated beef might be responsible for a recent increase in the number of cases of Creutzfeldt-Jakob Disease. In 1994 England and Wales had seen 55 cases of CJD—more than twice the number reported a decade earlier. A couple of months before Vicky first started showing symptoms, newspapers reported the CJD death of a dairy farmer whose herd had been infected with mad cow disease, and a second farmer's death was reported a month before she entered the hospital.

"Vicky was mad on animals," Beryl said. "She was horse-riding from the age of four. The doctors asked if she'd had any cuts because she might have caught the disease that way. Of course she had: she worked in kennels after school and on weekends. But I knew it had to be something she had eaten. Her diet was like any other teenager's: hamburgers, sausages, curries, lasagna—

she'd make that herself. . . . And I always bought Bird's Eye beefburgers. They're the best, aren't they?"

The government's CJD surveillance unit in Edinburgh sent down a specialist to take a look at Vicky and to try to talk Beryl into keeping quiet about her condition. "He told me to think of what I was doing to Britain's economy," she recalled later.

"I knew then that they had something to hide," Beryl said. "It made me determined to find out how Vicky got the disease and to try to get the government to admit people could get mad cow disease."[2]

❈ ❈ ❈

Ever since the first cases of BSE were detected in England, the British government had insisted that the disease posed no threat to the human population. By the time Vicky fell ill, Britons had already heard too many of these failed predictions aimed at reassuring the public. An early government advisory committee had stated that cattle would be a "dead end host" for the disease, leading many to believe that the disease would not affect other species. A few years later, experiments showed that mad cow disease could be transmitted to goats, sheep, mice, monkeys, pigs and mink—in fact, to almost every species tested. The government pointed out that these experiments did not prove a risk from eating beef because rather than *feeding* them the infectious agent, researchers injected it directly into their brains, which was considered a much more dangerous route of exposure. Then house cats began dying from beef byproducts in their pet food, and it turned out that zoo animals were dying from *their* feed: a nyala, a gemsbok, an Arabian oryx, a kudu, and an eland. A puma died, and three cheetahs.

Through all these tribulations, the government continued adamantly to insist that British beef was perfectly safe. There was absolutely no connection between mad cows and disease in humans, declared Prime Minister John Major. In December 1995, agriculture minister Angela Browning told reporters that her government's stance was "ultra precautionary" and accused the media of an "unprincipled" effort to "whip this up to a frenzy of public alarm where there is simply nothing there."[3]

During the time that Vicky lay in the hospital, however, another nine cases emerged like hers, all involving unusually young victims of CJD with similar unusual symptoms and pathology, which would eventually be labeled "new variant Creutzfeldt-Jakob Disease" or "nvCJD" for short. All nine of those cases surfaced and died while Vicky remained alive.

On March 20, 1996, British Health Secretary Stephen Dorrell, who had also steadfastly denied that BSE posed any danger to humans, appeared ashen-faced before the British House of Commons to announce that mad cow disease was "the most likely explanation at present" for "10 cases of CJD which have been identified in people aged under 42."[4] Vicky Rimmer, still living in a vegetative coma, was one of those 10 cases.

"We have thought this through over and over because it would have been much more reassuring to come to a different conclusion," explained Dr. John

Pattison, the head of the government's Spongiform Encephalopathy Advisory Committee (SEAC). "But putting the unusual symptoms together with the different pathology made it inescapable."[5] Pattison admitted that Richard Lacey's nightmare scenario—*millions* of deaths—now seemed like a real possibility. Anyone who had eaten British beef was potentially at risk, especially people who ate it during the 1980s.

The transmissible spongiform encephalopathies are very different from Acquired Immunodeficiency Syndrome (AIDS), but they share two characteristics that prompted observers to draw frightening parallels. In the first place, both were considered virtually 100% fatal. In the second place, both had an incredibly long incubation period. The known human TSEs seemed to take an average of approximately 12 years to kill their victims. This parallel was noted by Luc Montagnier, the French scientist who first discovered the infectious agent that causes AIDS. At the time of his discovery in 1983, France had only seen a total of 200 AIDS cases. "I did not realize the epidemic could spread so fast and so widely in the world," Montagnier recalled. He warned that the handful of early human victims from mad cow disease could be the harbinger of a much larger epidemic. "It is very difficult to predict, as it was for HIV in 1983," he said. The total number of human deaths might be very small—a few dozen—or it might be enormous, echoing the epidemic that had already been seen in cattle. It would be years before scientists could expect to have enough data to make meaningful predictions, and in the meantime people would just have to bite their nails and wait.

In fact, the TSEs differed from AIDS in one respect that made predictions even more difficult. At least with AIDS, you could test someone early on to see if they were infected. With the TSEs, however, there were no tests capable of detecting the infectious agent during the long incubation period before symptoms started showing.

The British government's announcement triggered, finally, the financial catastrophe that farmers and the government had been fearing. Since 1990, when public fears first emerged that the disease could spread to humans, the market for British beef had fallen by 25 percent. In the days following the March 20 announcement, the market plunged into oblivion—"collapsing like a house of cards," in the words of the International Meat Trade Association.[6]

In addition to Vicky Rimmer and the other victims of new variant Creutzfeldt-Jakob Disease, the mad cow crisis was claiming other human victims—people like Robert Cowburn, a 40-year-old beef and dairy farmer in the southwestern British county of Cornwall. On the evening of May 30, 1996, two months after the British government's announcement, Cowburn's family found his car parked by the dairy, its engine running. A pipe led from the exhaust into the car, with Cowburn's lifeless body sitting in the driver's seat.

"This whole BSE thing proved too much for him," explained Cowburn's brother David. Shortly before the mad cow crisis broke, the two brothers had purchased land to double the size of their 100-acre milk and dairy operation, but the "BSE thing" had torn the heart out of their dreams. Two days before his suicide, Robert Cowburn had taken a shipment of cattle to market and come back disheartened. "The prices for the animals he took to market last week meant it was a waste of time him going," his wife said. "I suppose it was the BSE crisis that claimed his life."[7]

And Cowburn was not alone. John Capp, a 58-year-old farmer in the eastern county of Lincolnshire, was another suicide, found dead in April of carbon monoxide poisoning. According to his friends, the beef scare had "tipped him over the edge." Since it began, he had been unable to sell any of his 200 cattle and was facing financial ruin. The following month Bill Rodney, a 49-year-old father of three teenagers, killed himself with a shotgun blast to the head.[8] Coroners are often reluctant to record suicide verdicts, so other cases were probably not being reported. Knowledgeable observers estimated that three British farmers per week were killing themselves, the highest suicide rate of any profession in the country. Alarmed, the Royal Agricultural Society of England and the National Farmers Union launched a counseling service to assist distressed farmers. "A lot of people who have contacted me are not so much angry as bloody frightened," said Charles Runge, chief executive of the Royal Agricultural Society. "They see their livelihoods being taken away from them for reasons they don't understand."[9]

Farmers and their organizations clung desperately to the official "party line": This was nothing but a groundless food scare. Consumers simply needed to be "educated" to understand that British beef was safe. Then the crisis would pass. "However bad things are economically we can get through this crisis, and in six months or a year's time this could all be a rather unpleasant memory," argued National Farmers' Union regional director Anthony Gibson. "However difficult things are at the moment, for heaven's sake hang on and we will all pull through this together."[10]

Consumers, however, were proving hard to educate. And the fears did not end at England's national borders. In Ireland, police normally responsible for blocking guerrilla arms shipments were deployed to keep out cows from British-ruled Northern Ireland.[11] In France, the National Bovine Federation warned that consumers could turn violent unless the government took firm action to prevent the importation of British beef.[12] In Germany, beef consumption fell by a third. People ate pork, poultry, fish and even horse meat—anything but beef. A German goodwill visit to the English farming community of Wellington turned hostile when the German visitors informed their hosts that they wanted to avoid eating beef during their stay. In order to avoid ugly confrontations between the visitors and outraged farmers, the Germans had to be smuggled into the homes of the local families with whom they were staying.

Desperate to end the crisis, British Prime Minister John Major summoned senior ministers to consider means of restoring confidence in British beef. A proposal from the National Farmers Union (NFU) called for the government to oversee the slaughter and incineration of more than 800,000 animals, with government payments to compensate farmers for their losses. "We have no market at all for that beef now," said Ian Gardiner, the NFU's director of policy.[13] As a practical matter, however, destroying that many animals was impossible. Existing incineration facilities were inadequate to handle the volume.

Relations between England and its European neighbors worsened when the European Commission imposed a strict ban on imports of British beef, effective throughout the European Union's 15 member states. In addition to beef itself, the ban extended to cattle semen and embryos, along with beef byproducts such as gelatin and tallow, which were used in the manufacture of a wide range of products including food, cosmetics and medicines. British officials denounced the ban as "ramshackle, hasty, ill thought out and having no basis in science."[14] In reality, the Europeans had no choice. Since the British announcement, their own beef sales had fallen by up to 30 percent, and they were desperate to prevent a total market collapse. "Governments are clearly not prepared to do anything at this stage to jeopardize fragile consumer confidence," explained a spokesman for the European farm commissioner.[15]

The crisis was not limited to Europe. In the United States, the USDA and the National Cattlemen rushed to assure the public that there had never been a case of mad cow disease in U.S. cattle. In Texas, agriculture officials responded to the news of human deaths in England with a publicity stunt, organizing a cookout and offering reporters slices of smoked brisket while Agriculture Commissioner Rick Perry criticized the media for stirring up public fears. A spokesman for the meat industry stood alongside him and moralized about the need to avoid "hysteria in the U.S. about domestic beef." Additional reassurances came from the nutritional supplement industry, which uses cow glandular materials, and the Cosmetic, Toiletry, and Fragrance Association (CTFA), whose members use rendered animal fat and protein in facial creams and other products. CTFA spokesperson Irene Malbin pleaded "for U.S. consumers to listen to what the leading health authorities continue to state, which is that BSE is simply not a safety issue in this country."[16]

Of course, that is what the leading health authorities in England had said also—until teenagers started dying.

❋ ❋ ❋

In the United States, unlike England or Europe, the government's reassurances were based on the fact that mad cow disease had never been detected here. "USDA has been monitoring for BSE for ten years and has never identified a single case. In addition, no beef from England has been imported into the United States since at least 1985," stated a news release issued jointly by the U.S. Department of Agriculture, the Food and Drug Administration and the Centers for Disease Control.[17] Actually, the USDA had only been monitoring for *six* years, but that was a minor detail. The larger problem with the government's position was that *no* surveillance could hope to keep the disease out of the country. With other transmissible diseases, you could hope to keep them out by blocking imports from infected areas, but the transmissible spongiform encephalopathies play by their own rules. They seem to emerge "spontaneously," even in uninfected populations.

"If an evil force could devise an agent capable of damaging the human race, he would make it indestructible, distribute it as widely as possible in animal feed so that it would pass to man, and program it to cause disease slowly so that everyone would have been exposed to it before there was any awareness of its presence," observed British microbiologist Richard Lacey, a leading critic of his government's policies for dealing with BSE.[18] These characteristics of the TSEs were what had previously enabled mad cow disease to infect large numbers of British cattle. A disease this insidious was capable of slipping below the radar of even the most extensive surveillance, but the USDA didn't want to discuss that risk.

The unique characteristics of BSE and the gaps in scientific knowledge about its origin were part of the reason that people had such a hard time gauging its risks. "The issue of BSE is like the issue of nuclear power stations," a British medical advisor had opined in 1990. "In both cases most people with expert knowledge believe the risk is very low. But, if things go wrong, the result would be catastrophic."[19] Up until 1996, the scientists who advised government and industry had in fact been entirely correct when they stated that there was "no scientific proof of a link between BSE and disease in humans."

In the real world, however, governments and industries cannot always wait for proof of dangers, or even for a preponderance of evidence. In the absence of clear knowledge, someone has to bear the burden of the risk associated with that uncertainty. The issues raised by the mad cow crisis therefore go far beyond the immediate question of whether it is safe to eat beef. The deeper, longer-term questions center on how society should deal with dangers that often cannot be measured with mathematical precision. Who should bear the burden of those risks? Should we expect *industry* to bear the financial burden, by avoiding profitable practices which may turn out in the end to be entirely safe? Should industries have to prove that their products are safe before allowing them on the market? Or should we wait for proof of harm before imposing regulations? If we do, *consumers* bear the burden of proof, by exposing ourselves to risks which may later turn out to be deadly. In either case, the burden falls on *someone*.

In the case of mad cow disease, the burden of proof fell first and most heavily on the teenage shoulders of Vicky Rimmer and the other young victims of new variant Creutzfeldt-Jakob Disease.

In the year following the British government's first admission that there might be a link between eating beef and nvCJD, the evidence became so convincing that the government's own scientists began forecasting hundreds of additional deaths per year by the turn of the century. Twenty-one victims were confirmed by July 1997, and the government refused to release information about other unconfirmed cases under surveillance, which were rumored to number in the dozens.

Typical cases of CJD usually kill their victims within six to nine months after the first appearance of symptoms, but Vicky survived for more than four years. After she was transferred to a Liverpool Hospital, her grandmother Beryl moved into the home of a friend who lived near the hospital and began making daily visits to her bedside. She sat beside Vicky and told stories about her dog, Sophie. She brought fresh nightdresses for Vicky to wear, and took the soiled ones home. "I have to wash six or seven every day," she said. "She can't swallow, you see, so her saliva runs on to them and messes them up. This way, the nurses have fresh ones to put on her." Since Vicky was unable to feed herself, doctors kept her alive by surgically implanting a feeding tube into her stomach. Beryl continued her daily vigils, and on Vicky's birthday, family and friends held a party at her bedside.

"If there is a hell, this is it," Beryl said. "It makes me so angry. She'd just left school and was on the verge of doing what she wanted in life. She was my best mate and she never even said goodbye."

Food Fight

"You said this disease could make AIDS look like the common cold?" asked TV talk-show host Oprah Winfrey.

"Absolutely," said her guest, Howard Lyman of the Humane Society of the United States.

"That's an extreme statement, you know," Oprah said.

"Absolutely," Lyman said again, "and what we're looking at right now is that we're following exactly the same path that they followed in England. Ten years of dealing with it as public relations rather than doing something substantial about it. A hundred thousand cows per year in the United States are fine at night, dead in the morning. The majority of those cows are rounded up, ground up, fed back to other cows. If only one of them has mad cow disease, it has the potential to affect thousands."

"But cows are herbivores. They shouldn't be eating other cows," Oprah said.

"That's exactly right, and what we should be doing is exactly what nature says. We should have them eating grass, not other cows. We've not only turned them into carnivores, we've turned them into cannibals."[1]

It was easy to see why the National Cattlemen's Beef Association hated Howard Lyman. Many people within the meat industry regarded him as not just a critic but an outright traitor. A fourth-generation rancher, Lyman at age 54 still had a farmer's solid build and temperament. At the peak of the farm boom in the late 1970s, his Montana ranch had been a multi-million-dollar operation with 5,000 feedlot cattle and 1,000 range animals. Later, he had worked for a time as a Washington lobbyist for the National Farmers Union before converting to vegetarianism, organic farming and animal rights activism.

Two events in Lyman's life marked the turning points that led to his conversion. The first was the death of his brother from cancer following exposure to dioxin-contaminated herbicides. The other event occurred in 1979 when Lyman found himself in a hospital, paralyzed from the waist down. Doctors had found a tumor on the inside of his spine and warned that he would probably never walk again. "As I was lying there in that bed, I found myself remembering what our farm had looked like when I was a kid. I realized what it had become after twenty years of chemical addiction," Lyman said. "I made a vow that if I was ever able to walk again, I would do everything I could to make that farm sustainable and chemical-free."

Lyman recovered from the non-malignant tumor and began to make changes in his life. In 1983 he sold his ranch. He became convinced that excessive meat consumption lay at the heart of his health problems. "If I had not changed my diet, I'd be dead today," he declared in a 1996 interview. "I've dropped a hundred pounds since I stopped eating meat. I have more energy than ever before in my life now. I require less sleep, and my mind is clearer. I think back about a group of friends, ten of us that used to get together and play cards when I was living on the farm. Only one of the ten of us has not had heart disease, cancer or died. These were good friends, hard workers, slim and athletic, dying of heart disease and strokes. They were dying of a diet of affluence, dying from what they were eating."[2]

In 1992, Lyman signed on as executive director for activist Jeremy Rifkin's Beyond Beef campaign, which targeted the McDonald's restaurant chain with picketing and leaflets. "The reason I headed up the Beyond Beef campaign is that I believe factory production of food is an absolute disaster," Lyman said. "I'm still the greatest supporter in the world of the family farmers, the greatest resource that we have. The Beyond Beef campaign was not an assault on meat eating. We called for a 50 percent reduction, which seemed to have a greater chance of success than calling on people to remove all animal products from their diet. Beyond Beef was an impetus for what is happening today, a tremendous consumer awareness of health and diet issues."

For Lyman, the British government's announcement that mad cow disease could be linked to human fatalities came as no surprise at all. He had been following developments in England for years and had become convinced that the issue was being glossed over not only there but in the United States as well. In September 1993, he had attended a symposium on BSE at the University of Wisconsin–Madison and had been appalled at the treatment given to Richard Marsh, a UW–Madison professor whose research suggested that a BSE-like disease might already be infecting U.S. cattle. "It was like they walked him up to the gallows, put the rope around his neck, sprung the trap," Lyman said. "I believe the entire symposium was orchestrated simply to bring Dick Marsh to heel. I think it broke his heart. I think Marsh is a big teddy bear, a brilliant researcher, a wonderful human being, but he has no shell against that kind of attack. The university and industry just destroyed him. Some people when you pick on them they get tougher, others they wilt."

Marsh had expressed his views in the cautious and often inscrutable language of a scientist, language that was only dimly understood outside the circle of researchers who, like himself, specialized in the transmissible spongiform encephalopathies. The public was unlikely to become concerned by talk of "proteinaceous infectious particles," "heterozygosity at the 129th codon," "infectivity of corneal epithelium" or "pathogenicity in mink." Lyman, however, was not a scientist. An outspoken, commanding speaker with a wry sense of humor and a down-home cowboy-populist style, he knew how to use words that people understood. The general public might not understand the significance of proteinaceous infectious particles, but they *did* know what you meant when you talked about grinding up dead cows and feeding them to other cows. The chance to appear on Oprah was Lyman's first opportunity to take his message to a national audience, and he was determined to state his case in the simplest, most unmistakable terms.

"How do you know the cows are ground up and fed back to the other cows?" Oprah asked.

"Oh, I've seen it," Lyman said. "These are USDA statistics. They're not something we're making up."

"Now doesn't that concern you all a little bit, right here, hearing that?" Oprah asked her studio audience, which responded with supportive cheers.

"It has just stopped me cold from eating another burger," Oprah said. "I'm stopped!"

"Yeah!" answered the audience, clapping loudly.

Dr. Gary Weber, a policy director for the National Cattlemen's Beef Association, was the man charged with blunting Lyman's attack. Oprah had teamed him up with Will Hueston, a bearded scientist from the USDA. Weber and Hueston found themselves lined up not just against Lyman but also against Vicky Rimmer's grandmother and the father of a boy in the United States who had died of E. coli poisoning from the infamous Jack-in-the-Box hamburger outbreak. It was not the sort of debate that Weber could reasonably expect to win.

"Let me clarify that," Weber began. "There is a reason to be concerned. We've learned from the tragedy in Great Britain and made a decision here. . . . We started taking initiatives ten years ago to make sure this never happened here. Let me go back and correct a couple of things. Number one, we do not have BSE in this country and we have a ten-year history of surveillance to document that based on science. We do not have it. Also, we have not imported any beef in this country since 1985 from Great Britain."

"Are we feeding cattle to the cattle?" Oprah asked.

"There is a limited amount of that done in the United States," Weber admitted, to groans and sighs from the audience. "Hang on just a second now," he said. "The Food and Drug Administration—"

"I have to just tell you, that is alarming to me," Oprah said.

"Now keep in mind that before you view the ruminant animal—the cow— as simply vegetarian, remember that they drink milk," Weber said, floundering desperately. "I'm saying we do not have the disease here, we've got ten years of data, the best scientists in the world who are looking for this, over 250 trained technicians and veterinarians around the country. Everyone's watching for this."

"The same thing that we've heard here today is exactly what was heard for ten years in England," Lyman replied. " 'Not to worry, we're on top of this.' . . . If we continue to do what we're doing, feeding animals to animals, I believe we are going to be in exactly the same place. . . . Today we could do exactly what the English did and cease feeding cows to cows. Why in the world are we not doing that? Why are we skating around this and continuing to do it when everybody sitting here knows that would be the safest thing to do? Why is it, why is it? Because we have the greedy that are getting the ear of government instead of the needy and that's exactly why we're doing it," he thundered, again to audience applause.

"We don't want to just alarm you all, but I have to tell you, I'm thinking about the cattle being fed to the cattle and that's pretty upsetting to me," Oprah said.

"I just had one question," said an audience member. "I'm confused about why cattle are being fed lamb, and why are they being fed beef?"

"What it comes down to is about half of the slaughter of animals is non-sellable to humans," Lyman said. "They either have to pay to put it into the dump or they sell it for feed, so they grind it up, turn it into something that looks like brown sugar, add to it all of the animals that died unexpectedly, all of the road kills and the euthanized animals, add it to them, grind it up and feed it back to other animals. It's about as simple as it can be. We are doing something to an animal that was never intended to be done."

"Are the animals tested?" asked another audience member. "All of the animals that are ground into feed that are fed to the cows?"

"There is no test other than analyzing the brains, and since we don't have animals with these symptoms, not every brain is going to be evaluated," Weber admitted. "No animal can enter the plant that has any of these symptoms, by law. And there's veterinarians and . . . inspection and it doesn't happen, Howard and you know it. It doesn't happen."

"Oh come on, let's get real!" Lyman shot back. "Any animal that is not staggering around goes in there. You know as well as I do. We have a hundred thousand cows per year that die. . . . We ended up feeding downer cows to mink, the mink came down with the disease, transferred it to animals, the animals came down with it, and you're sitting here telling everybody that it's safe. Not true."

Weber sighed. This was *not* going well.

Why *not* stop feeding cows to cows? If you believed the official propaganda of the Cattlemen, you would think that the practice had already *been* stopped. Nine days after the British government's alarming admission of a BSE-CJD link, the National Cattlemen's Beef Association had joined other meat industry organizations in announcing a "voluntary ban" to assure that "ruminant-derived protein is not used in ruminant feed products." If you thought about it for a moment, of course, you might realize that a "voluntary ban" is a contradiction in terms, but aside from a few complaining consumer groups, no one bothered to think that hard. "For the most part, the media coverage has focused on the crisis in Great Britain and the media has not tried to import the crisis into the United States," exulted an internal memorandum by Jim Barr, CEO for the National Milk Producers Federation. "Thanks to prompt work on the part of USDA and industry groups, U.S.-focused coverage has talked mainly about the steps taken here since the mid-1980s to keep our country BSE-free."[3]

The Oprah Winfrey Show was the exception to the rule. It aired on Tuesday, April 16—less than a month after the British government's first admission that mad cow disease appeared to be spreading to humans. It was not the first time that U.S. viewers heard about the British troubles, but it was the first time that a major U.S. news program focused on the fact that U.S. cattle breeders were continuing the cannibalistic feeding practices which had created the epidemic in the first place.

The day of the broadcast, livestock traders on the floor of the Chicago Mercantile Exchange scrambled to sell off cattle futures, which fell a penny and a half a pound to 59 cents—the maximum allowable drop for a single day's trading.[4] Spokespersons for the NCBA angrily blasted the TV program, calling it "irresponsible and biased." In a letter to Winfrey, NCBA called the show "one more example of the irresponsible scare tactics with which much of American television has become identified. . . . The show was one of beef-bashing—not a reasonable discussion of BSE and the safety of the American beef supply. You took a complex technical issue and turned it into an hour of unjustified scare-mongering."[5] NCBA's Gary Weber complained that the show had selectively edited his comments, cutting out most of his "scientific" rebuttal of Lyman.

At first, Oprah stood her ground. "I am speaking as one consumer for millions of others," she said in a prepared statement. "Cows eating cows is alarming. Americans needed and wanted to know that—I certainly did. . . . I asked the questions that I think the American people deserved to have answered in light of what is happening in Britain. We gave them a chance to respond."[6]

Under pressure, however, Winfrey's staff issued a second statement promising to schedule "another program to address unanswered questions." The follow-up show, which aired a week later, featured a 10-minute one-on-one exchange between a cowed Oprah Winfrey and Gary Weber, who got to have his say this time without any fear of rebuttal from Lyman or other beef industry critics. As Weber issued reassurances, Oprah uttered weak half-apologies that seemed as though they were being forced through gritted teeth. "Our concern was for consumer safety and not about stock prices," she said. "I had no idea the stock prices were going to fall and I wasn't trying to influence them one way or another. You all need to know, you cattle people, that we're just dependent on y'all out there."[7]

Oprah's newfound humility reflected some cold financial realities. In the days following the original show, the beef industry had retaliated by pulling $600,000 in network advertising.[8] Even Oprah's follow-up fluff piece failed to appease. In Texas, State Agriculture Commissioner Rick Perry asked the attorney general to use the state's new "food disparagement law" to file a lawsuit against Lyman and the Oprah show. When the attorney general declined, beef feedlot operator Paul Engler and a company named Cactus Feeders stepped in to shoulder the burden, hiring a powerhouse L.A. attorney to file a lawsuit which sought $2 million in damages plus punitive fines. "We're taking the Israeli action on this thing," Engler said. "Get in there and just blow the hell out of somebody."[9] The lawsuit, filed on May 28, 1996, complained as follows:

The defendants allowed anti-meat activists to present biased, unsubstantiated, and irresponsible claims against beef, not only damaging the beef industry but also placing a tremendous amount of unwarranted fear in the public. Defendant Howard Lyman was negligently allowed to imply that the meat-consuming public should be very afraid of the beef that is produced in this country. . . . Plaintiffs own and operate one of the largest cattle feeding operations in the world. . . . As a direct result of defendants' false, slanderous, and defamatory statements, plaintiffs have endured shame, embarrassment, humiliation, and mental pain and anguish. Additionally, Plaintiffs are and will in the future be seriously injured in their good name and reputation in the community and exposed to the hatred, contempt, and ridicule of the general public. . . . Defendants' conduct in making the statements contained herein and allowing those statements to be aired without verifying the accuracy of such statements goes beyond all possible bounds of decency and is utterly intolerable in a civilized community.[10]

Interestingly, the lawsuit made no mention of Lyman's main point—the point he had hammered at repeatedly, and which had triggered the strongest negative reactions from Oprah's audience. Whatever science said about "bovine spongiform encephalopathy," the thing that stuck hardest in the craw of the audience—and of Oprah herself—was the simple fact that *cows had been turned into cannibals.* "That in itself is disturbing to me," Oprah had said. "Cows should not be eating other cows!"

The meat industry's "voluntary ban" was aimed at fooling the public into believing that this practice of "ruminant-to-ruminant" feeding had already ended. It was misleading, and deliberately so, but from the myopic viewpoint of the Cattlemen, their own attempt to manipulate the news was simply good public relations. Howard Lyman's attempt to warn the public, on the other hand, went "beyond all possible bounds of decency and is utterly intolerable in a civilized community."

Was mad cow disease the threat that Howard Lyman thought it was? Would it make "AIDS look like the common cold"? Probably not, according to most scientists who worked in the field of the spongiform encephalopathies—including even Richard Marsh, from whom Lyman had learned much of what he knew about the disease. In England, on the other hand, failure to recognize the unique nature of the disease *had* enabled BSE to grow into a problem of literally incalculable proportions.

For consumers in the United States, the most important immediate question was, "Is it safe to eat beef?" The cattle industry was determined to ensure that the answer they heard would be "yes, absolutely." From the industry's point of view, its campaign to silence Oprah Winfrey and Howard Lyman was a battle between "sound science" and "emotional fear-mongering." What the industry missed, or chose to miss, was that Lyman was raising a different and much more important question: "Are adequate measures being taken to guarantee the safety of our food?"

The lawsuit against Howard Lyman marked the first test case for a new legal standard which the agriculture industry had spent the previous half-decade introducing into more than a dozen U.S. states. "All agricultural eyes will be watching this one," observed one food industry lobbyist. Engler's attorney described the suit as "a historic case; it serves as a real bellwether. It should make reporters and journalists and entertainers—and whatever Oprah considers herself—more careful."[11]

Known as "agricultural product disparagement laws," the new legislation gave the food industry unprecedented powers to sue people who criticized their products, using standards of evidence which dramatically shifted the burden of proof in favor of the industry. "In them, American agribusiness has its mightiest tool yet against food-safety activists and environmentalists, whose campaigns can cost industry millions if they affect consumers' buying habits," observed *Village Voice* reporter Thomas Goetz.[12]

In the past, the food industry had been required to prove that its critics were deliberately and knowingly circulating false information. Under the new laws, it didn't matter whether Lyman believed in his statements, or even whether he could produce scientists who would support him. The industry would be able to convict him of spreading "false information" if it could convince a jury that his statements on the Oprah show deviated from "reasonable and reliable scientific inquiry, facts, or data"[13]—a standard of proof which gave a clear advantage to the beef industry, particularly in Texas cattle country.

The problem with this standard of proof is not simply that it makes juries comprised of non-scientists responsible for judging the validity of complex scientific theories. The deeper problem is that *not even scientists* agree on which scientific theories are valid and which are not. Indeed, the scientific method is *based* on hypothesis and conjecture, on best-guess speculations which change continually as new evidence becomes available. Until the 1950s, for example, smoking tobacco was not only considered safe by many scientists but was recommended as an aid to relaxation, digestion and weight loss. If "agricultural product disparagement laws" had existed in the 1960s, it would have been illegal to criticize pesticides such as DDT, which were believed "safe" for the environment according to data then considered "reasonable and reliable."

Mad cow disease in particular belongs to a class of diseases that have confounded farmers and researchers for more than 250 years. The transmissible spongiform encephalopathies have proven so immune to scientific inquiry that one researcher calls them "god in the guise of a virus"[14]—even though most researchers today do not believe the disease is a virus at all. The history of research into the TSEs has been littered with the bodies of dead theories. In centuries of study, no one has been able even to isolate the agent which causes the illness, let alone explain the remarkable characteristics which set it apart from every other known transmissible disease. In the 20th century alone, the infectious agent has been described at various times as a "sarcosporidia parasite," a "filterable virus," a "slow virus," a "provirus generating RNA," an "unconventional virus," a "replicating protein," "membrane-bound DNA," a "spiroplasma-like organism," a "viroid-like nucleic acid," a "virino," a "replicating polysaccharide," and a "prion."[15] These labels represent differing theories, and none of them has yet been able to explain all of the known evidence about the nature of the disease agent. The leading doctrine today is the "prion theory," which was itself labeled a "heresy" a decade ago because it seemed to violate what biologists consider the "central dogma of modern biology."

In demanding that Lyman and Winfrey confine their remarks about mad cow disease to proven facts, the beef industry was therefore attempting to impose a standard which no one previously had been able to meet—not even scientists, and certainly not the beef industry itself. As Lyman awaited his day in court, the number of theories still swirling left little doubt that scientists, industry and food-safety activists would continue to debate, speculate and disagree for decades to come, and that indeed centuries more might have to pass before they would reach a consensus on what was "reasonable and reliable."

THE THING
THAT EATS
YOUR BRAIN

First Tremors

In 1982, four years before the first known case of mad cow disease surfaced in England, the state of Oklahoma saw a perplexing outbreak of a rare but troubling disease in sheep. Known as scrapie, the disease was only reported in 12 flocks in the entire United States that year, but eight of them occurred in Oklahoma, and as a precautionary measure the U.S. Department of Agriculture ordered the destruction of some 3,300 animals, valued at almost $1 million.

"When we find it in a flock, we destroy the flock of sheep," said Dr. John Vogel, the USDA's assistant veterinarian in charge of Oklahoma. "They have to be either burned or buried."

Jack Pitcher, the USDA's chief staff veterinarian for viral diseases of sheep and goats, explained the reasoning behind these seemingly drastic measures. Although scrapie was rare in the United States, it was inevitably fatal. It was also known as a "slow virus," taking from 18 to 64 months to show its symptoms. This meant that once it got started it was very difficult to stop. A single infected sheep could literally spend years contaminating other animals, possibly moving through several flocks, before the infection was discovered. "There is no prevention, there is no diagnostic test in live animals and there is no known treatment," Pitcher said. "Scrapie is a difficult disease to work with."[1]

In other parts of the world, Pitcher pointed out, the disease had spread to the point that eradication no longer seemed feasible. "They make no effort to eliminate it in the British Isles," he said. "They live with it." As a result, he added, the British also lived with the possibility that scrapie might be linked to multiple sclerosis or to "kuru," an obscure and deadly dementia in humans which "demonstrated a marked similarity" to scrapie.

The British didn't seem very worried. They had lived with scrapie for more than 200 years, without observing a comparable outbreak of scrapie-like disease in humans. In fact, scrapie had been seen throughout Europe since 1732, when Spanish shepherds first reported a disease that they named "la trembladera" (the trembling) or "la enfermedad trotoria" (the trotting disease). In Germany, England and Scotland, it went at first by various names: "rickets," "goggles," "rubbers," "shakers," "scratchie," or "the trot." The French called it "la maladie folle" (the mad disease) or "la vertige" (staggers). Some shepherds simply called it "the plague."[2]

The disease usually occurred in middle-aged animals. Its early signs were so subtle that they could be mistaken for what we call absent-mindedness in humans. A shepherd might notice that one of his sheep was standing quietly, staring blankly into the distance, unresponsive to its surroundings. While the other sheep grazed happily on a pasture of good grass, an affected animal would wander erratically, eating only a few mouthfuls with each step. At the watering trough, it would also move repeatedly. It would visit the trough frequently, but would only drink a little water at each visit. Sometimes it would behave aggressively, charging at other animals. It would seem restless and display small jittery movements.

Later, the affected sheep would exhibit more serious problems. It would develop a clumsy gait and would tire easily, sometimes even collapsing in its tracks when being herded. A little later on, it would begin to behave as though it had an uncontrollable, severe itch, rubbing itself against posts and other solid objects, nibbling obsessively at its hair, or scratching itself with its hind feet. Its lack of stamina and its walking problems would get worse, and some animals would suffer waves of trembling or shivers. The itching behavior would get so bad that it would scrape away large portions of its wool, leaving the skin raw and sore. Noticing this behavior, the Scottish called it "scrapie," giving the disease the name by which it is best known today in English-speaking countries.

In the final stages, an animal with scrapie would lose weight rapidly. Unable to walk more than 50 yards at a time, it would spend most of its time lying down and would eventually lose the ability to stand altogether. It might lose its vision, suffer partial paralysis, or experience epileptic-like seizures. Death was the inevitable conclusion, usually within three to six months after the first symptoms appeared.

The available evidence suggests that scrapie appeared for the first time in several different parts of Europe, but its spread seemed to accelerate around the same time that other countries began importing merino sheep from Spain. Prized for their fine wool, the merinos were considered such national treasures that Spain originally forbade their export, but the decree began to break down in the 18th century when the Spanish crown began offering gifts of merinos as special tokens of royal favor. Gifts of this type helped establish merino flocks in Germany and France. England got its hands on a few, and in 1788 Mad King George, disappointed by the colonial rebellion in the Americas, turned his attention to agriculture and imported a large consignment of merinos. The improvement of wool became a major economic issue in Europe, with King George and other influential personages actively encouraging new efforts in agricultural improvement and livestock breeding.

Europe was entering the "Age of Enlightenment" which was destined to transform the world with its new faith in science, rational thought and technological innovation. Domestic animals were transformed genetically by the application of a new agricultural technique that was previously considered dangerous and unnatural—animal incest, or close inbreeding. To improve the performance of thoroughbred racehorses, for example, the British practiced what was called "breeding in-and-in," mating fathers to daughters, sons to mothers, and brothers to sisters. Similar practices were used to improve sheep flocks, often using Spanish merinos as studs. Many of the distinct breeds of sheep that exist today were created in the 1700s. For the most part, these inbreeding experiments worked as expected, reinforcing desired animal traits without adverse consequences. The science of genetics had not yet been invented, and animal breeders had no way of knowing that inbreeding could accidentally increase the emergence of rare genetic defects by encouraging the reproduction of harmful recessive genes.

Today, 250 years later, scientists are still unable to explain exactly what caused the emergence and spread of scrapie in sheep. Did the merinos help it spread? Did they carry and transmit an infection to other animals? Was scrapie caused by an infectious agent? Was it triggered by a genetic defect? If so, did the merinos carry a genetic predisposition to scrapie, or did inbreeding encourage the emergence of genetic potential that was already found in other sheep as well?

Most diseases can be traced clearly to either a genetic or an infectious cause. Infectious diseases are typically caused by either a virus or a bacteria. Viral infections can cause illnesses as common and mundane as colds and influenza, or as deadly and exotic as AIDS and ebola. Other infectious diseases are caused by bacteria such as salmonella, staphylococcus, or E. coli. In either case—bacteria or virus—the disease is recognized by the body as a foreign intruder, and the body's immune system mobilizes to fight off the infection by forming antibodies against it.

Prior to the 20th century, hereditary diseases were recognized primarily by their method of dispersal. Infectious diseases primarily disperse horizontally throughout the population, sometimes with extraordinary speed. Hereditary diseases, by contrast, tend to spread slowly because they can only be transmitted *vertically,* from parent to child.

At first, farmers believed that scrapie was an infectious disease, based on its growth to epidemic levels in several countries within 50 years of its first known appearance. Other characteristics of the disease, however, seemed to argue against an infectious agent. For one thing, it almost never appeared in young sheep. Affected animals showed no signs of inflammation or fever, and there was no obvious link between occurrence of the disease in one animal and its emergence in its neighbors. A healthy sheep could rub against an animal with scrapie without developing the illness. It could share food or water. There was no evidence of transmission through sexual intercourse. Shepherds experienced some success in controlling the disease through careful breeding, slaughtering sick animals and using rams from healthy herds as stud animals in affected flocks.

In Wessex, England, scrapie was unknown until the mid-1700s, but by the 1770s it was widespread. The Agricultural Improvement Society of Bath reported, in its first communication on livestock, that the disease "within these few years has destroyed some in every flock around the County and made great havoc in many."[3] Careful culling and breeding seemed to have virtually eliminated the disease by 1850, but it continued to spread elsewhere. By 1868 scrapie was prevalent throughout Germany and middle Europe, and did not disappear in Germany until 1945—"but so had most of the German sheep, and scrapie was a major factor in their decimation," observed scrapie researcher Gordon Hunter in his 1993 book on the disease. In Hungary, farmers reacted to outbreaks of scrapie with a ruthless but effective policy of destroying all affected animals and their relatives. In France, widespread outbreaks were occurring by the late 1700s and have continued until the present, although Hunter and others noted that French farmers attempted to cover up the extent of the disease through "much concealment."[4]

In Great Britain, scrapie emerged again in force in the early 20th century, appearing first in the Suffolk flocks of east England. "Well recognized in 1920, by 1950 it had become a serious cause of concern," Hunter stated. "The period since 1950 has seen closer veterinary inspection of sheep and many spontaneous outbreaks of disease have been reported, cases occurring in most of the recognized breeds. Severe epidemics have occurred in Swaledale and Welsh Mountain sheep. The Swaledale breeders reckoned even in the early 1970s that their losses had already run into several million pounds over a five-year period. Scrapie may also occur extensively in some other breeds, but firm information is lacking and there is still today widespread concealment of the disease."[5]

England's problem was not limited to its own borders. According to Hunter's listing of recorded outbreaks, sheep imported from Great Britain could be traced to eight out of ten outbreaks of scrapie recorded in other parts of the world between the years of 1937 and 1987, including the earliest known cases in North America. Scrapie first appeared in the United States shortly after World War II, prompting a vigorous eradication policy. "This policy does seem to have been crowned eventually with some success, and there are now few outbreaks of the disease reported in the U.S.," Hunter stated. He added, however, that the "Canadians are somewhat less optimistic about progress in the eradication programme, and some U.S. outbreaks may have been concealed."[6]

Scrapie was hard to fight because no one could figure out what was causing it. Knowledge of the cause of a disease is obviously important in order to take effective control measures. You stop an infection from spreading by isolating or killing affected animals. To stop an inherited disease, however, you have to alter breeding practices. Neither of these approaches seemed very effective when dealing with scrapie, whose behavior seemed calculated to defy every expectation. By the time the 20th century dawned, most animal scientists had concluded that the disease was an inherited illness. Then, in the 1940s, two French scientists showed that it was transmissible by performing experiments in which they ground up the brains of scrapie-infected sheep and injected them into other animals.

The French findings were confirmed accidentally at about the same time by Bill Gordon, a Scottish scientist who directed the Compton Laboratory of England's Institute for Research on Animal Diseases. While developing a vaccine against another sheep disease called Louping Ill, Gordon unwittingly prepared the vaccine using tissues obtained from sheep that had grazed on pasture previously occupied by scrapie-infected sheep. He stabilized the vaccine using formalin, a potent disinfectant made from formaldehyde and alcohol. Normally this treatment would be expected to kill foreign infections, but the scrapie agent survived and went on to kill several hundred of the sheep treated with Gordon's vaccine. Gordon realized that he had accidentally performed a massive experimental transmission, with disastrous results. He had proven that scrapie was not only transmissible, but incredibly persistent. The sheep used to prepare his vaccine had apparently gotten the disease simply by grazing on the same ground where infected animals had previously grazed, and the infectious agent had even withstood prolonged exposure to formalin.[7]

As he began to study scrapie in earnest in the 1950s, Gordon ran into opposition from the British government's Agricultural Research Council (ARC), which took the position that scrapie was an unimportant disease. After the ARC refused to allocate funding for research, Gordon obtained funding from the United States and asked the ARC for authorization to buy three dozen sheep from different flocks so he could investigate their susceptibility to infection. The ARC head office refused to grant permission, but Gordon bought the sheep anyway, using local farm funds. The head office was not amused or impressed by his persistence. They ordered him to abandon the experiment and sell the sheep. Gordon defied the order, went ahead with his plans, and inoculated the sheep with scrapie. At this point, the ARC's only way of stopping the experiment would be to take the controversial step of firing Gordon outright, and the head office backed down. Irked by his rebellion, however, they continued to starve the Compton Laboratory for funding.[8]

Initially, Gordon hoped to develop a vaccine for the disease whose spread he had unintentionally assisted. The first step in developing a vaccine is to identify the organism that carries the disease. In the case of scrapie, scientists were consistently frustrated in their attempts to isolate the disease agent. They knew that inoculating healthy sheep with tissue from sick animals would induce the illness. They knew that sheep seemed to also get the disease by eating contaminated grass. But what *was* the disease agent? Was it a virus or bacteria? What did it look like? What was its structure, its genetic design and manner of function?

Research showed that the infectious agent could be found throughout the body of an infected sheep, but it concentrated in the brain and the nerves, where it did its damage by disrupting the brain's ability to function. Unlike other infections, it seemed to provoke absolutely no response from the body's immune system. Immune system activity creates inflammation and fevers, and doctors can usually identify the specific infectious agent by testing blood samples to see what antibodies their patients are producing. Scrapie failed to trigger any detectable antibody response, further complicating efforts to identify the infectious agent or even to diagnose the disease. Without antibodies, the only way to confirm that an animal had scrapie was to examine its brain after death. Under a microscope, it was possible to see the damage the disease inflicted: tiny, spongelike holes that riddled the brain. Scrapie destroyed the brain by wiping out neurons, the main cells responsible for carrying nerve impulses thoughout the body.

The disease took an extraordinarily long time to kill its victims. Whereas other known infectious diseases showed symptoms within days or weeks after exposure, scrapie took at least six months to emerge. The length of time between exposure and onset of symptoms ranged from two to four *years*. This, of course, explained why scrapie almost never appeared in young sheep. It also meant that research into the disease was painfully slow. Most research involved efforts to induce scrapie in experimental animals, and scientists had lots of time on their hands while they waited for the experiments to bear results.

"A Barrier of Silence"

The scientists also faced human obstacles. The government wasn't alone in its reluctance to assist with their research. Since the disease was inevitably fatal, shepherds came to realize that they had little to gain by calling in a veterinarian, and in fact they had a great deal to lose if others learned that their sheep were infected. The atmosphere of secrecy surrounding the disease was so intense in East Anglia that James Parry, a professor of veterinary medicine at Oxford University, discovered farmers didn't want him around "on the grounds that other farm staff and neighbors would assume there must be 'disease trouble' in any flock I was seen to be visiting." In order to soften their paranoia, he undertook "repeated visits and long enquiries and discussion on non-veterinary matters of sheep breeding," gradually winning their acceptance by posing as someone who was "not really a veterinarian but merely an odd eccentric, interested in all aspects of sheep breeding, who had some practical aid to offer." [9]

Parry spent 25 years working with farmers to document scrapie's spread, and became a controversial critic of the government's "official" assessments which, in his opinion, underestimated the extent to which the disease had infected British sheep. "Owners and shepherds will go to great lengths to hide the occurrence of the disease from enquirers," he observed. "To attempt to establish freedom from scrapie in a flock or an animal on the basis of verbal enquiries would be a hazardous undertaking. . . . The recorded occurrences of the disorder are hence not a reliable guide to actual occurrence . . . the totality of which may be likened to an iceberg, of which these recorded cases represent the tips visible above the sea-surface. . . . Most knowledgeable flock-masters and shepherds had deliberately erected a barrier of silence, and refused to admit to any knowledge of the disease; only the inexperienced talked openly or sought advice. Owners, many highly respected, often clearly indicated to their shepherds that they did not wish to be informed about any possible cases in their own flocks, which were to be put down and unobtrusively buried. They were then free to say they knew nothing about the disease. . . . It is an ancient craft, this weaving of a web of deception to protect one's cherished flock from outsiders' knowledge." [10]

In Iceland, meanwhile, scrapie demonstrated once again its remarkable ability to persist in the natural environment under conditions that would kill most other diseases. Iceland had suffered limited outbreaks of scrapie in the late 1800s after importing an English ram from Denmark, but the disease grew to epidemic proportions following the importation in 1933 of a batch of apparently healthy sheep from Germany. "What happened in Iceland is a warning against the careless introduction of new genetic stock into an unrelated group of animals," Hunter stated. "Within a few years Icelandic sheep, which had been isolated for centuries, became prey to a whole range of diseases."[11] In addition to scrapie, they began succumbing to jaagsiekte, a transmissible cancer of the lung, and visna-maedi, the sheep equivalent of AIDS. Iceland made a desperate attempt to save its sheep industry by dividing the entire country into quarantine areas and slaughtering entire flocks of sheep, even when they only harbored a single sick animal. This policy of extermination succeeded in eradicating jaagsiekte and visna-maedi, and for awhile the Icelanders thought they had also gotten rid of scrapie. After killing the infected animals, the government brought in new flocks of healthy sheep. A few years later, they were amazed when scrapie began to reappear, even on farms which had been left without sheep for three years. The disease had somehow survived, and within the space of a decade it became more widespread in Iceland than ever. It spread both horizontally and vertically. An infected ewe, even before she began to show symptoms, could pass the disease on to her newborn lamb, possibly through the exchange of blood. The placenta left over from the birthing process was also shown to be highly infectious, and scientists theorized that birthing ewes were contaminating the grass eaten by other sheep.[12]

Crossing the Species Barrier

At the Compton Laboratory, Bill Gordon's first breakthrough came in 1950, when he discovered that scrapie could be transmitted from sheep to goats. A decade later another Compton scientist, Dick Chandler, managed to transmit it into mice. In these first cross-species experiments, the scientists discovered another surprising characteristic of the disease agent. It seemed to change every time it passed into a new species. The first attempts to pass scrapie from sheep into mice, for example, were slow and inconsistent. There was some sort of "species barrier." Some mice injected with sheep's brain would get sick, while others stayed healthy. Once a mouse caught the disease, however, the infectious agent in its brain tissue seemed to adapt itself so that it could infect other mice faster and more reliably. Mouse-to-mouse transmission could take place in as little as four months, which was still a long wait but a significant advance over the two years required with sheep. Experiments with mice, moreover, were a lot cheaper than experiments with sheep. Once adapted to mice, the scrapie agent acted with almost clockwork precision—especially when working with highly inbred mice that were genetically virtually identical. "Scrapie disease became very predictable when working with pure strains of the scrapie agent in infected mice, and it became possible at the time of disease injection to predict the death of an animal to within a few days, even when the signs of disease would not actually be evident for more than a year," Hunter noted.[13]

The discovery that they could transmit the disease reliably in mice gave scientists a faster way of testing tissue samples to determine whether they carried the infection. The next step, however, proved even more difficult. Attempts to isolate the mysterious disease agent by filtering it out from other brain tissue showed that the agent was incredibly tiny. It passed through filters as small as 30 nanometers. This meant that it was smaller than any bacteria, smaller even than the smallest known viruses. Chandler began studying scrapie samples under an electron microscope, but even the most extreme magnifications failed to reveal any recognizable shapes that might be the virus.

Another pair of scientists, David Haig and Tikvah Alper, conducted experiments in which they attempted to deactivate the scrapie agent by bombarding it with radiation. Bombardments of this type operate on a "target" basis. Large molecules make larger targets and are more easily destroyed than small molecules. The experiments by Haig and Alper showed that scrapie was remarkably resistant to radiation, suggesting that it was only one-hundredth the size of the smallest viruses. It was small enough, in fact, to survive bombardment by radiation capable of destroying nucleic acids—the DNA and RNA molecules which carry the genetic blueprints used by all living organisms to reproduce themselves. Even bacteria and viruses contain nucleic acids. Following the discovery of DNA in the 1950s, its essential role in cell reproduction had become known as "the central dogma of modern biology." Scrapie seemed to violate this central dogma. It was too small even to carry its own genetic blueprint. How, then, did it manage to reproduce?

Other experiments showed that the scrapie agent resisted treatments that would easily destroy other living organisms. Bill Gordon discovered that a sheep's brain would remain infective even after being boiled for half an hour. It survived dry heat also, and proved resistant to household bleach, along with a range of other solvents, detergents and enzymes known to destroy most known viruses.[14] Scientists joked that the disease agent must be made of linoleum or kryptonite, the mythical green substance that can kill Superman.[15]

These results offered little hope that the disease could be cured, and researchers continued to chafe at the slow pace of progress. Even in mice, experiments could take years to yield results. "Incubation periods of years give scientists ample time for reflection, and tension mounts during the prolonged wait for the seemingly interminable experiments to yield results," observed researcher Gordon Hunter. "The tension has been reflected in rich displays of temperament and character by the research workers involved." One researcher suffered a nervous breakdown after five years of unsuccessful attempts to get the scrapie agent to grow in tissue culture. In Canada, a scientist who had successfully isolated a disease virus in mink decided to take a stab at scrapie. In due time he published a report complete with electron microscope photographs of what he claimed was the scrapie virus. He was forced to admit error after other researchers showed that the same particles could be found in the brains of healthy sheep.

From his outpost at the Compton Laboratory, Bill Gordon became embroiled in a feud with John Stamp, who had started his own scrapie research program at another laboratory, the Moredun Research Institute. The Agricultural Research Council attempted to improve communications by organizing a "Scrapie Working Party" which was supposed to bring the Compton and

Moredun scientists together every six months for the purpose of sharing information. Gordon and Stamp hated each other so much that the ARC excluded them from the meetings, but in their absence the feuding continued among their underlings, terrifying the bureaucrats from the head office who attempted to mediate. Iain Pattison, a pathologist from the Compton lab, clashed especially with Ivan Zlotnik, a Polish scientist engaged in similar pathological research at Moredun. Fights also broke out between researchers from other institutions, notably between Alan Dickinson, a geneticist at the Edinburgh Animal Breeding Research Organization, and James Parry, the veterinarian at Oxford University. Parry continued to insist that scrapie was primarily controlled by genetics, a view that Dickinson thought was pure rubbish. The British scientists carried their warfare to the United States at a 1964 research symposium that came to be known as the "Battle of Washington." According to Hunter, "The American sponsors were astonished to witness the violent arguments between the British scrapie workers, which included dramatic walkouts and scathing criticism of each other's work." [16]

Within the small, ingrown circle of scrapie researchers, violent hostility seemed to be as infectious as the disease itself. Professor E.J. Field, the director of a research unit sponsored by England's Medical Research Council at Newcastle-upon-Tyne, waded into the field determined to earn a name for himself and began reporting significant advances in research into scrapie, along with other medical conditions including cancer, aging and multiple sclerosis. Scepticism about his claims prompted an investigation which collapsed into farce when Field had a union representative bodily thrown out of his lab. As Hunter relates the tale, the union rep "promptly issued a note calling all the technicians out on a one-day strike. E.J. intercepted the note and tore it into little pieces. The union representative then managed to smuggle a message through to the investigating committee and called everyone out for two weeks. E.J. meanwhile enlisted the support of the *Sunday Times,* and he was featured as the scientist who worked day and night (as he did) and was being pilloried merely for expecting his staff to do a good day's work too." In the end, Field's scrapie research produced little of substance. [17]

Dickinson, meanwhile, began to criticize the researchers at the Compton Laboratory, which suffered serious reversals when an overzealous research assistant at Compton announced that he had managed to isolate the scrapie virus. His breakthrough was considered so important that it was published in considerable detail, and other workers were brought in to study his findings. Upon further examination, however, the student's results turned out to be unrepeatable, creating suspicions that the Compton scientists were fudging data or, at best, guilty of sloppy research. Unfortunately, the embarrassment came at a moment when the Agricultural Research Council was coming under pressure to cut its research budget. Dickinson persuaded the ARC to "rationalize" its scrapie program by closing down research at Compton and bringing it under his authority at Edinburgh. "Scrapie work ceased at Compton soon afterwards," Hunter recalled. The work at Edinburgh, moreover, limped along and was further disrupted when Dickinson retired earlier than expected. Hunter concluded sadly that "a committee, reminiscent of so much in British science, had destroyed the lead we held in scrapie, and the British initiative, already being challenged, passed finally across the Atlantic to the U.S."[18]

The American challenge had already begun in the 1960s, led by Daniel Carleton Gajdusek, a virologist whose brilliance and eccentricities were destined to reach mythic proportions. Gajdusek was even more adept than the British at stirring up bitter antagonisms among his colleagues, but by 1976 no one doubted that he richly deserved the Nobel Prize which he received for research that took scrapie in an entirely new direction. Prior to his arrival on the scene, scrapie had seemed to be an animal disease with no implications for human health. Gajdusek's investigations in the remote, cannibal-inhabited jungles of Papua New Guinea helped link scrapie to a previously-unknown human disease which, like its animal counterpart, was incurable, horrible in its effects and inevitably, unremittingly fatal.

Kuru

The chain of events that culminated in Carleton Gajdusek's scientific adventure began in the spring of 1955, in the fledgling South Pacific island nation of Papua New Guinea. Dr. Vincent Zigas, a young Lithuanian physician, had attended the birth of a child and felt obliged to attend the christening party hosted by its parents, members of the Australian upper class who still ruled the island in the years prior to its formal independence. Personally, Zigas had come to detest the Australians' social gatherings, where "ice tinkled in the glasses, beer foamed, champagne spouted, and . . . erotic puppetry . . . was in abundant evidence." To him, their affairs seemed like cheap imitations of the European culture he had left behind. In his memoirs describing the circumstances that brought him together with Gajdusek, Zigas disparaged the Australian elite as a "shabby gentility" who "live in self-imposed seclusion, succumbing to frustration, neurosis, and the inability to enjoy living." [1] He preferred the company of other doctors, and of New Guinea's Highlander natives, whose lives by comparison seemed vital and authentic.

Tall, fair-haired and emotionally sensitive (some people thought he resembled the actor Danny Kaye), Zigas had arrived on the island with his own set of Western biases—"blinded and made halt of mind," as he put it, "by the cruel doctrine of racial prejudice." [2] He had been told that the Highlanders were savage warriors and cannibals. As he came to know them personally, however, he began to admire the region's "inhabitants so separated and durable, its rituals so essential and so graceful, that being here feels like purification." At night he would listen to "the melody of New Guinea's waters . . . a tune rising from every rock, root and rapids . . . rivers and cascades. . . . Then on still nights when the campfire is low and the moon amid Aurora Australis has climbed above the rimrocks, one needs to sit quietly and listen for a distant beat of drums and the wailing cry of bamboo flutes. . . . Then you may hear it—a vast undulatory harmony; the score inscribed on a thousand hills and mountains, its notes like the life and death of humanity. . . . There I was among martial people no one knew: this people, unscarred by civilization, capable of inhabiting a natural realm without disturbing the harmony of its life." [3]

Zigas found the Highlanders remarkably friendly, and charmingly free from the inhibitions that afflicted the Europeans. Their customary greeting was considerably more intimate than a handshake: a standing embrace in which both men and women handled each other's genitals. "It appeared that they were in need of continual exposure to the possessiveness that characterized their relationship by direct physical contact with other people," Zigas observed. "Even in the villages, among people who saw one another every day, hands were continually reaching out to caress a thigh, arms, and searching mouths hung over a child's lips or nuzzled a baby's penis."[4]

The sensuality of the indigenous culture seemed to appeal to some of the European settlers, who took advantage of the opportunity to indulge in behaviors that would not be allowed in "civilized" society. On one occasion a Highlander showed Zigas an abandoned hut where a white man had lived some years previously. The man had been tolerated, even though he was not well liked. "He did no harm," the villager explained, "but this man did not make love to women—he liked small boys."

Another white man—like Zigas, a physician from Lithuania—found happiness in his reputation among the natives as a peculiar kind of faith healer: "His respective enjoyments were focused on gastronomy, tippling, and, as he called it, 'roasted coffee beans'—the fawn-colored maiden's bosom on the topless brown supple body with long, firm nipples. . . . During his Sunday promenade in the local market there would be a number of pubescent girls, either in the company of elders or alone in groups, showering him with demonstrative affection and solicitously proferring their young virgin breasts at the first cast of his touch. The natives were convinced that his 'magic touch' would enrich the supply of milk after marriage." Zigas considered the man a friend and colleague, and insisted that "his fondness for caressing the firm young breast was more for the pleasure of being 'privileged' rather than from any carnal intent. His every 'magic touch' was accompanied by a soft chant in a language alien to the native, which they regarded as a beneficial spell."[5]

The Australians gathered at the christening party, by contrast, struck Zigas as a bunch of boring, sexually frustrated bigots. Distraction came in the form of an argument among several of the men gathering around the host's well-stocked bar. For the first time, Zigas noticed a young Australian patrol officer. Fortified by several glasses of rum, the officer was vigorously challenging other members of the group as they mocked the character and merits of their Highlander servants.

"They don't really want a job, they don't want to work, any of them, lazy bastards; no loyalty, no responsibility," argued one of the drunken Australians.[6]

"For two dollars and fifty cents a month you would be lazy too," countered the patrol officer, whose name was John McArthur. The others replied that native labor wasn't even worth two-fifty a *year*. McArthur maintained his lonely defense of the natives, and Zigas found himself taking a liking to the young man. After the argument ended, the two struck up a personal conversation.

McArthur, it turned out, was stationed in the North Fore (pronounced FOR-ae) region of the Highlands, a remote outpost still considered "uncontrolled" by the colonial administration. Although his job was to pacify the natives, he had taken a personal interest in the region and its people. Turning to the topic of health, McArthur asked if Zigas had seen his patrol report describing a form of local sorcery called "kuru," a word that meant chill, trembling or laughter. Zigas replied that the report had not reached his desk, drawing a stream of profane commentary from McArthur. He had been trying for two years to interest the colonial authorities in kuru, which was killing large numbers of Fore tribespeople, but no one in authority seemed to "give a bloody damn." Zigas said he'd be interested in taking a look, and three months later a native guide arrived at his hospital, with directions leading to a rendezvous in the Fore region that McArthur described as "mountains fretted with evil spell."

The Kuru Curse

It was a two-day hike to the village where McArthur was waiting. On the first day of the journey, Zigas saw his first kuru victim, a middle-aged woman sitting incapacitated in her dilapidated hut. "She looked odd, not ill, rather emaciated, looking up with blank eyes and a mask-like expression. There was an occasional fine tremor of her head and trunk, as if she were shivering from cold, though the day was very warm."

The Highlanders believed powerfully in magic spells and taboos. Their superstitions were so strong that Zigas had seen a man collapse and die simply from the psychosomatic impact of the suggestion that he had violated a taboo. Beginning with the assumption that kuru sorcery was either psychosomatic or treatable, Zigas had brought medicines that he hoped would enable him to work his own brand of counter-magic. "The sorcerer has put a bad spirit inside the woman," he told the natives who gathered to watch him work. "I am going to burn this spirit so that it comes out of her and leaves her." To make his magic convincing, he rubbed her legs and stomach with warming liniment. When he commanded her to walk, however, she just looked back at him, unable to rise. "I took her by the arms and lifted her; she sank limply back to the ground," he recalled. "In an even sterner tone I let out: 'Stand up!' The woman struggled feebly as if to rise, then, exhausted, started to tremble more violently, making a kind of foolish laughter, akin to a titter. I lifted her again; again she sank back. Only now I realized I was helpless. . . . The audience looked at me triumphantly and cackled, and I suddenly felt as naked as a conjurer whose white rabbit had burrowed too far up his sleeve and fallen down his trouser leg."[7]

By the time he reached McArthur's village, Zigas had concluded that there was more to kuru than native superstition. McArthur led him to other cases of the disease in various stages of its progression: a young boy, staggering clumsily as he walked, showing the first symptom of impaired coordination; another boy, further advanced, "a limp figure grossly emaciated to little more than skin and protruding bone, the shivering skeleton of a boy, looking up at me with blank crossed eyes. On both his hips were large bed-sores, and when I tried to apply a dressing to protect them against blowflies his tremor became more pronounced and from his cracked lips came a moan-like sound. He could not utter a single word." McArthur pointed out another boy, stumbling along a path, his facial expression rigid as though frozen. According to McArthur, the boy had been perfectly fine a month before. Now he was barely able to speak and remain upright. "He stood, erect on a wide base, holding his hands together in an attempt to control the involuntary tremors and maintain his equilibrium," Zigas wrote. "As if he sensed, in a very slow motion, some threat from behind, he gradually turned his head to one side. With his outstretched arms, he uttered a single rasping inarticulated shriek of laughter. He couldn't keep his balance any longer—I caught him before he fell."[8]

Zigas saw more cases of kuru in the women's huts. Middle-aged and elderly women were succumbing, along with adolescents and children. All of them showed similar signs of trembling, awkward movements and progressive paralysis, combined with the frozen, mask-like smiles and occasional spasms of uncontrollable, humorless laughter that were the basis for the name "kuru." Zigas was transfixed by the sight of a young girl who "got up, though very awkwardly, and bracing herself with a stick, studied me. With the corner of her little mouth lifted, a slight tremor of her slender body, and with the shadow of a timid smile, she looked forlorn. She could not yet be eleven." He witnessed the grotesque mourning of a middle-aged woman as she cleaned the body of her small son, who had died hours previously: "With one hand she was wiping off brown porridge-like feces from the boy's puny buttocks with a handful of grass. Each soiled grassy wad was tossed to the pig waiting eagerly for the flings. Her other hand was fondling the boy's penis and she was talking to him. There was no response from the still figure. . . . Interrupting her action, she busily tried to chase two wretched dogs away from the boy's stiff body. One beast had managed to lap up quite a bit of the gray-yellow maggot-filled slough from a huge bedsore on the boy's hip. The other beast was obstinately trying to follow suit, but was driven away by a kick."[9]

Zigas became obsessed with finding a cure for kuru. He scoured books for information on diseases of the central nervous system, and made additional trips into Fore territory, collecting information about the disease and its symptoms. He sought out colleagues for their advice, but found that they showed little interest in kuru and knew even less than he did about what might be causing it. He took advantage of rare visits to New Guinea by medical experts from England and the Netherlands, who theorized that the symptoms he was seeing might be related to malaria, measles, pneumonia, encephalitis, meningitis, Parkinson's Disorder, brain tumors or tuberculosis. The most famous visitor to hear his harangue was Sir Macfarlane Burnet, the "pope of Australian virology," who was soon to receive the Nobel Prize for his research into the body's reactions to skin grafting and organ transplants. Zigas passionately expounded on kuru while Burnet "pretended to look adequately interested, nodding and smiling whenever he guessed it to be appropriate. . . . I felt he must look upon me as a freak, obviously unbalanced. Perhaps, I thought, my description of kuru was delivered with too much gusto, giving an impression to this austere figure that my discovery was just a new obsession. The days of his visit frittered away, leaving me in doubt about his promised cooperation in the investigation."[10]

Early in 1957, however, letters arrived giving the green light for kuru research, with the assistance of facilities at Burnet's laboratory in Melbourne.

An anthropologist visited and interviewed a number of Fore clansmen about their customs and their experiences with the disease. In February a letter came from Burnet stating that he had agreed to send a scientist to undertake an epidemiological investigation, although Burnet worried about "the possible dangers from hostile native reaction" and cautioned that he "should not be justified in consenting to the project" if the natives turned against it.[11]

"Atom Bomb" Gajdusek

Carleton Gajdusek was not the scientist that Burnet was planning to send. *His* arrival, on March 13, came unannounced and uninvited. Gajdusek simply showed up at the hospital and began asking questions. "At first glance he looked like a hippie, though shorn of beard and long hair," Zigas said. "He wore much-worn shorts, an unbuttoned brownish-plaid shirt revealing a dirty T-shirt, and tattered sneakers. He was tall and lean, and one of those people whose age was hard to guess, looking boyish with a soot-black crewcut unevenly trimmed, as if done by himself. He was just plain shabby. He was a well-built man with a remarkably shaped head, curiously piercing eyes, and ears that stood out from his head. It gave him the surprised, alert air of someone taking in all aspects of new subjects with thirst." Gajdusek said he had worked in Melbourne with Macfarlane Burnet, whom he referred to as "Sir Mac." He had heard about Zigas and his work with kuru from Roy Scragg, the acting director of New Guinea's Public Health Department. This introduction struck Zigas as odd. Why hadn't Sir Mac himself told Gajdusek about kuru?

In any case, Gajdusek was finally showing the type of interest in the disease that Zigas thought it deserved. "I was machine-gunned by his numerous questions. I had barely answered one when another would be asked. . . . My suggestion that he accompany us the following day to Okapa and my assurance that he would be in a position to observe several dozen kuru victims of different sex, age, and phases of the disease was met with shining, eager eyes full of enthusiasm."[12]

In fact, Macfarlane Burnet *did* have a reason for declining to tell Gajdusek about kuru. At age 33, Gajdusek had already earned a reputation both for his genius and for his eccentric personality, and Sir Mac considered him something of a loose cannon. "His personality . . . is almost legendary among my colleagues in the U.S.," Burnet would later write. "Enders told me that Gajdusek was very bright but you never knew when he would leave off work for a week to study Hegel or a month to go off to work with Hopi Indians. Smadel at Washington said the only way to handle him was to kick him in the tail, hard. Somebody else told me he was fine, but there just wasn't anything human about him. . . . My own summing up was that he had an intelligence quotient up in the 180s and the emotional immaturity of a fifteen-year-old. He is quite manically energetic when his enthusiasm is roused and can inspire enthusiasm in his technical assistants. He is completely self-centered, thick-skinned, and inconsiderate, but equally won't let danger, physical difficulty, or other people's feelings interfere in the least with what he wants to do. He apparently has no interest in women but an almost obsessional interest in children, none whatever in clothes and cleanliness; and he can live cheerfully in a slum or a grass hut." [13]

Gajdusek's scholarly accomplishments included studies in physics and mathematics before entering Harvard Medical School at age nineteen, where he studied pediatrics, neurology and biophysics. Among his professors, his brilliance and explosive passions had won him the nickname, "Atom Bomb Gajdusek." Since then he had traveled to all corners of the globe, working with some of the world's leading scientists on laboratory and field research into rabies, plague, hemorrhagic fevers, arborvirus infections, scurvy and other epidemiological problems in exotic and isolated populations. He had studied problems of survival on life rafts during World War II and developed techniques for purifying blood products. During the Korean War, he had helped study an epidemic of hemorrhagic fever among the troops. Those studies were followed by medical and anthropological explorations in Iran, Afghanistan and the Amazon jungles of Bolivia, and then a two-year stint studying hepatitis and autoimmunity at Burnet's institute in Australia.

Since his days at Harvard, Gajdusek had been especially fascinated with diseases affecting children. During medical school, he had virtually lived at Boston Children's Hospital, where he was famous for his devotion to young patients, often maintaining round-the-clock vigils at the bedsides of stricken children. After finishing his work with Burnet, he was planning to combine his passion for children with his passion for exotic travels by developing a research project called the "Program for the Study of Child Growth and Development and Disease Patterns in Primitive Cultures." He believed that studying pre-industrial societies could provide valuable insights into human health problems. While based in Australia, Gajudsek had made medical expeditions to Australian aboriginal communities with the Royal Flying Doctor Service, and in 1956 a medical survey of several remote populations in New Guinea and New Britain. In keeping with his desire to study some "primitive cultures," he had arranged to join Mac Burnet's son, Ian, on a New Guinea expedition to previously unvisited groups and to spend several months on pediatric studies with Stone Age peoples.

Other than this brief tour, though, the Australians had no intention of letting their eccentric American guest run amok and unchaperoned among the Highlanders. They were dismayed to discover how quickly he was capable of developing his own agenda. One night's talk with Dr. Zigas was enough to convince Gajdusek that the Fore were suffering from a new, lethal neurological disease—exactly the type of scientific challenge he was looking for. He immediately abandoned his plans to travel with Ian Burnet and joined Zigas on a trek into Fore territory. After seeing the ravages of kuru firsthand, he became completely obsessed with the disease. Within a week he had drafted a letter to Joe Smadel, his former superior at the Walter Reed Army Medical Center, providing detailed and graphic descriptions of the kuru cases he had witnessed.

"I am in one of the most remote, recently opened regions of New Guinea," Gajdusek wrote, "in the center of tribal groups of cannibals only contacted in the last ten years and controlled for five years—still spearing each other as of a few days ago, and only a few weeks ago cooking and feeding the children the body of a kuru case, the disease I am studying. This is a sorcery-induced disease, according to the local people; and that it has been the major disease problem of the region, as well as a social problem for the past five years, is certain. It is so astonishing an illness that clinical description can only be read with skepticism; and I was highly skeptical until two days ago, when I arrived and began to see the cases on every side. Classical advancing 'parkinsonism' involving every age—found overwhelmingly in females although many boys and a few men also have had it—is a mighty strange syndrome. To see whole groups of well-nourished healthy young adults dancing about, with athetoid tremors which look far more hysterical than organic, is a real sight. But to see them, however, regularly progress to neurological degeneration in three to six months (usually three) and to death is another matter and cannot be shrugged off." [14]

The Australians, meanwhile, were not pleased. Suddenly they felt that *they* had first claim on any investigations into the disease. Gajdusek received a cordial but blunt letter from Sir Mac, thanking him for his "extremely interesting" reports and "invaluable" help, and asking when he intended leaving "Australian New Guinea" so that kuru research could become an "Australian affair." [15]

In reply, Gajdusek dashed off a lengthy letter providing more details about the cases he had seen. "I should like to remain in Australian New Guinea until I have exhausted what little I can contribute to this kuru problem on the spot," he wrote. "At the moment, I consider myself the most qualified pediatrician—both clinical and investigative—in the Territory. . . . I doubt that there is anyone around or likely to soon be around who can complete these studies any better than I. I therefore consider it a duty both to kuru patients and to my intellectual curiosity to stick to it for a month or longer, as the matter works out."

As for Sir Mac's suggestion that he had invaded the territory of other researchers, Gajdusek diplomatically alluded to the complete absence of any other actual researchers on the scene. "Here on kuru research," he stated, "we could immediately use a dozen workers—epidemiologists, microbiologists, and pathologists; two dozen would not hurt or exhaust the problem, and the quicker they arrive, the better. . . . The problem of medical investigation is an open field, and one that to me has always been noncompetitive." [16]

In a letter some months later to Joe Smadel, Gajdusek expressed himself more frankly: "Zigas and I are now preparing a paper for submission to the U.S. journals. . . . We both see clearly that unless we work out and publish our preliminary and very extensive studies, Zigas will be cheated out of anything by administrative super-structure. Secondly, I suspect a good deal of jealousy by the Australian sources shortly, as the word crops out. The fact is, that besides Zigas and myself, no other medical man in the world has investigated or seen the disease, excepting for a few administrative M.D.'s who saw some cases for a few hours, when Zigas brought them out of the region to 'civilization.' " In short, Gajdusek said, Sir Mac's "interests are here, but no one is doing a thing." [17]

Come hell or high water, Gajdusek planned to stay. "I have the 'real thing' in my hands," he told Smadel. "I tell you Joe, this is no wild goose chase, but a really big thing. . . . I stake my entire medical reputation on the matter." He was prepared, if necessary, to support the research out of his own pocket, figuring that "on my own I can hold out for one or two months and still have enough to get home via Europe." He was hoping, however, that Smadel could come up with some money to buy axes, beads, tobacco and other items that the natives would take in trade so Gajdusek and Zigas could "purchase bodies (along with autopsy permission) and food for our patients." [18]

By this time, the Australians were livid. As far as they were concerned, Gajdusek was a sneaky interloper, a medical pirate who had used the pretext of a brief visit to New Guinea as an excuse to intrude where he had not been invited. Roy Scragg, New Guinea's recently-appointed Director of Public Health, sent a bluntly worded radiogram stating that the Australians would be sending a doctor of their own soon to look into the matter. Scragg reminded Gajdusek that he had not received authorization to undertake research among the Fore, and advised him "on ethical grounds" to "discontinue your investigations." [19]

Impossible, Gajdusek shot back in a hastily-scribbled reply: "Intensive investigation uninterruptible. Will remain at work with patients to whom we are responsible." [20]

The next letter came from Scragg's superior, Dr. John Gunther, who expressed amazement "that you had the discourtesy not to call upon me or make some contact with me while you were in Port Moresby. . . . Without sponsorship by Sir Macfarlane Burnet or his Institute, you have come to this Territory and are working in a field that we had proposed for Sir Macfarlane. . . . Whilst I agree that there may be scope for more and more research within this area, I believe it was grossly unethical for you to enter the area, as you have done, without the approval of either Sir Macfarlane, Dr. Scragg, or myself." [21]

The Australians could fume and sputter all they liked. As a practical matter, they knew it would be difficult to absolutely force Gajdusek to leave. Simply *finding* him could be a challenge as he moved about in the eastern Highlands of New Guinea, which comprised several thousand square miles of largely uncharted, mountainous terrain inhabited by warring tribes of cannibals. And Gajdusek was moving around a *lot*. Over the course of the next eight months, he performed one of the most remarkable feats ever undertaken in medicine, a two-thousand-mile marathon trek by foot through Fore territory. Since geographic maps of the territory did not exist, Gajdusek drew up maps himself along the way, as well as recording native customs in the process of drawing a detailed clinical and epidemiological profile of kuru. He was also rapidly teaching himself to communicate in the eleven native languages spoken by the groups afflicted with the disease. (Among his other talents, Gajdusek was a brilliant linguist who would eventually boast of speaking a dozen languages.)

Zigas, who accompanied Gajdusek, found this odyssey "the most trying experience in my seven years in the mountainous jungles." During a single six-day sojourn, for example, "the climb of about 7,000 feet was such that we had to ascend hand over hand. Once attaining the ridge, we then had to descend to 3,000 feet, and then climb another ridge for about 6,000 feet; like a yoyo, straight up and down for long, strenuous hours. There we encountered the major environmental hazard—the swampy sago country. Here we all suffered badly from leeches, which were extremely numerous and aggressive. Every member of our party also developed bleeding legs and feet each day from the trek. Another hazard was afforded by wild bees. . . . Mosquitoes were also a problem. . . . The final hazard was the long, razor-sharp elephant grass. Try as we did to avoid contact, when we lightly brushed against it the sharp edges would cause deep cuts."

During these travels, Zigas was amazed by Gajdusek's strength and endurance. "Upon our arrival in a village after the most strenuous 'thrills,' soaked to the skin, numbed and short-winded, Jack and I would have to rest for a while. Carleton, however, would immediately commence to interview the villagers and collect blood specimens. There was a smack of fanaticism in the way he collected blood from every willing person, including infants, regardless of sex or age." [22]

Gajdusek's remarkable charisma with children helped him recruit a "cargo line"—an entourage of boys, some as young as five or ten, who volunteered to help carry supplies and who served as interpreters of the native languages. They enabled Gajdusek to cross streams and ravines by constructing suspension bridges of vine or by balancing tree trunks on rocky outcrops. Without their assistance, he would have been helpless. With them, he achieved miracles. He came to see himself as their "Pied Piper," enticing the children to follow him with "the sincerest notes in my repertoire. All else is but exercise for these tunes, and all work is but practice for the pipes." [23]

In the absence of a proper laboratory, Gajdusek set up makeshift facilities at first in the one-room home of Patrol Officer Jack Baker. They used the dining table to examine patients and perform autopsies. Unwashed plates and bottles of rum from dinner sat on the table alongside a typewriter, a microscope, and enamel wash basins containing the human brains that Gajdusek was extracting from kuru victims. Later the natives built a separate house for Gajdusek, along with a field laboratory. They were simple, thatched-roof structures with bamboo mat floors, lacking running water and electricity, but Gajdusek and Zigas managed to obtain laboratory reagents and essential equipment that they used to carry out a host of tests: blood counts, hemoglobin determinations, urine tests, and assays of brain and spinal fluids.

After tempers cooled, the Australians began to supply valuable laboratory backup at Macfarlane Burnet's Hall Institute. Although Sir Mac said he was "still considerably irked at Gajdusek's actions," he admitted that "there is little doubt that he has the technical competence to do a first-rate job. . . . I have a sort of exasperated affection for Gajdusek and a great admiration of his drive, courage, and capacity for hard work. Also, there is probably no one else anywhere with the combination of linguistic ability, anthropological interest, and medical training who could have tackled this problem so well." [24]

In the space of five months, Gajdusek identified 750 people suffering from kuru, 50 of whom had died since his arrival. The disease was responsible for half of all deaths occurring among the Fore. A clear pattern was emerging, confirming his early observation that kuru tended primarily to afflict children and women. Through numerous interviews, Gajdusek concluded that the disease was a relatively new phenomenon. It had emerged some decades before first European contact, which had been made by German Lutheran missionaries just before World War II. In the space of a few decades, it had grown from a rare problem into a devastating plague. It was killing so many women that it was jeopardizing the ability of the Fore to reproduce themselves. Extinction of the tribe was beginning to seem like a real possibility.[25]

For therapy, Gajdusek tried every medicine he could secure: antibiotics, antimalarials, antifungal drugs, aspirin, vitamins, anticonvulsives, detoxifiers, tranquilizers, drugs against roundworms, parasites and multiple sclerosis. On the theory that male hormones might account for the low rate of incidence in men, he tried injections of testosterone. He tested Fore food and water for toxic substances and found nothing. He treated them with nutritional supplements, to no avail. His patients suffered with stoicism as he loaded them with painful shots of everything from crude liver extract to cortisone to antibiotics. None of these treatments showed any ability whatsoever to halt or even slow the inevitable fatal course of the disease.

Efforts to identify the cause of kuru were equally frustrating. Gajdusek took samples of blood, urine and feces, as well as culture swabs for fungi, bacteria and viruses. If patients agreed he would also perform lumbar punctures to examine their cerebro-spinal fluid. He scoured the native landscape in search of unusual plants, spiders, fleas or mites that might carry some previously unknown neurotoxin. He carefully sifted epidemiological data in hopes of finding some factor common to all the victims. The disease was occurring in clusters of people, suggesting that it was probably infectious. But the classic symptoms of infection never showed—no fevers, sweats or changes in white blood cells or in cerebrospinal fluid. He sent back tissue samples to labs in Melbourne, Port Moresby and the National Institutes of Health (NIH) in the United States. Clinical tests in those labs found no antibodies that could be linked to the disease. He arranged for small laboratory animal inoculations using ground-up autopsy tissue samples from kuru victims and injecting them into mice and other test animals, but the animals all stayed healthy.

The Fore, meanwhile, had developed their own theories about the disease. They believed that sorcerers cast their spells by stealing items intimately associated with their intended victims—their excrement or leftover scraps of food—binding it up in a "magic bundle" with special pieces of bark, twigs and leaves, and burying it to the accompaniment of a chanted curse. Periodically the sorcerer would return to the spot and beat the bundle with a stick, causing the victim's symptoms to intensify.

The Fore punished suspected sorcerers with a ritual revenge called "tukabu"—brutal, murderous beatings, bashing in heads and crushing genitals with stones and wooden clubs. As the number of kuru cases rose, so did the level of desperation among the Fore, until ritual murders were causing as many deaths as the disease. "With the disease progressing relentlessly to speedy

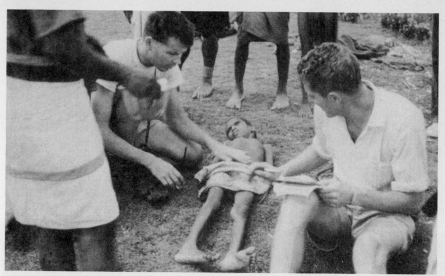

Drs. Carleton Gajdusek (left) and Vincent Zigas (right) examine a child victim of kuru. *(D. Carleton Gajdusek, archive #57-369B. Used with permission)*

complete helplessness and death before our eyes, the Fore nation in turmoil because of it, and with ritual murders and savage killings in reprisal for kuru sorcery comprising the major administrative problems in the region at the moment, we certainly feel we should be doing more for our patients—even if these trials are based on the most remote chances of benefit," Gajdusek wrote. "Therapeutically, we are licked. Sorcery seems as good an explanation for kuru as any we can offer them." [26]

Gajdusek was certain that victims' brains held the key to understanding the disease. Whenever possible, he performed autopsies in which he extracted the brains, preserving them in formalin for later laboratory examination. For lack of proper equipment, he performed his first autopsy using a carving knife, working at 2:00 A.M. by lantern light in a native hut surrounded by a howling storm. Until then, the natives had been friendly and cooperative as he poked and prodded and stuck them with needles. It was another thing entirely, however, to watch him cut open someone's skull and plop the brain into a smelly jar of chemicals. Other victims' survivors were reluctant to let him remove tissue from their family members, and some of the Fore suspected that he was taking the brains so other people could eat them. He advised his colleagues back at the National Institutes of Health to treat each brain they received as though it would be their last. By August, 1955, his relationship with the Fore had begun to deteriorate, and some families were turning angry. It was difficult to stay calm when surrounded by angry cannibals, but Gajdusek and Zigas struggled on. "It looks as though further autopsy materials may be unobtainable," Gajdusek wrote in a November letter to Joe Smadel. "The natives have given up on our medicine; they know damn well it does not work, and I am fighting verbal battles in Fore, bribing, cajoling, begging, pleading, and bargaining for every opportunity to see a patient, and strenuously working tongue muscles for hours, for every day we get a patient to stay in the hospital, accept thera-peutic trials, etc., etc." [27]

By December, Gajdusek was preparing to leave New Guinea, discouraged by the absence of visible progress toward identifying the cause of the disease. As he packed, another spat erupted with the Australians, who thought they should be entitled to retain possession of his field notes. Wearily, Gajdusek pointed out that not only did they belong to him, but it would be impossible for anyone else to decipher his handwriting.

Spongy Brains

At the National Institutes of Health (NIH) in Washington, neuropathologist Igor Klatzo was assigned to examine the sixteen kuru brains that Gajdusek had managed to obtain. Klatzo was dismayed at the condition of some of the brains, which Gajdusek had removed without proper tools. Twelve of the brains, however, were in remarkably good condition. Klatzo and his techni-cian photographed them, impregnated them with wax, and pared them into microscopically thin slices which were placed on slides and stained. Under the microscope, Klatzo saw for the first time the visible evidence that some-thing unusual had happened. The brains were riddled with gaping holes and strange plaques—flower-shaped waxy buildups of a protein called amyloid. Kuru brains had holes where neurons used to be, accompanied by enlarged astrocytes, the star-shaped cells that attach themselves to blood vessels inside the brain. Klatzo had never seen anything like it before.

"Whatever the problem was, it didn't look to me as though it was caused by toxicity, or by heredity, or by infection," Klatzo recalled. "I was forced to think very hard about what the condition did resemble, and suddenly, some-thing clicked." [28] He remembered an obscure neurological disease that he had heard about back in his days as a medical student in Germany. It was so obscure that he had to search the German medical literature to find any ref-erence to it—Creutzfeldt-Jakob Disease, a condition so rare that only 20 cases had ever been reported. Microscopic examinations of the brains of CJD victims had shown similar signs—enlarged astrocytes, holes, and amyloid plaques.

Klatzo's insight led to another in the spring of 1959, when a museum in London hosted an exhibition based on Gajdusek's kuru research. By chance, one of the visitors to the exhibit was William Hadlow, a young American vet-erinarian working on scrapie research at Bill Gordon's research laboratory in Compton. Looking at Klatzo's microphotographs of kuru brain sections, Hadlow was struck by their similarity to the spongy holes he had observed for years in the brains of sheep afflicted with scrapie. As he read Klatzo's pathology report and case studies of kuru, he was struck by other parallels: similar behav-ioral changes; the absence of antibodies or other response from the immune system; the inability to isolate a causal agent; and, of course, the untreatable nature of the disease on its irreversible trajectory toward death. Hadlow became the first person to theorize that kuru might be a human version of scrapie.

In the absence of other explanations, the scientists studying kuru were moving steadily toward the opinion that it was a genetic disease transmitted by inheritance. This explanation was hard to reconcile with the rapid way the

within the Fore population, but
ıtal attempt to induce the illness by
ound with scrapie research, Hadlow
their methodology. They were test-
a normal virus or bacteria—the type
ute infection." Acute infections show
osure. Accordingly, Gajdusek's team
a few weeks after inoculation. But
nfection, a "slow virus" like scrapie?
ıld happen within the time frame of

ajdusek and published a letter detail-
al, *The Lancet.* In late 1959, he toured
armers about methods for controlling
t lecture and began pressing him for
ıd's experience with scrapie, Gajdusek
slow viruses. Following their model,
nch a new series of tests—expensive
anzees as test animals. It was impor-
similarity to humans and because they
rm observation. To oversee the exper-
Joseph Gibbs, Jr., a career scientist
the perfect counterpart to Gajdusek's
nt the job. "Goddamn it," Smadel told
ıre going to give stability to an otherwise unstable program."

While Gajdusek continued his travels to the South Seas and other exotic
locales, Gibbs held down the fort at the National Institutes of Health. He over-
saw the creation of the Patuxent Wildlife Center, a research lab occupying 5,000
acres of secluded park in the Maryland countryside. Caretakers were hired,
and Gibbs purchased a colony of 54 chimpanzees, squirrel, macaque and other
monkeys. In August of 1963, scientists began their attempt to kill these animals by injecting them intracerebrally with ground-up brains of human kuru
victims. They were lively, likeable animals, and the researchers gave them
human names—Daisy, Hermann, George, Georgette.

In New Guinea, meanwhile, a husband-and-wife team of anthropologists,
Shirley Lindenbaum and Robert Glasse, carried out further investigations among
the Fore. Their sponsor was Dr. John Bennett, a specialist in mathematical
genetics who was convinced that kuru was caused by the presence of a single,
dominant gene. In previous encounters, Zigas had come to perceive Bennett
as one of the conspirators in the Australian intrigues against Gajdusek. Zigas
even hated Bennett's handshake, which "was like a wet cloth, cold and clammy.
I dropped it as one would a burning coal. He looked to me more like a garden
gnome than an academician." Worse, Bennett had offered to make Zigas
"director of kuru research," on condition that he disassociate himself from
"Gajdusek and his collaborators." Zigas considered this offer "the most blatant

piece of bribery I had ever seen. His ill-mannered address and offensive over-
ture stunned me. I felt stricken by emotional dysphoria at the thought of selling out one's friend." [30]

On the basis of his genetic theory, Bennett was proposing a "eugenic"
solution to the kuru problem, placing the Fore under strict quarantine and prohibiting migration of tribal leaders from their own ethnic areas. The policy was
supported by Roy Scragg, the director of public health for New Guinea who
had clashed previously with Gajdusek. Zigas became embroiled in a heated
argument when Scragg ordered him to "submit a written statement that no
accommodation was available for Gajdusek" as a "pretext for the postpone-
ment of Carleton's return." Zigas protested, but Scragg "simply smirked. And
the faster I advanced arguments against his policy relating to Carleton and
eugenics, the more he smirked. As it dawned on me that I was in fact struggling for the right to proper research, I became more vocal. . . . An exchange
developed with charges and countercharges made on both sides. Scragg had
finally said that now as in the past I had acted in a cowardly way toward 'controlling Gajdusek.' I contained my anger with difficulty. He dared to judge and
accuse me of cowardice. Why and how was I to 'control' Gajdusek, the genuine researcher? My impulse was to charge Scragg, choke him, blind him." [31]

Lindenbaum and Glasse, however, proved to be the genuine article—
careful researchers, respectful of the Fore, and adept at forging relationships
with the natives. After nine months in the field, they had amassed genealogi-
cal and chronological data that thoroughly exploded Bennett's genetic theories.
As recently as fifty years previously, the Fore said, kuru had not existed at
all. It first appeared in the north Fore territory around the turn of the century, and since then had spread southward. It had spread so rapidly in living
memory that there was no way a genetic model could explain it. Bennett
accepted their report with polite disappointment and encouraged them to continue their research.

The Cannibal Connection

The team's next breakthrough was inspired by a suggestion from R.W.
Hornabrook, an epidemiologist from New Zealand. Hornabrook had also
clashed with Zigas and Gajdusek, but his advice to Lindenbaum and Glasse
provided precisely the focus they needed. "Go and find out," he said, "what
it is that the adult women and children of both sexes in the Fore tribe are
doing that the adult men are *not* doing." [32]

Lindenbaum had formed a close relationship with a number of Fore
women and began to interrogate them more closely. Gradually, the anthropologists realized that there were important differences in the way men and
women practiced cannibalism. The practice of eating dead relatives was not
an ancient tradition but a newly introduced custom, practiced first around the
turn of the century by a group of elder women. Over the years the practice
had caught on, especially among women. Partly this was because women had
less access to other food sources than Fore men.

The Highlanders in general showed a social pattern marked by constant warfare and severe sexual discrimination. They cultivated food in vegetable gardens, and kept pigs which were a constant source of friction between neighbors who quarreled over whose pig belonged to whom, and who was responsible for the destruction of whose garden. They had no formal way of resolving their disputes. Instead, they engaged in perpetual, intermittent clan warfare based on continually shifting alliances among neighbors. Their leaders were called "Big Men," and their authority stemmed in large measure from their fearless leadership in acts of aggression against rival groups. During battles, which were fought up close and personal, they would verbally abuse their opponents with insults similar to the ones you might expect to hear among feuding boys on a school playground: "You are weak like babies, we are strong like wild pigs." "We make you eat woman's vulva." "We make you eat our shit and drink our piss."

Big Men would also broker marriage arrangements, in which the groom's kin would purchase the bride through payment of pigs or other valuables. The rules against marriage within a clan meant that women were often sent to marry members of neighboring, warring tribes, and the fact that your sister was likely to someday marry your enemy contributed to attitudes of suspicion and discrimination against women. In some of the Highlander societies, men learned to shun female companionship from an early age. Adolescent males and young men went into periodic seclusion to free themselves from the polluting aspects of female contact. They especially feared contact with menstruating women, believing that it could sicken a man, cause vomiting, turn his blood black, corrupt his vital juices, wrinkle his skin, dull his wits and eventually lead to a slow decline and death. [33]

Outside of marriage, men and women lived largely separate lives. Boys beyond eight or ten years lived in separate houses with the men, who hunted wild animals and kept the meat for themselves. Women raised pigs, but the men ate the better meat, leaving the entrails for women and children, who supplemented their diet with vegetables, frogs, insects or rats. They were also responsible for preparing bodies for burial, and although eating of the dead was a rite of respect, love and mourning, simple hunger also seemed to play a role. Older widows even began attending funerals of people to whom they were only distantly related, joining in the mourning rituals so they could catch a bite of the deceased afterward. Men rarely joined in the feast, and when they did, they ate the good parts, leaving the women with the brains and other internal organs. [34]

With these facts established, Gajdusek and Gibbs had a theory capable of explaining how kuru had originated and spread. In 1965, Gibbs attended a meeting on scrapie in France and explained the hypothesis: Creutzfeldt-Jakob Disease, which was similar to kuru, appeared to occur "spontaneously" at very low rates of incidence in the human population. No one knew what caused these cases, but they seemed to occur everywhere in the world. Normally, these spontaneous cases would die without infecting anyone else. Among the Fore, however, the unique context of ritual cannibalism had given the disease an opportunity to multiply and develop into an epidemic.

Of course, Gibbs admitted, all of this was hypothetical, simply a theory. The experiments with monkeys had been initiated almost two years previously, and so far they had shown no signs of illness. Without sick monkeys, there was no direct evidence that the disease could be transmitted infectiously. Moral considerations precluded the possibility of attempting experimental transmission directly on humans. If the monkey experiments failed, Gajdusek and Gibbs would have no way of testing the theory further.

Upon conclusion of the conference, Gibbs flew back home from France. He had barely walked in his front door when a phone call came from the Patuxent Wildlife Center. Something odd was happening with Georgette, one of the chimpanzees.

Gibbs didn't bother to unpack. He drove straight to the laboratory to see for himself.

The Virus that Wasn't There

Georgette was indeed shaking with kuru tremors, and she wasn't alone. Daisy was also showing signs. Both of their faces had taken on the frozen, blank expression that Zigas and Gajdusek had noted as one of the classic symptoms. The similarities to kuru were so striking that at first Gibbs could barely believe what he was seeing.

Over the next several weeks, Gibbs watched as Georgette and Daisy deteriorated. Then Hermann fell sick, and then George. Gajdusek was in Australia, but he made his manic presence felt by phone, issuing a stream of directives for autopsies and examinations. Georgette's brain was flown to England for examination by Dr. Elizabeth Beck, a neuropathologist. Her report confirmed that Georgette's brain showed the same type of microscopic lesions as in brains affected by kuru. Autopsies of the other animals showed identical results. Under the microscope, the brains were so full of holes that they looked like Swiss cheese. The results provided dramatic, unambiguous proof that kuru could be transmitted as an infectious disease.

"Often in science successful experiments cannot be easily reproduced," Zigas said. "Never, however, have experiments succeeded so prettily and so progressively. Our research continued those rare rewards for the researcher whose bane and usual experience is a succession of experiments that are negative, go haywire, or contradict one another. Gajdusek, Gibbs, and Alpers were like happy boys telling each other, 'We have got the virus, we have got it!' "[1]

Epidemiological evidence provided further confirmation. Beginning in the 1950s, the government of New Guinea had used arrests and other actions to discourage the practice of cannibalism. The impact of those measures became evident in the mid-1960s when the number of new kuru cases began to decline. In 1963, kuru had been so widespread that the Fore began to fear extinction. By 1970, the number of cases among children was declining dramatically. New cases were still appearing, but only among older people who had engaged in cannibalism before the practice was outlawed. These cases showed that kuru had an amazingly long incubation period. New cases of the disease would continue to emerge more than *40 years* after the victims had eaten human flesh.

The breakthrough with kuru inspired a series of experimental attempts to prove that other progressive neurological diseases could also be transmitted.

To begin with, what about Creutzfeldt-Jakob Disease, the rare human dementia that produced spongy holes in the brain similar to the holes found in kuru victims? Gajdusek's team began collecting brain tissue from CJD victims and injecting it into monkeys. Once again, the experiments were successful. With CJD, the time from inoculation to onset of symptoms was shorter—12 to 16 months, approximately half the time required with kuru.

Attempts were also made to inoculate primates with tissues from people with a variety of other neurological diseases, including presenile dementia, multiple sclerosis, Alzheimer's and Parkinson's disease. None of the animals exposed to these diseases developed signs of spongiform disease, but some of the animals receiving extracts from Alzheimer's brains showed other types of pathologic changes in their brain tissues. The evidence was inconclusive, but Gajdusek, Gibbs and Alpers continued to suspect some link, noting that brains of Alzheimer's patients showed amyloid plaques similar to the ones that Klatzo had observed in kuru brains.

By the mid-1970s, scientists had identified four conditions which they categorized as "transmissible spongiform encephalopathies" (TSEs) or "scrapie-like diseases." In addition to scrapie, kuru and CJD, a fourth TSE had been observed in herds of commercially-raised mink. Transmissible mink encephalopathy was extremely rare, but when it did appear, a single outbreak could wipe out all of the animals on an entire mink ranch.

Gajdusek's success at identifying the source of kuru brought worldwide renown. At the National Institutes of Health, he continued to direct his Program for the Study of Child Growth and Development and Disease Patterns in Primitive Cultures, and to oversee research into TSEs as director of a program he established called the Laboratory of Slow, Latent and Temperate Virus Infections. Both of these NIH programs operated under the umbrella of the National Institute of Neurological and Communicative Disorders and Stroke, where Gajdusek was appointed chief of the Laboratory of Central Nervous System Studies. "These are titles of fearsome length," commented writer Roger Bingham, in an admiring 1984 profile. "What they boil down to is that Gajdusek is at home in pediatrics, virology, epidemiology, neurology, and anthropology; sits at the hub of what has been called an empire of perhaps two hundred collaborating laboratories worldwide; and has a remarkable way with children." [2]

As a researcher, Gajdusek continued his field trips to exotic cultures. "In fact, hardly a year has passed since his first trip without a return visit to Micronesia or Melanesia," Bingham stated. "When Gajdusek says, 'I have more experience than probably anyone else in the world with Stone Age man,' he has good reason. To the natives, '*Kaoten blong mipella*' (pidgin for 'Carleton belong me fella' or 'Our Carleton') has become something of a legend, a cross between Lord Jim and David Livingstone." [3]

Gajdusek's emotional bond with the children who had helped carry his equipment and served as his translators blossomed into what writer June Goodfield called "a long love affair with the mystery of kuru and its victims." [4] A lifelong bachelor, he built an unconventional family by informally adopting dozens of children from New Guinea and other Micronesian and Melanesian cultures. To smooth the way for their entry into the United States, he provided letters of transit on the prestigious stationery of the National Institutes of Health, stating that he would be responsible for their support during their stay. Eight of the boys stood beside him in Stockholm in 1976, as the King of Sweden awarded his Nobel Prize. The Nobel committee described his research as "an extraordinarily fundamental advance in human neurology and in mammalian biology and microbiology." Gajdusek announced that he planned to use the prize money to pay for education of the children, whom he affectionately described as his "little savages." Much of his $110,000 annual salary also went into supporting them, including paying their college tuitions as they matured.

"Visiting Carleton Gajdusek's house in Washington is like attending a meeting of the United Nations held in the Metropolitan Museum," observed scrapie researcher Gordon Hunter. "In addition to the continual traffic of visiting scientists of all nationalities, he has adopted over the last twenty or thirty years two or three dozen orphan boys from various tribes in the South Seas. You sit down to dine with a boy from the New Guinea Kuku-Kuku just out of the Stone Age on one side of you, a Solomon Islander on the other, and the mathematician who invented Algol opposite. The house is full of artifacts from the South Pacific and elsewhere, on their way to the many museum collections that have been enriched by Carleton's generosity."[5]

As the years passed, Gajdusek put on weight and saw his unkempt black hair turned into unkempt gray hair. These signs of age set him apart physically, but not emotionally, from the children he had come to love. "To me, everything beyond the twenties is 'aged'—and though I am well in the thirties myself, I consider it closer to senility than youth," he had written in a journal entry during the period of his field research into kuru. A few years later he mused that he had "lived in a world of children and of child humor, child fantasy, and child passions for four decades."

As a physician, he had never liked geriatrics. "I would not be a good doctor with old people," he wrote. "I do not make enough concessions to the decline of the human organism . . . to be properly humane with the aged." He found it ironic that his research into kuru had led him into close study of senile dementias like Alzheimer's Disease and CJD, which almost always occurred in patients past the age of 50. "That's a beautiful way of the gods getting even with you," he joked. "A person like me, who, with such great confidence, focuses entirely on childhood, picks a child problem, loads up the hospital with child patients, gets pulled into *geriatrics!*"[6]

Age and scientific celebrity did little to dim Gajdusek's childlike enthusiasms and endless curiosity for exploration. During one of his visits to England, he spent time with Hunter, who recalled "becoming slightly unpopular by declining to drive Carleton down from Newbury to London at six in the morning after we had been up until three o'clock discussing scrapie. He wanted to be at the British Museum in time for its opening at eight o'clock, because the rest of his day included a visit to Keats's house in Hampstead (he was studying the poet Keats at the time), then calling at the Imperial Cancer Research

Fund Laboratories at Lincoln's Inn Fields, then back to Cambridge, finally a visit to Stonehenge, and a flight back to the U.S.A. the following morning."[7]

Other Slow Viruses

Gajdusek's theory that spongiform encephalopathies were caused by "slow virus" infections inspired new research and insights into other diseases. Until then, virology had seemed to be a backwater in scientific research. The major viral infections of the past—smallpox, polio, mumps and measles—had been virtually wiped out as a result of the development of vaccines. Following Gajdusek's success, the field exploded. "We are seeing associations of viruses with cancers, neurological diseases and immune disorders," said Dr. Joseph McCormick of the virology lab at the Centers for Disease Control. In a 1986 interview, he described it as "one of the most exciting areas in science."[8]

Measles, for example, turned out to have a dual personality. Ordinarily, it had an incubation period of one to two weeks, followed by symptoms that ended in less than a week. In rare cases, however, the measles virus survived within the body after the conventional measles attack had run its course. It could lurk undetected in a victim for seven or eight years, and then erupt again as a fatal brain disease called subacute sclerosing panencephalitis (SSPE). A child with SSPE would begin having difficulties in school. Declining mental abilities and loss of coordination would be followed by uncontrollable jerking movements of the limbs and seizures. Following onset of symptoms, the disease would take years to run its course, leaving the patient mindless, mute and helpless by the time death occurred.

Early in the 20th century, the discovery of a virus that causes leukemia in chickens had inspired numerous unsuccessful attempts to find viral links to human cancers. The realization that *slow* viruses might be responsible reopened the inquiry. In 1980, Dr. Robert Gallo at the National Cancer Institute provided concrete evidence for a viral link to cancer when he identified "human T-lymphotrophic virus type 1" (HTLV-1) as a "retrovirus" capable of triggering leukemia by genetically transforming T-cells in the body's immune defense system. A closely related virus called HTLV-2 produced a rare variant called "hairy cell" leukemia. Other researchers found links between the hepatitis-B virus and liver cancer. Traces of the virus that causes venereal warts were identified in victims of cervical cancer. The Epstein-Barr virus, usually associated with mononucleosis, was linked to cancers of the nose and throat and to Burkitt's lymphoma, a rare cancer that primarily strikes children in Kenya and Uganda.

Acquired Immunodeficiency Syndrome (AIDS) became the most notorious slow virus to emerge from this welter of research. First discovered in France by Dr. Luc Montagnier, the virus became the center of controversy and accusations of scientific theft against Robert Gallo at the National Cancer Institute, who claimed in 1984 that he had discovered it independently and that it was a variant of the leukemia viruses. Gallo called the virus HTLV-3, while Montagnier called it "Lymphadenopathy-Associated Virus" (LAV). They resolved the dispute by claiming joint credit for the discovery and adopting the name Human Immunodeficiency Virus (HIV).

Like the leukemia viruses, HIV infects T-cells in the immune system. It is also associated with a rare form of cancer called Kaposi's sarcoma. Researchers have found a variety of closely related viruses in other species: in cows, bovine leukemia and bovine immunodeficiency virus; visna-maedi in sheep (which had been described as a "slow virus" by researchers in Iceland even before Gajdusek appeared on the scene); feline leukemia and feline immunodeficiency virus in cats; and simian immunodeficiency virus in monkeys. Classed as "lentiviruses," they cause immune system failure in their hosts in addition to slow, progressive wasting disorders, brain degeneration and death.

Gajdusek was credited with popularizing the concept of slow viruses, thereby helping scientists to envision the possibility of diseases like AIDS. He participated himself in AIDS research, as well as inspiring others. Jaap Goudsmit, a leading AIDS researcher at the University of Amsterdam, said his experience at Gajdusek's lab had inspired him to undertake research that showed how the virus penetrates the immune system. "Gajdusek taught me to look for exceptional things in your field," Goudsmit said. "AIDS is exceptional in its field." [9]

From his post at NIH, Gajdusek was treated as an elder stateman, a Big Man within the scientific community whose opinions were eagerly sought by others. Harvard Medical School chose its 200th anniversary to present him with an honorary degree. In 1993, he joined an international team of researchers who visited Cuba to investigate an unusual epidemic causing blindness and other neurological disorders. His exploits in New Guinea even inspired a fictional play, a comedy titled *Kuru* in which a doctor loosely modeled after Gajdusek takes a child bride from among the natives to the dismay of his former fiancée, an Iowa cooking instructor. [10]

Eminence did not mean that Gajdusek lacked critics. Some, like scrapie researcher Alan Dickinson, felt that some of his work lacked depth. His kuru studies inspired breakthrough discoveries of other slow viruses, but the kuru virus itself—if it *was* a virus—proved maddeningly elusive. Like scrapie and the other spongiform encephalopathies, kuru victims showed no immune system response and no antibodies that could be used as signals of infection. The brains of kuru victims were clearly infectious, and Gajdusek had *assumed* the cause was a virus, but three decades of research failed to identify the specific agent within the brain that carried the disease.

Even Gajdusek's admirers had questions about some of his conclusions. In *The Enigma of Slow Viruses,* a book published to honor Gajdusek on his 70th birthday, author Pawel Liberski questioned the validity of Gajdusek's slow virus theory. Liberski said he had written the book with the goal of summarizing "almost all existing data on scrapie and related infections, asking . . . whether they fit one complete pattern." After reviewing the research, Liberski concluded that "such a task is not possible." [11]

Gajdusek also came under criticism following publication of his Nobel Prize lecture in *Science* magazine. The article included a photograph of Fore natives seated around a feast, with a caption that implied they were eating a relative. When pressed, Gajdusek admitted they were actually eating roast pork. He had photographs of actual cannibalism, he said, but chose not to publish them because they were too offensive. A leftist anthropologist argued that reports of cannibalism in Africa and the South Sea islands were fabrications, part of the ideology used by imperialism to justify its domination of native cultures by labeling them "barbaric" and "primitive."

Gajdusek found this accusation particularly galling. He felt a deep personal affection for the native peoples among whom he had lived and worked. He had even adopted their children. During the days of his kuru research, Gajdusek had complained about newspaper reports that described the New Guinea Highlanders as "Stone Age cannibals" and referred to kuru as the "laughing disease."

As for the question of whether the Fore had practiced cannibalism, Gajdusek considered the evidence to be so clear as to be above debate. Zigas, in his memoirs, had described personally witnessing an instance of cannibalism, and had spoken with tribal chieftains who readily discussed the practice. Perhaps the most telling proof was the gradual disappearance of kuru after cannibalism was outlawed. "Kuru is gone," Gajdusek told an interviewer. "All you have to do to avoid kuru is be born after they stopped opening up the bodies. You can still live in a house with a sister and mother who are incubating kuru, you can nurse at their breasts, you can eat with them, share food with them, copulate with them, stay and nurse them through their disease until they die . . . and never get kuru." [12]

The link between cannibalism and spongiform encephalopathy was further strengthened by the discovery of a number of cases of accidental medical transmission of Creutzfeldt-Jakob Disease. At least 25 cases had occurred that could be traced to what Gajdusek described as "high-technology cannibalism," in which people acquired the disease when they received transplants or injections of body tissue from other people. These accidental transmissions of CJD led to lawsuits and to changes in medical policies and procedures. [13] But researchers paid no heed to another type of "high-technology cannibalism"—an innovation that was being introduced outside the laboratories and hospitals, in a bloody realm where people performed inhumane acts on nonhuman beings, and where cannibalism on a truly massive scale was not only being practiced but preached as an example of the latest miracle in modern agricultural efficiency and scientific progress.

THE
INTERESTS OF
INDUSTRY

Cannibal Meat

Prior to the discovery of mad cow disease, most people thought that "rendering" was something juries did with verdicts or architects did with drawings. The public at large remained blissfully unaware that something called a "rendering industry" even existed, let alone that it played a crucial role within the larger meat industry. Prior to the 1980s, rendering was rarely mentioned even in the most biting meat-industry exposés, an omission which the industry felt little desire to rectify.

Then, as now, rendering—the practice of converting waste animal parts into marketable products—played an indispensable role within the livestock industry. It served as the least objectionable means available for disposing of the stray body parts and bacteria-laden corpses that are the inevitable byproducts of large-scale animal husbandry. Like any disposal operation, renderers dealt with the gross, putrid stuff that corporations didn't like to advertise and consumers didn't like to hear about.

The silence which shrouded the industry was so total, in fact, that it shocked writer Frank Burnham when he was hired in 1971 to create an industry trade publication called *Render* magazine. "Most appalling," he wrote, "was finding—during a literature search—that not a single book about the rendering industry was available, even in such huge libraries as those maintained by the City of Los Angeles and the University of California." Seven years later, Burnham attempted to address that gap with a book of his own titled *Rendering: The Invisible Industry,* which set out "to inform the general public about its contributions to society and to correct a number of major areas of misinformation . . . an industry that has remained almost invisible for more than 150 years quietly doing its thing on the back streets of America . . . an industry which today contributes more than $2 billion to the GNP."[1]

Burnham's effort notwithstanding, the rendering industry remained largely invisible until the 1990s, when it found itself thrust into public view as a result of its role in the spread of mad cow disease. The publicity tended to either blame the industry for causing the epidemic or to dwell on sensationalistic, gory details about its workings. In September 1995, reporter Van Smith of Baltimore's weekly *City Paper* gave the following account of his visit to Valley Proteins, Inc., a local rendering plant:

> Consider these items: Bozman, the Baltimore City Police Department quarterhorse who died last summer in the line of duty. The grill grease and used frying

oil from Camden yards, the city's summer ethnic festivals, and nearly all Balti-more-area . . . restaurants and hotels. A baby circus elephant who died while in Baltimore this summer. Millions of tons of waste meat and inedible animal parts from the region's supermarkets and slaughterhouses. Carcasses from the Baltimore Zoo. The thousands of dead dogs, cats, raccoons, possums, deer, foxes, snakes and the rest that local animal shelters and road-kill patrols must dispose of each month.

These are the raw materials . . . which are processed into marketable prod-ucts for high profit at the region's only rendering plant. . . . In a gruesomely ironic twist . . . most inedible dead-animal parts, including dead pets, end up in feed used to fatten up future generations of their kind. Others are transmo-grified into paint, car wax, rubber, and industrial lubricants. . . .

During a midsummer day's visit to the plant, I gag upon first contact with the hot, putrescent air. My throat immediately becomes coated with the suety taste of decayed, frying flesh. "You picked a bad day to visit a rendering plant," [plant manager Neil] Gagnon says. . . . "By the time we get [dead horses] they're soup. Summertime is bad around here."

A load of guts, heads and legs, recently retrieved from a local slaughter-house, sits stewing in one of the raw materials bins at the plant's receiving bay. . . . It will be fed into "the hogger," a shredder that grinds up the tissues and filters out trash, before it is deep-fried in cookers charged with spent restau-rant grease and blood. . . . Blood and body fluids leak out from under the trailer gate. . . . Suddenly a hot gust of wind blows droplets of it on our bare legs. As the bloated stomachs and broken body parts slide en masse from the trailer bed to the bin, Bud shouts out, "Watch out for the splatter!" . . .

Following Valley Proteins' route driver Milton McCroy on his rounds is a colorful tour of Baltimore's fat and protein sources. Every Monday, Wednes-day and Friday, McCroy enters the . . . city animal shelter and loads dead ani-mals into his truck. He then continues his rounds to Parks Sausage, the city's lone remaining meat-packing plant, where he picks up waste meat, and to the slaughterhouse in Penn-North, where he loads up with offal, before taking the shipment back . . . and dumping it in the raw materials bin.

[A]t the slaughterhouse . . . he backs the truck up to a storage shed, hauls a bloated sheep carcass onto the lift, and dumps it in the trailer, then starts preparing to empty many barrels full of heads, legs, hides and guts. . . . [T]he plant's owner catches wind that the press has entered the property. . . . He ushers us off to the adjacent sidewalk. . . . "There just is no good publicity for us right now," he explains.[2]

This stomach-churning passage was actually part of a serious, in-depth and fair article. Still, the people who earned their living in the rendering pro-fession were bound to regard this type of publicity as not only unflattering but unfair. They knew the sights and smells of putrefying flesh better than any journalist ever could. After all, they were the people who had to live with those sights and smells on a daily basis. They also knew what would happen if they *weren't* around to do their job. In the words of the old cliché, theirs was a dirty and thankless job, but *someone* had to do it.

The harsh eye of public scrutiny, however, could not be ignored. Ren-derers began to realize that unless they became more aggressive about defin-ing their public image, others would define it for them. In 1996, the industry

A sheep's head and other animal parts await rendering at Valley Proteins, Inc. in Baltimore. *(photo © Michelle Gienow. Used with permission)*

published a replacement for Frank Burnham's book which dropped the term "invisible industry" and instead referred to renderers as *The Original Recyclers*. "The buffalo exemplifies the rendering industry because the American Plains Indian appreciated the value of utilizing the whole animal," argued Dennis Mullane in the introduction. "In the early 1990s it became obvious . . . that we needed to promote our industry. People . . . need to know that we renderers provide safe products, that we are environmentally aware, that we are the original recyclers."[3]

Frank Burnham contributed a chapter to the new book, again emphasizing the theme of environmental responsibility by pointing out that rendering provided an economical way of dealing with huge quantities of material that would otherwise have to be incinerated or dumped into landfills. "In 1992, for instance, . . . thanks to the highly specialized rendering industry another 15 million tons of material never entered the waste stream," he observed. "Diverted before it could be considered waste, this material consists of the unused animal parts from our huge meat and poultry industry—highly perishable material that in a matter of hours can become infested with microbiological pathogens and pose a tremendous health and sanitation problem. The rendering industry, quietly and with little fanfare, has collected this potential waste and converted it into usable, in fact, essential products."[4]

"You can make all types of stories, that it is enough to fill boxcars from Miami to Seattle and back part of the way," said Fred Bisplinghoff of the National Renderers Association (NRA), the industry's U.S. trade and lobby organization. "It is a large volume of material. It is a high moisture-content material that cannot find its way into the landfill. It would be very expensive to think about landfilling the product. The most economical and sensible process is converting it, recycling it. We call ourselves the original recyclers, recycling this material into useful commodities."

According to Bisplinghoff, this practice of converting animal byproducts into animal feed and other commodities was an ancient, time-tested and venerable tradition that "started with the cave man. . . . The Indians—we learned a lot from the Indians about recycling, how we utilize the byproducts from the slaughter of animals. . . . The driving force, again, in animal protein ingredients, vegetable protein ingredients, is to improve the quality so we can continue to have the best agriculture economy in the entire world, so we can grow our chickens faster, better, more efficiently and have lower-cost poultry meat, lower-cost beef, lower-cost pork for the American public than any other country in the world. We have made grand strides."[5]

This description neatly reconciled two contradictory notions about the nature of the rendering industry: first, that it was merely carrying on a time-honored tradition as old as humanity; second, that it represented the latest in scientific progress and innovation. There was some truth in each of these notions, but neither was entirely true. Like most institutions in modern society, the rendering industry was a synthesis of inherited traditions and recent innovations. During the 20th century, it had undergone a particularly dramatic evolution, although each step along the way was so subtle and seemingly minor that it was easy to miss the fact that something new, different and potentially dangerous was developing.

Rendering Since Caesar

Descriptions of rendering go back to the days of the ancient Greeks, and rendered animal products first came into significant use in the manufacture of soap and candles during the Middle Ages. Butchers' fat trimmings were cut into pieces and melted down in pots so that the fats could be skimmed off. Soap was produced by mixing ashes with the fat and heating them to induce a transformation that chemists would later describe as "saponification." Candles were made by dipping the wicks in tallow, a heavier fat which turned solid when cooled. After the fats were skimmed off, the rendering process left behind a residue of meat-derived tissues known as "greaves" or "cracklings" used for feeding dogs and ducks.

The industrial revolution transformed these traditional practices, as scientific methods of production did with agriculture what Henry Ford accomplished with the automobile industry. Small farms, farmers' markets and regional agricultural economies became transformed into a factory farming system dominated by giant transnational corporations. Applications of new technology brought dramatic changes in animal husbandry and farming. The 19th century brought railways and other innovations in mass transportation, coupled with the availability of ice which made it easier to refrigerate and store meat. New economies of scale in particular favored increased production of cattle, which were larger animals and yielded more edible meat than smaller animals such as hogs, sheep or goats.

Exploding production meant a burgeoning disposal problem. "Only about 60 percent of the beef animal produces edible products," Burnham stated. "The hides, bones, entrails, hooves, horns, fat, gristle and tough membranes are, by law, not permitted to be used in food. In other words, 400 or more pounds of a 1,000-pound steer is inedible. Consider also that animal tissue, once the animal is no longer alive, is perhaps one of the world's most perishable substances. As the kill rate rose in the nation's slaughter houses from tens to hundreds, even thousands of animals per week, without the renderer the problem of disposing of these inedible byproducts of the beef industry would have become one of horrendous proportions. . . . Virtually no one is unacquainted with the nuisance, health and disease problems associated with decayed animal flesh. Unless refrigerated and preserved in some manner, animal flesh rapidly putrefies, not only giving off the most sickening and disagreeable of odors but also providing a perfect environment for the development of disease-propagating bacteria and protozoa."[6]

As the scale of the disposal operation expanded, rendering technology also changed. Instead of boiling their raw materials in open kettles, renderers began using autoclaves—metal vessels which were filled with fat, bones and other animal parts, sealed off, and heated under pressure. "As we got more sophisticated over the years, we went to a wet rendering process where all the raw material was added to a closed vessel with water," said Fred Bisplinghoff. "The fat would actually float on the top. The water would be drained and go to the water-treatment facility. . . . The protein product was called tankage. For many years, this tankage was used as a fertilizer. It wasn't until 1912 that Swift and Company in Chicago decided to take the tankage and add some blood meal to it and make a product called digester tankage that was 60% protein and decide, perhaps, it could be used as a food ingredient versus a fertilizer, and fed it to hogs. So they did, and the animals responded remarkably. It was the first instance of feeding hogs something other than garbage and corn. . . . The hogs grew remarkably well, and they won first prize at the International Livestock Show in Chicago in 1914."[7]

World Wars I and II further accelerated the transition from agrarian societies to urbanized life, spurring further expansion and innovations in the rendering business. In England, the need for food self-sufficiency during wartime prompted farmers to feed their cattle with cheap, high-protein sources derived largely from slaughterhouse waste. In the United States, World War II created a huge demand for rendered glycerine, which was used in the manufacture of nitroglycerine explosives. "As with most modern technologies, it took the demands of a major world conflict to really accelerate development," Burnham observed in *Rendering: The Invisible Industry*.

You Eat What You Are

Peace brought the dawn of a new age characterized by ever-more-intensive farming. Innovations pioneered during the war continued, as protein supplements offered an opportunity for accelerating the growth of young calves that was too good to resist. Rendered animal fats, along with meat and bone

meal, were incorporated in ready-made feeds supplied by large-scale manufacturers. They were also available separately by the bag, so that farmers could
add as much as they liked to the feed. "While it took a world war to push the
development of the fatty acid industry and thus to open up new markets for
tallow and animal oils, it took the tremendous world growth in population
stimulating the need for food to provide the forcing factor in the development
of animal nutrition technology," Burnham stated. "Over the years it became
common practice to use this material to feed livestock and poultry."[8]

In 1947, researchers succeeded in accelerating the growth of chickens by
supplementing their rations with meat and bone meal derived from fish, cattle
and from other chickens. "About this time the rendering industry was seeking
new markets," noted Henry Fuller, a scientist at the University of Georgia. "The
concentration of the broiler industry in the Southeast made it feasible for the
rendering industry to collect and process the offal from the poultry processing plants. This introduced new products, including poultry byproduct meal
and feather meal. . . . Dr. O.H.M. Wilder at the American Meat Institute Foundation (1956) was among the first to demonstrate the extent to which meat
and bone meal could be used in broiler rations. . . . The feeding value of poultry byproduct meal for poultry was established in the beginning of the 1950s."[9]

Meanwhile, other changes threatened the rendering industry's traditional
markets. Prior to 1950, more than 70 percent of the fat derived from animal
sources was used in the manufacture of soap. That market disappeared with
the advent of petroleum-based synthetic soaps. "Renderers were forced to seek
new markets for their products," Burnham stated. "The largest market for rendered products was drying up and crash research programs were required to
develop new markets."[10]

In 1962 the rendering industry launched the Fats and Proteins Research
Foundation (FPRF) to stimulate research and development of new end uses
for the industry's products. Dr. Conwell Johnson, FPRF's director of product
development, was an animal nutritionist who focused in particular on promoting the use of feed fats, along with rendered protein supplements derived from
other animal parts, including meat and bone meal, blood meal and feather
meal. "Basically, the feed industry today is our single biggest customer," Johnson said, "and if we aren't familiar with its problems we are going to miss the
mark when it comes to servicing that market."[11]

"During the 1960s, prices for animal fats decreased dramatically, reflecting decreased demand," said FPRF President Gary G. Pearl. "These changes
emphatically illustrated the necessity to find new uses for animal fats. The industry focused on funding research that would broaden its product base. . . . Past
and current projects involve virtually all species, all products produced by the
rendering industry, and all disciplines of use or potential use." Pearl recited
examples of FPRF-sponsored research showing the vast scope of feeding
options pursued: "beef, growing pigs, dairy cattle, broilers, beef calves, cat-
fish, single-cell protein, turkeys, piglets, ruminants, pets, horses, layers, sows,
racehorses, poultry, light growing steers, Western Hemisphere shrimp, growing turkeys, laying hens, nursery pigs, early weaned pigs, segregated early

weaned pigs, feeder pigs, dogs, adult cats, high-temperature horses, salmonid fish, high-producing dairy cows and high-lean pigs."

The success of these research efforts could be measured in the growth of market demand for rendered feed. During the 1960s and early 1970s, fats derived from rendering began to be used extensively as cattle feed. Rendered products also found a market in the pet food industry, which tripled its sales between the years of 1965 and 1974. "When the Foundation was formed, only 300,000 pounds of feeding fat were used by all of animal agriculture," Pearl stated. "The ensuing basic research, followed by applied research and its implementation into practical feed formulations via a dedicated product awareness program, resulted in growth that approaches four billion pounds, its present annual usage in the United States." [12]

The rendering industry's research and marketing programs dovetailed neatly with the livestock industry's own concerns, as competitive market pressures drove the industry to maximize "efficiency," seeking simultaneously to cut costs while accelerating growth rates and increasing yields. Innovations in genetics and artificial insemination created super-producing breeds of cows, pigs and chickens. Synthetic hormones and antibiotics also helped maximize growth and production levels, while drugs helped fend off diseases that might hinder production in growth-stressed animal populations.

Protein Efficiency

In order to reach ever-higher production levels of meat and milk, animals needed to consume optimum levels of carefully-formulated rations. Cattle, which previously had grazed on summer grass and winter hay, were moved indoors. "The feedlot was introduced," Burnham stated. "This essentially consists of force feeding scientifically-blended rations to selected cattle held under controlled conditions, telescoping the time period needed to bring the cattle to marketable weight. Thus, more quality beef can be made available . . . over a given period than is possible when allowed to attain their full growth on range grass." [13]

So far, however, cattle were mostly consuming rendered *fats,* while rendered *proteins* went to feed chickens and pigs. Feedlots achieved faster growth rates by feeding proteins in the form of grains and soybeans. By the 1970s, this practice came to be viewed as costly and wasteful, leading to a search for alternative substances. According to *Consumers Research* food editor Beatrice Trum Hunter, rendered animal parts were only one of the unlikely new materials introduced into the animal feed supply:

> It has taken us from grass and hay feeding to such non-traditional ingredients in animal feed as sewage sludge and treated manure. The search for alternative substances in animal feed suited the new conditions that arose from agricultural changes. . . . A plethora of substances found their way into animal feed. They included agricultural wastes. . . . They included retail food wastes. . . . Slaughterhouses and tanneries provided blood, entrails, hoofs, bristles, and feathers for use in animal feed. Some alternative substances were . . . industrial wastes such as sawdust, wood chips, twigs, and even ground-up newspapers

and cardboard boxes. Others were cement dust from kilns, sludge from municipal composting plants, water from electric generating plants that used fluidized bed combustion of coal, and waste water from nuclear power stations. . . . "The Four Ds"—dead, dying, disabled, and diseased animals . . . moisture-damaged or maggot-infested grains; foods contaminated by rodents, roaches, or bird excreta.[14]

By 1978, more than 2.6 billion pounds of rendered tallow and grease were going into animal and poultry feed, along with *billions of pounds* of meat, bone and feather meals. "The amount of rendered products utilized in livestock and poultry rations continues to grow each year as new research by colleges, universities and independent scientists continues to reveal more and better applications," Burnham wrote happily in a 1979 issue of *Render* magazine.[15]

The industry's enthusiasm for these productivity-enhancing and cost-cutting innovations met few obstacles. "Some have said that with our growing management sophistication and heavy concentration of animals in small areas, there's a danger of some entirely new disease popping up—not unlike the *Andromeda Strain* in science fiction," observed a contributor to the March 1978 *Farm Journal*.[16] But cautionary voices like these were few and went largely unheeded. The benefits seemed to outweigh the risks.

At the beginning of the 1980s, FPRF-funded studies by University of Nebraska researcher Terry Klopfenstein helped the rendering industry to develop and promote the widespread use of rendered animal protein as a feed ration specifically for cattle. The secret to this new market was the "bypass protein effect." Proteins from rendered meat and bone meal tended to withstand digestion in the first stomach chamber, called the rumen, of ruminant animals such as sheep and cows. By escaping degradation in the rumen, bypass proteins could deliver enough proteins to the small intestine to achieve maximum growth and lactation in high-yield dairy animals. "The value of these byproducts for ruminant animals is perhaps the biggest thing that has happened in years," Klopfenstein said. "The secret is that the amount of protein in the ration that bypasses the first stomach . . . varies with the kind of protein fed, and the more that bypasses the better." [17] By the mid-1980s, the bypass protein concept had begun to win wide acceptance. "Feeding of meat and bone meal to U.S. dairy cattle became significant after 1987, and reached its highest level in 1989 and 1990," noted the USDA in 1991.[18]

The practice of feeding animal protein to cattle rose in importance at the same time that another technological innovation made it possible to render larger quantities of material at lower temperatures. The old system of cooking in autoclaves was known as "batch cooking." Renderers would dump in a batch of material, heat it until thoroughly cooked, then empty out the finished product and start over again with a new batch. In the 1960s, a rendering company in Los Angeles pioneered a "continuous" cooking process. Several systems were developed, but the basic idea was similar in all cases. A continuous cooker was basically a long cylinder into which raw materials could be continuously added at one end, while cooked materials emerged from the other. Paddles or screw conveyors kept the materials moving through the cooker at a

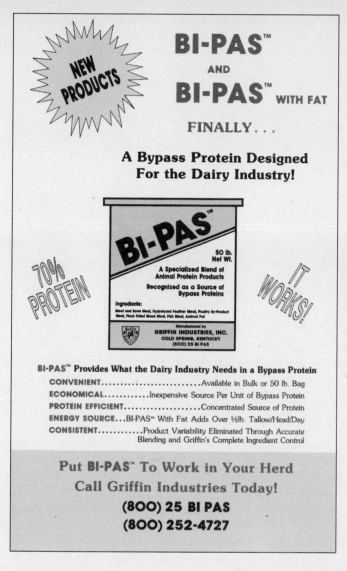

This 1990s promotional flyer, circulated at the World Dairy Expo, touted animal byproducts as a source of "bypass protein" for dairy cows.

controlled rate. Among its other advantages, this system made it easier to heat everything more or less equally, enabling rendering to take place at lower temperatures. It was more energy-efficient, and lower temperatures meant that more animal proteins would survive the rendering process without degrading, resulting in what the industry considered a "higher-quality product." The older batch cookers remained in significant use into the 1980s, but continuous cookers increasingly became the standard.[19]

Downwinders

None of these technological advances changed the fact that rendering "was a dirty and foul-smelling business," as Frank Burnham acknowledged in *The Invisible Industry*. "It wasn't a job for men with weak stomachs. It wasn't pleasant for those whose station in life caused them to live downwind of a rendering plant. In fact, it was this olfactory visibility which caused the renderer to quietly go about his business shunning public attention and actively seeking anonymity. . . . In locating his plant, the renderer usually had to strike a happy medium—be as far away from the rest of the community as possible and still keep his lines of supply as short as possible. At the very least, the rendering plant always ended up on the 'wrong side of the tracks.' " [20]

Being on the "wrong side of the tracks," of course, was a euphemism for being located in a low-income or minority community. Rendering plants also tended to draw many of their employees from low-income or minority sectors, including immigrant laborers—people whose "station in life" obliged them to earn a living working in surroundings that combined the unique charms of the slaughterhouse and the sewer. Heat and humidity created health problems including exhaustion, muscle cramps, fainting and rashes. Hazardous chemicals used in rendering included sulfuric acid, potassium permanganate, liquid chlorine, sodium hypochlorite, lime, formaldehyde, phosphoric and acetic acids, and lye. In the 1980s, worker safety concerns prompted changes in the rendering process which eliminated the use of hydrocarbon solvents to extract fat from meat and bone meal. Ironically, this change in the rendering process, combined with the lower temperatures used in continuous cookers, is now thought to have contributed to the mad cow epidemic by making it easier for the infectious agent to survive the rendering process.

Safety problems inside the plant were exacerbated by the fact that aerosolized fat mists tended to accumulate on every surface—walls, flooring, stairs, walkways—creating inevitable problems with employee slips and falls. "Fire can be a major hazard in rendering plants," noted a 1976 safety manual published by the U.S. Department of Health, Education and Welfare. "Some wooden buildings have become so fat-saturated through the years that they can ignite like tinder." Indeed, three separate rendering plants were destroyed by fire during 1973 alone. [21]

Foul odors were the major problem generating complaints from people who lived outside the plant walls. Renderers attempted to minimize the problem by using air scrubbers, even though the scrubbers used chemicals which presented another safety risk to employees. There was no scientific way of measuring odors, so renderers used a "Scentometer"—a "small rectangular chamber that contains two sniffing tubes for insertion into the nostrils." Using the tubes, a plant manager could inhale filtered, theoretically odor-free air to get a sense of how it compared with "ambient air odors." [22]

This measurement system was highly subjective and did little to answer community concerns. Complaints continued, prompting a psycho-sociological analysis from food-industry consultant James Cox, who explained that complainers simply lacked the "proper attitude. . . . Odor problems often are misleading. There are many cases where a slight odor problem is attended by drastic measures against a processor by authorities, media and public outcry. At the root of this situation is often found what we have termed the 'hypermotivated complainant,' or HMC. This complainer may be reacting abnormally.

. . . This form of Parkinsonian madness often yields complaints from otherwise uncomplaining individuals. . . . The complaints of the HMC may in turn generate additional complaints by relatives, friends, business dependents, or by just plain suggestion." [23]

Rendered products also had a bad rap among many farmers. "Meat and bone meal has had a nasty reputation for a long time because of the issue of salmonella and whether it is a source," said Ric Grummer, a professor of dairy science at the University of Wisconsin. [24] The industry admitted that rendered feeds carried detectable levels of salmonella and other disease organisms, notwithstanding all efforts at disinfection. "Animal proteins have been identified as having the highest incidence level of most feed ingredients," admitted the NRA's Fred Bisplinghoff, although he argued that the amounts fed were too small to cause a problem. "There is no direct link between between the outbreaks of Salmonellosis in dairy cattle and meat and bone meal," he insisted.[25]

The salmonella issue illustrated one of the ways that rendering had changed over the years. Originally, it was a small-scale activity carried on by frugal farmers and local butchers. Over the course of a century, capitalism and industrialization concentrated these activities in mechanized factories where thousands of tons of waste animal parts were dumped by the truckload to be ground together and blended in huge cooking machines. Rendering plants had become central collection points for any diseases or persistent toxins that these animals carried. Infected tissue from a single animal had the potential to mingle with tissues from thousands of others, and then to be distributed widely in feeds.

The transmissible spongiform encephalopathies were naturally rare, but when large quantities of animal tissue are pooled, even a rare disease can pose significant dangers—particularly a disease which is resistant to most normal disinfection procedures. This fact came to light in a particularly poignant way in 1985 when three unusual deaths from Creutzfeldt-Jakob Disease came to the attention of authorities in the United States. All three cases were people who had been treated in their youth with human growth hormone derived from the bodies of dead people. Worldwide, 30,000 people had received the hormone, which was extracted from pituitary glands harvested from 1.4 million human cadavers. "Retrospective evaluation indicates a high likelihood that a batch of between 5,000 and 20,000 cadaveric pituitary glands would include at least one gland from a patient dying of CJD," concluded CJD expert Paul Brown. The hormone treatments, therefore, had multiplied patients' risk of contracting the disease. The three cases detected in 1985 turned out to be only the beginning. Following dozens of additional deaths worldwide, researchers concluded that hormone recipients' risk of dying from CJD had risen from one in a million to one in a hundred.[26]

If these human deaths had surfaced sooner, they might have given someone pause to reconsider the risk involved with cooking up huge batches of dead animals and then feeding them back to their own species. In all likelihood, however, the risk would have been dismissed by industry analysts as inconsequential. After all, sheep were the only meat animals known to suffer from a transmissible spongiform encephalopathy, and there appeared to be no measurable correlation between the incidence of scrapie and CJD rates in humans. No one had seriously considered the possibility that cattle might develop their own TSE, or that cannibalistic feeding practices could cause such a hypothetical disease to explode out of control.

Besides, the industry had other worries. When it came to food safety, the TSEs seemed like the *least* of their concerns.

Acceptable Risks

Everything we do in life involves some kind of gamble, as the pundits who work for government and industry never tire of reminding us. If you drive a car, there's a certain statistical probability that you will die in a traffic accident. If you stay at home, you might die in a fire or at the hands of a burglar. You can get zapped with lightning, flattened with a meteor, eaten by bears, crushed in an earthquake, or asphyxiated by invisible deadly gases. You can die from failing to eat the right foods, or from eating the wrong ones. The news carries endless, often contradictory warnings about toxic chemicals, carcinogens and other hidden dangers that lurk in mushrooms, apple cider, tea, and even mother's milk. While the general public struggles to cope with this bewildering barrage of conflicting advice, representatives of government and industry struggle to persuade consumers that the risks occurring under *their* watch are "minimal" and "acceptable."

The problem is finding a definition of "acceptable" that everyone can agree upon. "Risk analysis is a subtle discipline," observes mathematics professor Ian Stewart. "It is an elaborate and rather naive procedure, that can be abused in several ways. One abuse is to exaggerate benefits and tone down risks. A particularly nasty kind occurs when one group takes the risk but a different group reaps the benefit."[1] The political realities of power, politics and vested interests therefore lurk beneath the seemingly objective language of "balancing risks against benefits." The question of which risks are acceptable depends ultimately on where the person passing judgment stands in relation to those risks. Take, for example, the case of Alvin Biscoe.

On September 27, 1979, bank robbers stole $3,000 from a savings-and-loan office in Arlington, Virginia. An alarm was triggered as they fled, and a lookout was posted for a green Dodge Dart. Officer Michael Kyle, a 10-year veteran of the Arlington police force, spotted a vehicle matching that description on Route 50, heading toward Washington, DC. A chase ensued, with the robbers firing shots in Kyle's direction as he followed them in close pursuit, lights flashing and siren sounding, across the Theodore Roosevelt Bridge and through the E Street tunnel leading to the heart of downtown Washington. Kyle radioed for help, and city police officers joined in the chase, which reached speeds of 80 miles per hour in a posted 25-mile zone.

At the corner of 19th and E Streets, the green car attempted to run a red light, colliding with a south-bound car. The robbers' car ricocheted off the other vehicle, spun out of control and slammed into a man standing at the corner, pinning him against a lamppost. Still spinning, the green car rammed two other parked vehicles and then came to a halt.

The man they had hit was Alvin Biscoe, a 47-year-old economist and associate vice president of the University of Tennessee. Miraculously, hundreds of other noontime bystanders escaped unscathed. Quick action by others probably saved Biscoe from bleeding to death on the spot. The impact had completely severed one of his legs; the other was crushed so badly that it would have to be amputated four days later. As he lay on the sidewalk, surrounded by broken glass and smashed fenders, a security guard from a nearby building ran to the scene and used his belt for a tourniquet to stop the bleeding until paramedics arrived and he could be helicoptered to surgery.

After six months of painful recovery and physical therapy, Biscoe filed a lawsuit charging that the police chase had unnecessarily and recklessly violated public safety.

In their defense, the police argued that the risks they had taken were acceptable and necessary. According to Arlington attorney William Dolan III, Officer Kyle had acted reasonably in trying to protect himself and the public "against bank robbers who would shoot police officers in a minute."[2]

Biscoe's attorneys argued differently, as did consumer advocate Ralph Nader, who commented on the case by citing a study which showed that 500 innocent bystanders died each year during police-led hot pursuits of criminals. "You're unleashing a missile when you let a policeman drive above the speed limit, yet no one does anything about it," Nader said. "Without public pressure, there is no reason for police department to change their policies."[3] The jury ruled in Biscoe's favor. After appealing unsuccessfully all the way to the Supreme Court, Arlington County paid damages of $5 million—the largest award ever granted to a hot pursuit victim in the United States.

From Al Biscoe's point of view, the moral of the story was that human safety was more important than money. "In my case, the thieves had stolen $3,000, and let me tell you, $3,000 does not replace my legs," he said. "I hope this verdict is loud and clear—that the duty of a police department is to protect the public first and catch criminals secondly."[4]

If matters had ended there, Biscoe's ordeal might have simply become another cautionary tale told by attorneys, police trainers and consumer advocates. Ironically, however, his court settlement seems to have helped finance a business partnership which is helping corporate America to engage in reckless endangerment of the public on a far larger scale than the Arlington County police could ever have contemplated. Victim-crusader Al Biscoe became the middle name on the door of the notorious Washington, DC firm of Mongoven, Biscoe and Duchin (MBD for short).

MBD calls itself a "public affairs firm," but it specializes in helping corporations compile dossiers on their enemies. Its promotional brochure boasts of maintaining "extensive files on organizations and their leadership," particularly "environmental and consumer groups, churches and other organizations which seek changes in public policy" regarding issues including "acid rain, clean air, clean water, hazardous and toxic wastes, nuclear energy, recycling, South Africa, the United Nations, developments in Eastern Europe, dioxin, organic farming, pesticides, biotechnology, vegetarianism, consumer groups, product safety, endangered species, oil spills."[5] Clients have included the tobacco industry, oil companies, chemical manufacturers, the National Pork Producers Council, and the National Cattlemen's Beef Association. The bond with NCBA is strengthened by the fact that MBD partner Ronald Duchin raises cattle himself. Also, the Cattlemen have found that they share common ground with MBD's other clients on a surprising range of issues.

The Infant Formula War

MBD company president Jack Mongoven is a hardened veteran of past food wars, beginning in the early 1980s when he helped the Nestlé corporation cope with a massive protest against Nestlé's infant formula marketing practices in the Third World. Nestlé was the world's largest seller of infant formula, which provided a profitable outlet for surplus milk produced in Europe and the United States. Using advertisements, brochures, and free product samples distributed in hospitals, Nestlé and other multinational corporations had successfully persuaded some 50 percent of Third World mothers to switch from breastfeeding to formula use. The advertisements argued that use of store-bought infant formula was supported by medical experts, that it was more "scientific," that it was healthier for babies, and that mothers who cared about their children would use modern formula instead of the "old-fashioned" breast method.

What the propaganda failed to mention was that powdered infant formula could be fatal to children when used in the Third World, where people often lacked the clean drinking water needed to dilute it, let alone facilities to sterilize feeding utensils. Cecily Williams, a pediatric physician in Africa, was one of the first to identify the problematic nature of the practice. After "seeing day after day this massacre of the infants by unsuitable feeding," she stated bluntly that "misguided propaganda on infant feeding should be punished as the most criminal form of sedition, and that these deaths should be regarded as murder."[6]

Nestlé responded with a broadside accusing its critics of "an indirect attack on the free world's economic system."[7] As vice-president of the Nestlé Coordination Center for Nutrition (NCCN), Jack Mongoven began collecting files on the activities of the various churches, student groups, trade unions, women's organizations and health workers who had joined a boycott of Nestlé products. The strategy behind this surveillance, according to NCCN president Rafael Pagan, was "to separate the fanatic activist leaders—people who deny that wealth-creating institutions have any legitimate role to play in helping the Third World to develop—from the overwhelming majority of their followers."[8]

This notion that critics were simply dupes of "fanatic activists" served as the prototype for Mongoven, Biscoe & Duchin's subsequent work for other corporate and food-industry clients. In the 1980s, MBD conducted similar surveillance for the Monsanto Company aimed at identifying "radical" critics of the company's genetically-engineered bovine growth hormone. In the 1990s, it developed PR plans for chemical and meat-industry clients anxious to counter the work of consumer and environmental groups that were raising concerns about the harmful effects of dioxin and other chlorine-based chemicals.

The dioxin debate intensified when the U.S. Environnmental Protection Agency undertook a risk reassessment of mounting evidence linking dioxin to long-term health problems. "EPA's study indicated that there is no safe level of dioxin exposure and that any dose no matter how low can result in health damage," admitted a 1994 MBD advisory to the Chlorine Chemistry Council. "New findings on the mechanism of dioxin toxicity show that tiny doses of dioxin disrupt the action of the body's natural hormones and other biochemicals, leading to complex and severe effects including cancer, feminization of males and reduced sperm counts, endometriosis and reproductive impairment in females, birth defects, impaired intellectual development in children, and impaired immune defense against infectious disease. . . . Further, dioxin is so persistent that even small releases build up over time in the environment and in the human body."[9]

Dioxin also accumulates in nonhuman animal tissues, including cattle. In fact, EPA's study showed that consumption of beef and milk products accounted for more than three-fourths of human daily exposure to dioxin-like compounds. Most of the remaining exposure came from consumption of other meats—chicken, pork and fish. The meat industry responded to this information in typical fashion—by forming an alliance aimed at preventing recognition of the dangers associated with its products.

"The National Cattlemen's Association (NCA)* is coordinating a group of affected industries to respond to the EPA's report on the reassessment of dioxin," reported the MBD advisory. "The group—called the Dioxin Working Group—currently includes the National Milk Producers Federation, American Society of Animal Science, National Broiler Council, National Turkey Federation, International Dairy Foods Association, American Sheep Industry, National Pork Producers Council, American Meat Institute, National Renderers Association, American Farm Bureau Federation and the National Food Processors Association. . . . The industry groups have met with United States Department of Agriculture (USDA)/Animal Research Service and Food Safety and Inspection Service to discuss USDA's plans for looking at levels of dioxin in cattle. . . . The Dioxin Working Group also is talking to hill staffers about its view of the report and it has met with other groups that are affected by the report, such as [the Chemical Manufacturers Association] and the Incinerator Industry to ascertain what each is doing and what messages they are sending out. At this time, the dioxin source industry groups are concentrating on questioning the toxicology data the report relies on. . . . NCA and its allies in the working group have a history of strong relations with the Agriculture depart-

---

* In 1994 the National Cattlemen's Association (NCA) merged with the National Live Stock and Meat Board, becoming the National Cattlemen's Beef Association (NCBA).

ment, and it's certain they will use these solid ties to put pressure on EPA through Agriculture." [10]

Thanks to a corporate whistleblower, details of MBD's work on the chlorine issue were leaked to the environmental group Greenpeace. The documents revealed a cynical disregard for human health that stunned even jaded political activists. In one memo, Mongoven complained that environmentalists were using "the issue of fertility as a vehicle to play on the emotions of the public and its concern for future generations. . . . Anti-chlorine activists are also using children and their need for protection to compel stricter regulation of toxic substances. This tactic is very effective because children-based appeals touch the public's protective nature for a vulnerable group. . . . For most substances, the tolerances of babies and children, which includes fetal development, are obviously much lower than in the general adult population. Thus, 'environmental policies based on health standards that address the special needs of children' would reduce all exposure standards to the lowest possible levels." [11]

Most *sane* human beings, of course, would regard "concern for future generations" and "the special needs of children" as something more than emotional claptrap. By the 1990s, however, corporate propaganda had become a sieve designed to effectively filter out these concerns. In their campaigns against environmentalists and consumer groups, corporations and their public relations consultants had created a mythology so pervasive that they believed it themselves. According to the myth, industry was an innocent, hapless giant under attack from innumerable evil Lilliputians known as "activists"—manipulative fearmongers out to destroy the free enterprise system and civilization as we know it. In a 1991 speech to the National Cattlemen, MBD's Ronald Duchin thundered against "radicals" who "want to change the system; have underlying socio/political motives" and see multinational corporations as "inherently evil. . . . These organizations do not trust the . . . federal, state and local governments to protect them and to safeguard the environment. They believe, rather, that individuals and local groups should have direct power over industry." [12]

Throwing Precaution to the Wind

In MBD's worldview, conflicts between industry and activists boiled down to a stark struggle between rationality versus emotion, science versus superstition, good versus evil. At the center of this great divide stood a philosophical concept that Mongoven called "the precautionary principle." To win its war against activists, industry needed "to mobilize science against the precautionary principle. . . . The industry must identify the implications posed by the 'precautionary principle' and assist the public in understanding the damage it inflicts on the role of science in modern development and production." [13]

"The precautionary principle holds that a manufacturer must prove that its product does no harm, before it can be marketed," Mongoven wrote in the March 1995 issue of *Eco-logic*, an anti-environmentalist newsletter. "Activists want to use this weapon to control the behavior of other Americans . . . [to] revolutionize American thinking about regulation, constitutional law, and government's role in society." [14]

To the general public, the precautionary principle sounded like the essence of common sense: "better safe than sorry" or "look before you leap." Many members of the public, in fact, assumed that this principle was already the legal standard used to define the acceptable bounds of corporate behavior. In the real world, however, there were no clear boundaries separating acceptable and unacceptable risks. Standards for safety were fluid and ever-changing in response to public moods, evolving scientific knowledge, business requirements, and the unpredictable new risks that came with every innovation in technology and social behavior.

For corporate leaders, the precautionary principle was indeed a revolutionary concept. It was threatening precisely *because* it sounded so much like simple common sense. The principle was hard to argue against, and every time it was invoked, it had the potential to add new restrictions and expenses that threatened profit margins. Worse yet, the precautionary principle was unpredictable. Industries knew that they had to respond to *proven* risks, but feared the chaos and uncertainty implied by the idea that they should be forced to minimize risks for which the scientific evidence was still inconclusive. "The average American is ignorant of science and the scientific method," Mongoven complained, calling for "a national risk-assessment policy based on sound science. . . . If industry does not participate in the process and ensure that logic and sound science prevail, it will have to live with the consequences, including the kind of fuzzy thinking which brought us the likes of the Precautionary Principle." [15]

Meat Under the Microscope

These railings appealed to the meat industry for the same reason that similar ideas appealed to the tobacco industry in the 1950s. The rhetoric about sticking to "sound" science was actually a defensive posture in response to mounting scientific evidence against the safety of their product. Once hailed as all-star foods of champions, meat and dairy products were increasingly linked to diseases that ranged from bacterial infections to cancer, heart disease and other chronic problems.

Meat has been a common element in human diets for thousands of years, but for most of recorded history it has been a luxury item, available primarily to the upper classes and only in limited quantities to the rest of the population. In the United States and other affluent countries, the advance of scientific production techniques made meat commonly available at the same time that nutrition scientists were becoming more aware of the role that various foods played in supplying the body's needs. At the beginning of the 20th century, their research focused on alleviating nutritional *deficiencies*. Heart attacks and strokes were luxuries that few people lived long enough to experience, but deficiencies in vitamins and other nutrients caused diseases that crippled and killed. Tens of thousands of people in the United States developed pellagra, a disease caused by unsufficient niacin in the diet. Economists at the U.S. Department of Agriculture developed a food guide called the "Basic Seven." By choosing foods from each of the seven food groups, people could ensure that they received all the nutrients they needed. In 1956, the USDA pared the list down to a "Basic Four" consisting of (1) dairy, (2) meat, (3) fruits and vegetables, and (4) breads and cereals. The Basic Four met with enthusiastic support from farmers and the food industry—particularly from the National Dairy Council, which used the USDA's recommendations in scores of free nutrition educational materials distributed to schools and health programs.

Meat was indeed a rich source of protein and other nutrients, but by the 1950s nutritionists were beginning to realize that too much of a good thing could also be a problem. Fat is a nutrient, for example, but Americans were consuming way too much of it—particularly the saturated fats found at high levels in red meat. In 1958, two years after the introduction of the Basic Four, a private group called the National Health Education Committee issued the first scientific statement favoring dietary changes to prevent heart disease. Its signers included eight prominent physicians and 106 members of the American Society for the Study of Arteriosclerosis. Three years later, the American Heart Association recommended that people reduce consumption of saturated fats in order to achieve "a reduction in blood cholesterol" which "may lessen the development or extension of atherosclerosis and hence the risk of heart attacks or strokes." By the late 1960s, the World Health Organization had come to the same conclusion, as had the National Heart, Lung and Blood Institute and the White House Conference on Food, Nutrition and Health. In 1979, the U.S. Surgeon General joined the growing consensus, which by then had won the support of more than 80 percent of the world's leading heart experts.[16]

Health experts were not calling for outright vegetarianism, but meat and dairy products were major sources of saturated fat, and the evidence pointed clearly in favor of at least *reducing* meat intake. The evidence linking fat to heart disease was followed, a few years later, by evidence linking dietary fat to cancers of the breast, colon, ovary, uterus, prostate gland and pancreas. By 1977, the evidence had already become strong enough to prompt a report by the Senate Select Committee on Nutrition, titled *Dietary Goals for the United States*, which flatly advised the public to "decrease consumption of meat." Intense lobbying by the meat and dairy industries managed to change the wording in the final document to "Choose meats, poultry and fish which will reduce saturated fat intake."[17]

Even that hedged language failed to appease the meat lobby. "If all Americans were to adopt *Dietary Goals,* beef and other red meat consumption would be reduced by approximately 48%," complained a typical 1980s farmers' textbook, titled *Beef Production and the Beef Industry,* which warned of "a different consumer environment emerging. Beef producers have been challenged by consumer boycotts, rising production costs, the environmentalist movement, the consumer-oriented movement, competition from meat analogs, limited dollars going into needed research projects, potential health problems, and no doubt several others."[18]

Using reasoning similar to Jack Mongoven's rhetoric against the precautionary principle, *Beef Production and the Beef Industry* argued strenuously against the need for consumers to reduce their meat consumption. "Evidence supporting the proposed cholesterol-heart disease relationship is still theory," it stated. "There have been research reports linking meat consumption to cancer of the colon. Also, it has been reported that frying hamburgers too long at temperatures above 300°F may produce carcinogenic substances. Cause and effect relationships have not been clearly identified. One physician recently remarked, 'The evidence is very lean and shaky to say that meat causes cancer. It is preposterous to advocate dietary changes as preventive measures.' . . . There are claims that using antibiotics in cattle is dangerous to human health because microorganisms, exposed to antibiotics, can develop resistant strains. . . . There is no conclusive evidence that these antibiotic resistant strains can be easily transferred from livestock to man." [19]

Good Science vs. Bad Science

Accustomed to viewing science as an ally in their production and marketing efforts, meat producers now found themselves torn between what they considered "good" science and "bad" science. "Good" science had given them the Basic Four Food Groups and techniques for feeding and medicating their animals. "Bad" science, on the other hand, had become what one industry news release called "a launching pad for a new generation of food faddism and quackery." The National Live Stock and Meat Board, a leading industry lobby group, circulated brochures, pamphlets and position papers denouncing the warnings of doctors and scientists as "highly questionable" and "patent nonsense." For the farmers and other industry members who depended heavily on these pronouncements, time and science might as well have stopped in the 1950s. "To anyone who relied on the Meat Board for information, it looked like the American Heart Association had a few maniacs running its show while the vast majority of scientists thought the diet-heart connection was hopelessly off-base," observed Patricia Hausman of the Center for Science in the Public Interest. [20]

In addition to health concerns, the meat industry faced criticisms from vegetarians, animal rights activists and environmental groups. The first indication that these issues might become real problems for the industry came with the 1970 publication of Francis Moore Lappé's book, *Diet for a Small Planet,* which talked of the "incredible level of protein waste built into the American meat-centered diet" and raised questions about the tie between America's rich diet and hunger elsewhere in the world. Lappé also persuasively refuted industry arguments that meat-based protein was better than vegetarian sources. At first, the industry dismissed her book as food faddism, but it sold more than a million copies, marking the beginning of a new awareness of the links between diet, health and planetary ecology.

The decade of the eighties saw a dramatic increase in the number of vegetarians in the United States, up from 9 million to 15 million people. [21] In the same decade, membership in the Humane Society of the United States grew from 160,000 to 963,000. Baskin-Robbins ice cream heir John Robbins defected from the meat-and-dairy camp to write *Diet for a New America,* which advocated a vegetarian diet for moral, environmental and health reasons. The

National Cattlemen's Association responded by paying $25,000 to have scientists at Texas A&M University attempt a detailed rebuttal of Robbins' book and spent $100,000 for full-page ads in the *New York Times* and *USA Today* on Earth Day weekend to convince readers that "Every Day is Earth Day for American Cattlemen." [22] Industry PR efforts, however, suffered embarrassing setbacks when actor James Garner, hired to represent the National Cattlemen, suffered a heart attack and had to undergo quadruple bypass surgery. Garner's replacement, Cybill Shepherd, also had to be terminated after disclosing to a fashion magazine that one of her beauty tips was not eating meat.

By the late 1980s, the meat industry was clearly in a defensive, backlash mood. "There's a void in social movements right now," complained Steve Kopperud, executive director of the Washington, DC-based Animal Industry Foundation. "We've gone through women's issues, racial issues and abortion, and animal rights is the latest issue to be picked up as a movement." [23] According to Kopperud, *none* of the criticisms made against his industry had any basis in fact whatsoever. "In more than twenty speeches given in the last year, I have never said some of their points may be valid, because, in fact, I have yet to hear one that is," he stated in 1988. "Whatever the accusation, be it cruelty to animals, endangerment of human health, or destruction of the family farm by monolithic agribusiness, I have yet to see an animal rights group use science, statistics or an acknowledged expert on farm practices to make its point. The movement traffics in emotionalism, propaganda and scare tactics to win converts." [24]

The health risks associated with mad cow disease had not yet appeared on the public viewfinder. The issues involved in assessing the risk from bovine spongiform encephalopathy were far more scientifically complex than those associated with saturated fats or E. coli or even dioxin, but they would be discussed in an atmosphere of polarization and hostility shaped by past debates over food safety. As the issues gradually came into focus and the risks became evident, the beef industry would react once again with disbelief, denial and outrage against critics whom it considered practitioners of emotionalism, sensationalism and "junk science."

DANGER
SIGNS

Dick Marsh at work in the veterinary research facility of the University of Wisconsin–Madison. *(photo © Eric Tadsen Photography. Used with permission.)*

Outbreak in America's Dairyland

Richard Marsh was in many ways the opposite of Carleton Gajdusek, the brash eccentric who stirred up controversy everywhere he went. By contrast, Marsh was a mild-mannered, unassuming midwesterner, the sort of person you probably wouldn't notice in a crowd. He had worked on the transmissible spongiform encephalopathies since the 1960s, but had never garnered the type of accolades that adhered to Gajdusek. He was a worker bee within the scientific hive, steadily scoring progress and accumulating data without inventing any grand new theories or otherwise drawing attention to himself.

Marsh worked as a research veterinarian at the University of Wisconsin–Madison. In the 1960s, Madison was known as a hotbed of student radicalism. During the Vietnam War, the city literally became an armed camp, with the state government sending in rifle-wielding National Guardsmen to control the rebellion. Protesters broke so many windows that shopkeepers stopped replacing them, putting up permanent plywood panels where the glass had been. In August 1970, the university was shaken by the infamous "Sterling Hall bombing"—a massive fertilizer bomb, planted by a small group of radicals, which killed a graduate student and destroyed the building housing a math center engaged in contract research for the U.S. Army. Confrontations between students and police became so violent that they were featured in a documentary film titled "The War at Home."

Marsh didn't get involved in the protests, and fortunately nobody ever tried to bomb the veterinary research center. Agricultural research was the other face of the UW–Madison, the part that didn't usually generate passions or grab headlines. The ag department stayed out of the "war at home" and continued doing what it had done since the days of the university's first founding—serving as a resource for area farmers, studying and developing mundane but quietly revolutionary techniques of pest management, fertilizer application, irrigation, crop rotation, animal insemination and disease control. Wisconsin was a dairy state, and the UW–Madison was known especially for its contributions in the field of bovine management, but Marsh didn't study cows. Ever since his days as a graduate student under Professor Robert Hanson, he had worked on one of the most obscure of all animal diseases: transmissible mink encephalopathy, or TME.

The United States accounted for about a third of the world's total mink production, and Wisconsin happened to be the largest producer of commercially-raised mink pelts in the country, a legacy of the fur trappers who were the state's first European settlers. Like other indigenous animals, wild mink had seen their numbers dramatically reduced by hunting and other encroachments of the human population. By the middle of the 20th century, trapping and hunting accounted for less than 10 percent of the mink furs sold, with the remaining 90 percent raised on farms.

The change to commercial ranching also meant a change in diet. In the wild, mink were enthusiastic hunters, eating muskrats, fish, frogs and birds. In captivity, they ate leftovers from the human food chain—meat that was considered unsuitable for consumption by people. Early mink ranchers fed their animals with materials picked up at fish processing plants and slaughterhouses. Later, the development of the rendering industry produced fish and poultry meals and other animal byproducts, available in granules or dry food pellets that ranchers found easier to store, transport and ration. Some mink ranchers preferred to use dead stock animals from neighboring farms, particularly cattle which had died from a variety of causes and were deemed unfit for human consumption. Trapped in this unnatural food chain, commercially-raised mink became a sentinel species. Like coal-mine canaries, they tended to be among the first victims and indicators of toxic substances and diseases in the environment. Mink were the first species to reveal the harmful effects of PCBs on animal reproduction. From cattle, they picked up diseases including anthrax, botulism, black leg, brucellosis and tuberculosis.[1]

Given Wisconsin's concentration of mink, it was hardly surprising that the first known outbreak of transmissible mink encephalopathy originated in the state, striking in 1947 and killing every single mink on the affected ranch. At a ranch in Minnesota, the 1947 outbreak also killed 125 animals, all of which had been acquired seven months earlier from the Wisconsin ranch.

TME followed a clinical progression with obvious parallels to scrapie and kuru, with death usually occurring two to seven weeks after the first symptoms appeared. In the early stages, the mink became restless and aggressive, startled easily at loud noises, and made frenzied attempts to attack anything that came near their cages. They became careless about defecating and ate less. After awhile, they began to show signs of unsteadiness in their hind quarters, falling down repeatedly. Eventually the hyperexcitability faded and they began to seem drowsy, resting frequently with their heads down. Their faces took on a fixed, frozen expression. Their bodies would occasionally convulse with tremors or shivering. Some animals circled continually in their cages. Their vision deteriorated, progressing to almost complete blindness.

As the disease advanced, sick animals would lose control of their hind quarters and would have to use their front legs to drag themselves along on their abdomen. Eventually, the front legs would fail also. They would become increasingly unkempt and malnourished from lack of eating. In advanced stages of the disease, the mink would compulsively bite at themselves or at nearby objects. Sometimes they would bite at their own flanks or tails with sufficient ferocity to cause self-mutilation or death. They would slide into an increasingly stuporous state and would eventually be found dead one day, often with their teeth firmly clamped onto the wire mesh of their cages.[2]

Following the 1947 outbreak, the disease did not occur again for 14 years. Then, in 1961, it struck five ranches in Wisconsin, killing between 10 percent and 30 percent of the animals on each ranch. Other incidents occurred in 1963, this time on a single ranch in Idaho, a ranch in Canada, and two more in Wisconsin. Scientists Dieter Burger and G.R. Hartsough, two colleagues of Dick Marsh, identified the infectious nature of the disease, pointing out that every outbreak of mink encephalopathy had occurred simultaneously on more than one mink ranch, and in every case the affected ranches shared a common source of feed. It was obvious, therefore, that the animals were getting the disease from something they ate. Burger and Hartsough examined the brains of mink that had died in the 1963 outbreak and found spongy holes like those found in scrapie-infected sheep. Laboratory tests confirmed that the disease could be transmitted like scrapie by injecting healthy animals with ground-up brain tissue from diseased mink. Burger and Hartsough published their results in 1965, the same year that Gajdusek and Gibbs achieved the first experimental transmission of kuru to monkeys.[3]

In 1969, Marsh and Hanson undertook a comprehensive study aimed at identifying the physical and chemical properties of the infectious agent which causes transmissible mink encephalopathy. They found that TME was chemically indistinguishable from the scrapie agent and that its infectivity could be substantially reduced through treatment with proteases, enzymes that digest proteins. In other research, they found that the cornea and other parts of the eye were highly infectious, a discovery that proved sadly prophetic a few years later when a woman developed Creutzfeldt-Jakob Disease after receiving a cornea transplant from a man who had died from the disease.

In collaboration with other researchers—notably William Hadlow, the scientist who had first noticed the similarity between scrapie and kuru—Marsh began experiments with a variety of animals to test their susceptibility to the TME agent. Minks are members of the weasel family, and the scientists found that they could readily transmit the disease from mink into related animals: ferrets, skunks, sables and martens. TME also transmitted to raccoons, rhesus monkeys, squirrel monkeys, and stumptail macaques.[4]

In the early days, Marsh would recall later, scientists studying the transmissible spongiform diseases were far more careless than they are today in the way they handled tissues from infected animals. They would toss a brain into a blender without much fear of contracting the disease themselves. "It was a total lack of common sense," he said. "It was kind of a slow evolution of thinking. . . . We always thought that these things had a species barrier which would make it unlikely they could transmit to humans, but gradually over the years we began to realize as we did these experiments that the barrier wasn't as absolute as we imagined. We transmitted scrapie first to other sheep, and then to goats, into mink, into monkeys. I think it was when we found we could put it into monkeys that we started to worry."[5]

In collaboration with British scrapie researcher Richard Kimberlin, Marsh discovered that hamsters were also susceptible, and that they incubated spongiform encephalopathies more rapidly than mice and developed higher levels of infectivity—over 10,000 infectious units per gram of brain—than any other test animal. Mice, on the other hand, seemed immune to the mink encephalopathy, despite repeated attempts to infect them with the disease. Interestingly, TME lost its infectivity to *mink* after several passages through hamsters or ferrets. "These findings suggest that mink may provide an important model to study species barrier effects," Marsh observed. "Comparing . . . genes in mink and ferrets may disclose important information on why these two closely related mustelids have such different susceptibilities."[6]

It was clear that mink got the disease from something in their food, but it was hard to pin down the precise source. Sheep were the obvious suspect, since they were the only animal species known to be common carriers of a transmissible spongiform encephalopathy. Marsh tested this theory by experimentally exposing mink to tissues from sheep infected with scrapie. The experiments were complicated by British researcher Richard Kimberlin's discovery that there were different *strains* of the disease agent. In sheep alone, there were at least 23 different strains, which could be identified because they caused different symptoms. One strain, called "drowsy" scrapie, made affected animals act sleepy. Another, called "hyper," made them itchy and agitated, while one strain in mice made them get fat. Different strains took different amounts of time to induce illness, and upon autopsy they showed distinguishably different patterns of amyloid plaque buildup in the brain.[7]

In order to test the susceptibility of mink to scrapie, Marsh turned to Alan Dickinson, whose laboratory at Edinburgh had compiled an impressive collection of scrapie strains. Dickinson sent over six sources of sheep brain, one drowsy goat brain, and fourteen strains that had been passaged and adapted into mice. Marsh and Hanson injected samples from each of these sources directly into the brains of test mink, but only one developed the disease. They had somewhat better luck with scrapie-infected sheep obtained from the United States, but even so, injection directly into the brain seemed to be the only method of exposure that was strong enough to induce illness. In experiments with oral feeding, the mink stayed relentlessly healthy. Judging from the number of mink that went down every time an outbreak occurred, they would have to be *highly* susceptible to the infection, but they were unable to find a strain of sheep scrapie that met this requirement.

Marsh theorized that maybe there was another strain out there, a strain he hadn't yet tested, that was better at jumping the species barrier. It was a puzzle, though. At the Canada ranch where the outbreak occurred in 1963, the rancher said that sheep had never gone into his feed.[8] The 1963 outbreak had occurred simultaneously on two separate ranches, sharing a common feed source that was limited to dead and "downer" cows—animals unable to stand which were therefore deemed unfit for human consumption. This prompted speculation that a spongiform encephalopathy might exist in U.S. cattle as early as December 1964. At a conference organized that year by Carleton Gajdusek and

Clarence Gibbs, scientists presented the first research documenting the existence of spongiform brain disease in mink. "It would appear that these mink were fed beef, and it is conceivable that the disease is caused by a virus which is commonly present in cattle," commented one scientist at the conference. "This possibility of a silent host may also help to explain the varied epidemiological patterns which are found in scrapie; in sheep, the silent host may actually be cattle."[9]

Transmissible mink encephalopathy was so rare, however, that there were very few opportunities to confirm or disprove any theories about its origin. Following 1963, the disease did not appear again in the United States for over two decades. Another outbreak occurred in Finland in 1963. Reports appeared of cases in East Germany in 1970 and Russia in 1974, followed by a decade with no cases reported anywhere in the world.

Then, in April 1985, a phone call came from the owner of a mink ranch in Stetsonville, a tiny town in north central Wisconsin. He was calling to report that many of his animals were behaving abnormally and some had died. Marsh and Hartsough visited the ranch and quickly recognized the telltale signs. Approximately 400 animals were sick, and more cases were emerging every day. Over the course of the next five months, 60 percent of the 7,300 animals on the ranch came down with the disease and died. Analysis of feeding and breeding records showed that all of the infected animals had been exposed to the infectious agent sometime between the dates of June 1 and July 17, 1984—approximately seven months before they started showing symptoms.[10]

Marsh and Hartsough questioned the Stetsonville rancher carefully to find out what the mink had eaten, and were struck by the parallels to the Canadian outbreak 22 years earlier. In both cases, the ranchers insisted that they had never fed sheep to their mink, and the Stetsonville rancher had good reason to be certain, because he was not using rendered feed products. Instead, he was a "dead stock" feeder who used mostly dairy cows and a few horses which he collected daily within a 50-mile radius of his mink ranch.

Perhaps one of the cows fed to the Stetsonville mink had carried an undiagnosed neurological illness. Marsh asked the farmer if he had fed the mink any "rabies negative" animals—cows that showed symptoms of rabies but tested negative in the lab. Rabies, a disease of the central nervous system, produced symptoms that could resemble a scrapie-like illness, and a rabies-negative cow might therefore have actually been carrying a transmissible spongiform encephalopathy.

"He knew the number right off," Marsh said. "He told us that he had fed 17 rabies-negative cattle. He showed us his record-keeping system, and every one was precisely entered. This guy knew what he was doing. When you're using dead stock in your feed rations, you'd *better* know what you're doing, or disease will put you out of business before you know it."[11]

The 1985 case at Stetsonville involved one of the few dead stock feeders left in the state. "His major source of meat for his mink was downer cows," Marsh said. "He never fed sheep. Here was a fellow who formulated his own diet; he was not using any byproduct mixtures at all, so he knows what he's putting in his feed. His farm was the only one infected. He had no reason not to tell us the truth. For the first time we thought, 'Maybe this is coming from downer cows.' " [12]

If the disease *did* exist in cows, Marsh realized, there was a potential new danger on the horizon. "I went to the meeting of the U.S. Livestock Association later that year and reported that there is strong epidemiological evidence that mink encephalopathy is caused by feeding infected dairy cows to the mink. I tried to put them on the alert to look for such a disease in dairy cows." [13]

Marsh didn't know it at the time, but a case of spongiform encephalopathy had already been observed in a cow—not in the United States, but in England. The case occurred in April 1985, the same month that mink started dying in Stetsonville. It was such an oddity that the British farmers at first thought it was a fluke, a one-time curiosity. Two years would pass before the recognition dawned that they were looking at something much worse—and by then, the disease had already mushroomed into a devastating, unstoppable, invisibly incubating epidemic.

Mad Cows and Englishmen

"Looking back over the years since then, horror is the only word to describe my feelings—horror that we had got something that seemed to be out of control," recalled Tom Forsyth, the head stockman at Plurenden Manor, where the first cases of mad cow disease appeared in the mid-1980s.

Located near High Halden in the county of Kent in southeastern England, Plurenden Manor was a prosperous farm operated by the family of the late Lord Plurenden, a wealthy German expatriate. John Green, the stockman in charge of the farm's 300 Holstein Friesian dairy cows, first noticed the changes in a cow named Jonquil. She had always been a nice, quiet animal, but in April 1985, she became unsteady on her legs and began behaving strangely. "She turned into a nuisance in the milk parlour, acting aggressively towards the other cows," Green said. "She seemed to hallucinate." [1]

At first, Green thought Jonquil was suffering from "grass staggers," an ailment caused by magnesium deficiency with symptoms that include shivering and staggering. Colin Whitaker, the local cattle veterinarian, was summoned to the farm on April 25. He found nothing wrong except cystic ovaries. He treated those and they got better, but Jonquil's condition continued to worsen. Whitaker finally suggested that she might have a brain tumor. She was slaughtered, and her body was buried.

For awhile Forsyth imagined that Jonquil's death was simply an isolated curiosity. If not for later events, the question of what killed her would have remained buried with her body, not even earning a footnote in a veterinary journal. Regarding the safety of their food supply, the British remained blissfully complacent, even smug. In December 1985, the *Guardian,* a British newspaper, ran a story titled "It's dog eat dog on Swedish farms," which warned against buying imported meat. "Many of the Christmas hams now on sale here have come from pigs fed on the minced carcasses of sick animals," the story announced, detailing Sweden's practice of converting sick animals into feed for cows, pigs, poultry and domestic pets. Apparently unaware that the same practice was ongoing in England, the reporter questioned the wisdom of turning "the traditionally vegetarian cow" into a carnivore. [2]

Six months after Jonquil's death, Plurenden Farm saw several more cows go down with identical symptoms. "It was then that I began to think that perhaps we had got something new," Whitaker said. "Of course I had no inkling then of the potential scale of it. If someone had told me then of the panic that would be caused, or that there would be 150,000 cases of BSE in 10 years' time, I would have thought they were mad."[3]

"We considered a whole range of possible causes, from lead poisoning to rabies, but nothing made sense," Forsyth said. "We did not know where it was coming from and we did not know how to put it right."[4]

With the help of an investigative vet, Whitaker began tests on the animals at Plurenden Manor and on other farms in the area, where additional cases were beginning to crop up. After months of fruitless inquiry, they decided to send a head from an infected cow to the Central Veterinary Laboratory of England's Ministry of Agriculture, Fisheries and Food (MAFF)—the British equivalent of the USDA.

Pathologist Gerald Wells examined the brain in November of 1986—nineteen months after Jonquil's strange behavior had first been noticed. Under the microscope, the brain was riddled with spongy holes. Wells immediately recognized the telltale pattern of scrapie, and the discovery prompted an immediate and dramatic reaction within the ministry, although another eleven months would pass before the first news of the disease reached the public.

"I'll remember it till my dying day," recalled MAFF Chief Veterinary Officer Keith Meldrum. "I was just down the corridor when the guys from the Central Veterinary Laboratory came in. Quite a hubbub . . . they were talking about scrapie. I understood scrapie. But they were also talking about things I'd never heard of—Creutzfeldt-Jakob Disease, and something called kuru."[5]

Tracking the Cause

"The immediate priority was to sort out what to do about the disease purely in animal health terms," recalled Richard Kimberlin.[6] By all accounts an outstanding scientist, Kimberlin had worked at the Compton station since the days when scrapie research was a jousting-ground for small, warring cliques of British researchers. He specialized in pathogenesis—study of the mechanisms by which scrapie was able to multiply and spread inside a sheep during the incubation period before symptoms emerged. He had also conducted experimental transmissions of scrapie to other animals. In collaboration with Dick Marsh, he had contributed to speeding up the pace of scrapie research with their discovery that the disease could be transmitted to hamsters in as little as as 60 days. Unfortunately, Kimberlin had suffered the embarrassment in the early 1980s of supervising the graduate student whose publication of erroneous findings contributed to the demise of the Compton research program.[7] When the mad cow crisis began to emerge in 1987, he took the opportunity to get out when the getting was good, retiring early from his civil service job and setting up his own company called the Scrapie and Related Diseases Advisory Service, through which he worked as a consultant to food groups, the government, research groups and drug companies. Based on his background with scrapie, Kimberlin believed that BSE was unlikely to harm humans, and he quickly became one of the most influential scientists shaping the British government's policies for handling the situation.

In June 1987, the British government initiated a study led by John Wile-smith, a veterinary epidemiologist employed by MAFF. "It was a beautiful, I would say brilliant piece of classic epidemiology," Kimberlin said, "It established that BSE is associated with the feeding of meat and bone meal. . . . That is one of the best documented pieces of evidence that we have. I really can't emphasize it too strongly." Wilesmith believed BSE had originated when scrapie-infected sheep were rendered and fed to cows. After the initial infection occurred, the practice of cow cannibalism through the rendering process became the decisive factor enabling the disease to multiply. "The reason why the epidemic built up so dramatically," Kimberlin explained, "was because once infection had become established in cattle, and they were rendered or their waste tissues were rendered and entered the feed chain, then of course you had the potential for exponentially building up an increasing reservoir of BSE infection for which there was now no longer any kind of species barrier."

"It was really by the end of 1987 that the epidemiology came out clearly that said meat and bone meal is the vehicle of infection," Kimberlin said.[8] The government did not announce that mad cow disease even *existed,* however, until October 31, 1987. On that date, the "Short Communications" section of the British *Veterinary Record* published a two-page report by Gerald Wells, titled "A novel progressive spongiform encephalopathy in cattle." The report described the symptoms afflicting cattle, showed some photographs of brain sections, and noted that the first cases had appeared in cattle herds from as far apart as Cornwall, Bristol and Kent. What was causing it? So far, Wells reported, the cause of BSE "remains unknown and no connection with encephalopathies in other species has been established."[9]

Most people, of course, do not read the *Veterinary Record,* and the public at large remained unaware of the disease. Concerns were rising, however, among farmers. In Hampshire, a farmer named Anhur Rolf experienced a case of BSE on a farm he leased from Lord Montagu of Beaulieu, one of England's most prominent landowners. Rolf was shocked to discover that even with the disease, the cow could have been legally sold for human consumption. He became so concerned that he appealed to Lord Montagu to put pressure on the Ministry of Agriculture. In response to Montagu's complaint, Agriculture Minister John MacGregor replied that there was no evidence that humans could catch the disease, and therefore no action was necessary. "I am amazed at the slow reaction of the ministry and the complacent attitude it had at the beginning," Montagu said later.[10]

Outside of the *Veterinary Record,* the media response remained low-key. On December 29, 1987, the *Times* of London published a brief story by agriculture correspondent John Young, titled "Mystery Disease Strikes at Cattle," which downplayed the possibility of danger. "The arrival of an unknown disease is inevitably a subject of curiosity and concern," he wrote. "When that disease appears to be confined to a single country—Britain—there are bound to be calls for urgent investigations and for more information to be made public. So far, however, the veterinary profession has had to confess itself baffled." Citing government experts, Young noted that the disease "could be linked to a sheep disease called scrapie," and that it showed "some similarities with a brain affliction among an isolated group of cannibals in Papua New Guinea." Despite these peculiarities, Young quoted Dr. Tony Andrews, a professor at the Royal Veterinary College, who "does not as yet see BSE as a serious threat to cattle health." [11]

Andrews, however, would soon change his mind and begin warning not only about animal dangers but human dangers. By the time his statement appeared in the *Times,* 421 cases of BSE had been observed. This statistic was not made public until April 1988, prompting Andrews to join a number of other veterinarians in criticizing MAFF's failure to take action against the disease. "The Ministry has to come clean about this disease," Andrews said in an interview with the *Sunday Telegraph.* "We simply don't know if it is a danger to humans. I don't want to over-exaggerate the seriousness of this disease and I don't want to do anything to harm the industry, but I am deeply uneasy about it." [12]

Writing in the *British Medical Journal,* T.A. Holt and J. Phillips called for an end to the use of feed from rendered animals, noting the similarity to Creutzfeldt-Jakob Disease and the likely resistance of the infectious agent to high temperatures and other normal sterilization methods. "Many infected cattle have been used to make meat products, and the reported numbers only represent those animals with well established clinically manifest disease," they warned. They also advocated an end to the use of bovine brains and spinal cord in cooked meat products such as pies.[13]

In retrospect, Kimberlin concedes now, action should have been taken sooner, but hindsight is always easier than foresight. "I hate being wise after the event. It is too easy and it is too facile, and life is full of mistakes, and, God, I have made a few," he said in a 1996 presentation before a U.S. audience. "I always remember John Wilesmith's epidemiology study was done on less than 200 cases, . . . In those days, it really was hard, in fact, nobody honestly could foresee what was going to happen. Now it is all painfully clear, the sheer scale of the epidemic. At the time it was very uncertain, and the extent of recycling and the kind of numbers of cases were totally unpredictable." [14]

If BSE originated with the practice of "recycling" cows and sheep into feed for cows, the obvious implication was that this practice should be stopped, but this was easier said than done. Rendering had become so entrenched within the meat industry that ending it would have serious economic implications all by itself—a cost of $600 million in England alone, according to industry representatives. Rendered animal protein wasn't simply a cheap food supplement. It helped solve a nasty waste disposal problem. Eliminate it as an option, and you had to pass the added cost on to consumers. Raise the price of meat, and British beef would no longer be able to compete with beef from neighboring countries. The end result, industry analysts predicted, would be to transform England from a net exporter to an importer of beef.

In the absence of clear knowledge, political and economic factors became the determining factors shaping the government's policies. At stake was a market for beef and veal worth $3.1 billion in U.S. dollars. England employed 40,000 dairy farmers and 70,000 beef farmers, plus another 8,000 truckers engaged in the transportation of cattle to the country's 200 livestock markets, where auctioneers' commissions were based on a fixed percentage of the dollar value of cattle sales. From market, some 16,000 cattle per week went to slaughterhouses (called "abbatoirs" in England), and from there to butchers, restaurants and supermarkets. Bovine byproducts that did not end up in human stomachs were routed through rendering plants which transformed them into tallow, meat and bone meal, gelatin and other ingredients used in the manu-facture of everything from facial creams to medicines to pie fillers to industrial lubricants. A problem for the beef industry meant problems for every link in this chain of production and consumption.

"Cattle exports, which were worth pounds 58 million last year, may be at risk if the disease is not controlled soon," warned agriculture correspondent David Brown in the London *Sunday Telegraph*. "Britain has a high reputation for animal health and Ministry of Agriculture officials are anxious to avoid panic in the meat industry which could seriously harm the export trade."[15]

Some people, however, were asking hard questions. In April 1988, the *Veterinary Record* published a paper by K.L. Morgan, a lecturer at Bristol Uni-versity, who pointed out that tissue taken from patients with Creutzfeldt-Jakob Disease could induce disease in goats and cats, and that scrapie had been trans-mitted from sheep to monkeys. Moreover, experiments had shown that pas-sage from one species to another could alter the subsequent host range of the scrapie agent. In the process of jumping from sheep to cattle, therefore, the dis-ease might have become more infectious to humans.

Despite its own ignorance about the disease, the British government con-tinued to downplay dangers. Two weeks after Morgan's paper appeared, the *Veterinary Record* carried an article by the government's veterinary service. "BSE must be seen in perspective," it argued. "The number of confirmed cases (455) is very small compared with the total cattle population of 13 million. The number of cases is expected to increase but if, as anticipated, it behaves like similar diseases in other species, only small numbers of incidents relative to the total number of cattle disease incidents are likely to occur."[16]

The Southwood Committee

In response to charges of foot-dragging on BSE, the government adopted a time-worn public relations strategy: it appointed a committee to study the problem. Sir Richard Southwood, a prominent professor of zoology at Oxford University and chairman of the National Radiological Protection Board, was selected to chair the committee. The three other members were all retired fig-ures who had been eminent in their fields—a professor of pathology, a vet-erinarian, and a professor of neurology. None of them, however, had any expertise in the field of transmissible spongiform encephalopathies. As a result, they relied heavily on the advice of three government-supplied civil servants attached to the committee, particularly on the epidemiological data supplied by John Wilesmith.

Wilesmith was clearly correct in his conclusion that rendering had caused the disease to multiply, but he had no scientific evidence of where it came from in the first place. He *believed* that it originated from sheep, which seemed like a reasonable guess given the high rate of scrapie in England. Belief and proof, however, are two different things. The British were apparently so convinced sheep were the source that they never bothered to test the theory. A test would have been simple, of course: just feed scrapie-infected sheep to cows and wait to see if they get the disease. In practice, however, the slow incubation time of the disease meant that any such tests would be slow, expensive, and—given the large number of different scrapie strains known to exist—potentially inconclusive.

Wilesmith had not yet heard of Dick Marsh's work with mink in the United States and his theory that cows had their own version of spongiform encephalopathy. Marsh's evidence suggested that cattle themselves, not sheep, might be the source for BSE. The disease might arise naturally in cows the same way Creutzfeldt-Jakob Disease seemed to occur in humans—as a very rare, sporadic condition triggered by spontaneous mutation or some other unknown cause. If BSE was as rare in cows as CJD in humans, it might have existed since time immemorial and never been noticed until the rendering process—feeding cows to cows—enabled it to multiply out of control the same way that human cannibalism enabled kuru to multiply within the Fore tribespeople of Papua New Guinea.

The possibility that cows themselves were the source of mad cow disease raised more serious concerns than the assumption that sheep were the source. It implied, to begin with, that no one could predict whether, where or when BSE might emerge outside England. It also meant that no one could predict what dangers it might pose to people who ate beef from infected animals. If BSE came from sheep, scientists considered it likely that the disease would behave like scrapie and pose no threat to humans. If the disease came from something *other* than sheep, however, all bets were off. The government preferred not to dwell on this possibility.

Southwood's committee met for the first time on June 20, 1988. After two weeks of deliberations, it reported its first recommendation to the Secretary of State for Health and the Minister of Agriculture: "At least until more is known about BSE, the carcasses of affected animals should be destroyed."

This recommendation came more than three years after Jonquil went down with the first suspected case of mad cow disease, and more than 18 months after the government's veterinarians had concluded that the disease was caused by feeding rendered meat and bone meal to cows. The gap between discovery and action turned out to be critical, giving the disease the time it needed to multiply into a serious epidemic. By the time Southwood's committee made its announcement, BSE had already killed more than 600 cows, and thousands more were infected without showing symptoms.

On July 7, 1988, the government took its first action aimed at controlling the disease—a belated and inadequate measure. "Arrangements will be made for compulsory slaughter and destruction of carcasses," said a press release from British Agriculture Minister John MacGregor. "Compensation will be payable at 50 percent of market value subject to a ceiling." [17]

If the government was only willing to offer 50 percent compensation, farmers had an obvious incentive to sneak sick animals past inspection and into the human food chain. Some people would later charge that this policy was a deliberate attempt to discourage farmers from reporting the true extent of the disease.

To control the disease, the government imposed a ban on further feeding of rendered cattle protein to cows. Initially, the policy had loopholes, and years would pass before they would be plugged—a delay caused in part by the reluctance of farmers and the rendering industry to recognize the seriousness of the problem they were facing. The government was being "high-handed," complained the director of one rendering plant shortly after the ban was announced. "It is not a good thing for our image for any of our products to be questioned," said David MacKesack-Leitch of Elgin Animal Byproducts.[18]

These protestations failed to sway the Southwood Committee, which met again in November of 1988. Its report, which was withheld from publication until February 8, 1989, summarized its deliberations regarding the cause of the disease: "The only common feature in all the cases that have been investigated is the use of commercial concentrates, either as finished rations, such as pelleted calf feed and dairy calf cake, or protein supplements used in home mixed rations. This points to meat and bone meal as being the vehicle of infection. . . . In every case of BSE investigated so far, animal protein had been fed to the animal."[19]

The urgent question, in fact, was not what *caused* the epidemic. The question was what it would take to *end* it—and whether it would spread to humans. On both those points, the Southwood Committee expressed optimism that would later prove unfounded, spawning accusations of government complacency, incompetence and coverup.

With respect to stopping the disease, the report acknowledged that BSE belonged to "a group of unconventional transmissible agents . . . unlike any bacteria or known virus . . . unusually resistant to heat and to the normal sterilization process." For reassurance, the report noted that "there is no evidence of maternal [cow to calf] or horizontal [cow to cow] transmission of BSE. If these methods of transmission are assumed not to occur it is possible to make an estimate of the order of magnitude of future occurrence. . . . A constant number of cases, of the order of 350–400 per month, can be expected; this is an incidence of one case per 1,000 adult cows per year. . . . This rate of presentation of the disease will continue until 1993, a cumulative total of about 17,000-20,000 cases from cows currently alive and subclinically infected. Thereafter, if cattle-to-cattle transmission does not occur, then a reduction in incidence would follow with a very low incidence in 1996 and the subsequent disappearance of the disease."[20] As it turned out, the actual size of the epidemic would be roughly ten times this estimate.

"The Risk Appears Remote"

Regarding the danger to humans, the Southwood report admitted that it was impossible to be certain. "With the very long incubation period of spongiform encephalopathies in humans, it may be a decade or more before complete reassurance can be given. . . . The risk of transmission of BSE to humans appears remote. Nevertheless, because the possibility that BSE could be transmitted orally cannot be entirely ruled out, known affected cattle should not enter the human food chain and action now undertaken assures this." [21]

Actually, this was a misleading assurance. *Affected* cattle meant animals that were already showing noticeable symptoms. To anyone familiar with the long invisible incubation period of spongiform encephalopathies, it was obvious that plenty of infected but as-yet unaffected animals would continue entering the human food chain. Moreover, the committee had no scientific evidence —experimental, epidemiological or otherwise—to justify its opinion that the risk of transmission to humans "appears remote."

In fact, the British were making two opposite assumptions: (1) BSE came from sheep but was *different*; and (2) BSE came from sheep and was *the same*. Its ability to persist in cattle would be *different* from scrapie, which had proven its capacity for horizontal and vertical transmission by persisting for more than 200 years within the sheep population. On the other hand, its effect on people would be *the same* as scrapie, which had apparently failed to enter the human population during that same two centuries and was therefore presumed harmless.

The fact that these assumptions seemed to contradict each other didn't necessarily mean that they were wrong. The spongiform diseases showed baffling and diverse transmission characteristics. Scrapie, in fact, was the only one that seemed easy to transmit. Kuru and transmissible mink encephalopathy had only emerged under unnatural feeding conditions, and the only documented cases of CJD transmission were the result of equally unusual medical accidents or laboratory experiments. It was possible that the British would turn out to be correct on both counts. It was also possible that they were *wrong* on both counts—or they could be right on one, and wrong on the other. From a strictly scientific standpoint, their position was weak, but it made sense from a gambler's perspective. The British were pursuing the same strategy as a blackjack player who splits a bet on a bad hand, hoping that at least one of the new hands will turn out to be a winner.

Bet #1: Mad cow disease will quickly decline and disappear.

Bet #2: Mad cow disease will be harmless to humans.

If they lost on number one, they still had a good chance that number two would cover their losses. On the other hand, they could lose on number two and still hope that number one would keep their losses to a minimum. Most gamblers would say they were making a smart bet. The alternative would be to assume a worst-case scenario and immediately undertake a drastic and expensive slaughter of healthy cattle. In blackjack, this move would be called a "surrender," and it is something that skilled players only do when their hand is so bad that losing seems almost certain. The British didn't think that their hand was that bad, but every gambler knows that even a good hand turns sour sometimes, and the Southwood Committee recognized that this was a

(photo ©1988 by David Jackson. Used with permission.)

possibility: "From present evidence, it is likely that cattle will prove to a 'dead-end host' for the disease agent and most unlikely that BSE will have any implications for human health," the report concluded. "Nevertheless, if our assessments of these likelihoods are incorrect, the implications would be extremely serious." [22]

It was a good bet, in other words, until you stopped to think about the fact that they were gambling with human lives.

For the most part, these concerns remained largely the province of scientists and public officials, but they were beginning to spread. In September 1988, Israel and Australia banned imports of British beef, citing concerns for human safety. "Of course there is alarm because it's potentially a great threat to the livestock industry as well as to human health," admitted James Hope, the head of an independent research unit studying the disease. "Because it jumped from sheep to cow, it might better be fitted to jump from cow to human." [23]

Most of the British people, however, remained blissfully unaware that they were eating beef from animals that carried a deadly disease. The government disposed of known infected cattle as discreetly as possible, removing their heads for study and dousing their bodies with gasoline before setting them on fire. As the number of animals began to climb, the government's activities provoked objections from the public. "The stench from the open fires was appalling," complained June Veevers, who lived near one of the disposal sites. "The blood and gore on the road from the seepage from trucks bringing in diseased carcasses could be immensely dangerous to animals living nearby."

"At that time most of the general public was not aware of BSE," recalled David Jackson, a freelance photographer who lived near Lean Quarry in Cornwall. "I only became aware of it when local people who lived near the quarry complained to the local paper of burning flesh."

The newspaper sent Jackson to see if he could get a picture of the disposal operation. "After making some inquiries," he said, "I managed to gain entry into the quarry and was met by the manager, who then took me down a long path to the middle of an open site, where a huge pyre had been erected and about 16 carcasses were burning fiercely. Not only that, each one had been decapitated. It was a terrible sight."

Jackson's photograph of the scene remains unique to this day. Soon after it was taken, the government stopped burning cattle in the open and began using incinerators instead. "Since then the photograph has been used all over the U.K., including Northern Ireland," Jackson said. "Then to France, Germany, Denmark, Norway, Sweden, South Africa, New Zealand and Japan, finally ending up in the *New York Times*. The picture has been turned into a political vehicle widely used . . . against eating British beef, and our industry has suffered a great deal. But what can you expect when someone sanctions the use of sheep parts to be used in cattle feed? It makes you want to turn vegetarian for life." [24]

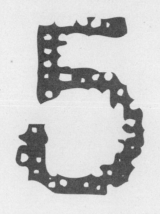

5

CRISIS
CONTAINMENT

Scrapie, American-Style

In the United States, responsibility for assessing the situation fell to the U.S. Department of Agriculture's Animal Research Service (ARS). The ARS quietly formed a "Task Force on Bovine Spongiform Encephalopathy," which met for the first time on April 24, 1989. The participants included ARS scientists John Gorham, Mark Robinson and Roger Breeze, along with William Hadlow, the U.S. researcher who had first linked scrapie to kuru, and Richard Marsh, the University of Wisconsin veterinarian whose research with mink had raised early warnings that U.S. cattle might carry a form of spongiform encephalopathy. The meeting began with a presentation from Gerald Wells, the pathologist who had first identified BSE in England. In addition to the Task Force, representatives from the government and the meat industry attended: the USDA's Animal and Plant Health Inspection Service (APHIS), Food Safety Inspection Service (FSIS), the National Institutes of Health (NIH), Food and Drug Administration (FDA), the Extension Service, and the American Sheep Industry Association, along with an aide to Iowa Republican Congressman Jim Leach, considered friendly to the meat and rendering industries located in his state.[1]

The committee developed a series of recommendations for research, such as an experiment to see how BSE affected mink, to learn whether it "is a 'scrapie-like' agent . . . or if it behaves more like a 'mink agent.'" It also recommended a program of ongoing surveillance to determine whether BSE was occurring in U.S. cattle. Under the direction of APHIS, state laboratories were already responsible for examining the brains of cattle diagnosed with rabies. On the possibility that mad cow cases might initially be misdiagnosed, the committee recommended "a careful evaluation of rabies submission data" to identify "increases in neurological cases that prove to be negative for rabies."[2]

Other researchers would inoculate cattle with U.S. strains of scrapie "to determine if the U.S. scrapie agent is capable of producing a syndrome in cattle similar to that observed with BSE in the United Kingdom." An experiment along those lines had already been performed a decade earlier, in Mission, Texas. Ten animals had been injected with scrapie, and although three developed signs of a neurological disease, the symptoms and brain pathology differed substantially from the pattern in England. The brains of those cows had been preserved, and the committee recommended that they undergo further examination.

Finally, the committee concluded that "it would be of great value to examine the activities of the rendering industry in the United States . . . what types of animals (particularly sheep) are rendered, how they are rendered, and where these products go. Also, we should try to correlate this information with the best information on geographical distribution of scrapie. We should investigate if any such sheep rendered products have ever been incorporated into animal feed, particularly for dairy. We do not know what the practices and regulations of the U.S. rendering industry are."[3]

In June 1989, NIH and Switzerland's International Association for Research and Education in Neurosciences sponsored an "International Roundtable on Bovine Spongiform Encephalopathy." Participants included Clarence Gibbs, Gajdusek's colleague at the NIH, who advised scientists to be on the lookout for mad cow-like diseases in countries outside of England. "It is highly probable that cattle and other species of ruminants, such as deer and elk, and possibly wild feral animals, have always been susceptible to spongiform encephalopathy (scrapie) at a frequency too low to be recognized," Gibbs warned. He called on the government to "legislate against the incorporation of meat and bonemeal supplements produced outside the United States into the foodstuffs of cattle, other domestic animals, and poultry intended for the human food chain." David Asher, another NIH scientist, went further by suggesting that "meat byproducts not be fed to U.S. cattle at all."[4]

In a list of consensus recommendations, the International Roundtable participants warned against continuing the practice of animal cannibalism: "The addition of rendered (tankage) meat and bonemeal supplements derived from bovine and ovine* carcasses, as is done in Great Britain, as a source of protein additive for cattle and sheep should be discontinued. In some countries, soya from the plentiful production of soybeans could replace animal protein supplements."[5]

Gibbs also expressed concern at "the alarming reemergence and rapid spread of scrapie in sheep flocks throughout the United States following USDA downgrading of control by condemnation of scrapie-affected sheep" and advocated "immediate reinstitution of the program on a national basis."[6]

William Hadlow expressed similar concerns. "The number of flocks in which scrapie has been diagnosed has increased greatly," Hadlow stated. "This alarming increase in prevalence of scrapie is well exemplified by its reported diagnosis in 52 flocks in 20 states from October 1988 to early June 1989. . . . In one flock of Suffolk sheep in Iowa, 50% of lambs born in 1986 have succumbed to the disease."[7]

From Total Depopulation to "Cost-Benefit Analysis"

Gibbs and Hadlow were responding to a disturbing "deregulation" trend within the United States which, since 1983, had largely dismantled the USDA's measures aimed at eradicating scrapie.

In the 1950s, the first reports of scrapie in the U.S. had prompted government officials to declare a "state of emergency" and a policy of "total flock

---

*Ovine means "of or pertaining to sheep."

depopulation." If even a single case of scrapie appeared in a flock of sheep, the entire flock was destroyed, with the government paying an indemnity to cover the cost of buying replacement animals. In 1957, the program was expanded further to include total depopulation of source flocks from which diseased sheep had been purchased, with funding coming from both federal and state governments.

In theory, these extreme measures ought to have succeeded, if not in eliminating the disease, at least in bringing it under control. In practice, however, they ran up against the realities of human greed, bureaucracy and the damn-fool stubbornness of sheep ranchers who had never seen scrapie before and didn't see why they should be forced to destroy entire flocks just because of some new-fangled government program. Animal inspectors who tried to enforce the program found themselves staring down the business end of shotguns wielded by angry ranchers who ordered them to get the hell off their land. Other farmers found creative ways to take advantage of the program. In Michigan, for example, one of the state's leading farmers was scheduled to receive $1,999,751 in compensation for his flock of 2,180 sheep when evidence came to light showing that he had deliberately infected his sheep and then inflated the size of his flock by secretly purchasing hundreds of cheap, low-quality animals.[8]

In 1983, a combination of sheep industry lobbying and Reagan-era preoccupation with government budget-cutting persuaded the USDA to drop the policy of destroying entire flocks. Under the new policy, called "bloodline indemnification," farmers were only supposed to kill animals that showed symptoms of the disease and their immediate relatives. Total flock depopulation became a measure of last resort, used only in cases where "a cost-benefit analysis establishes that it is more cost-effective to destroy the flock than to maintain it under surveillance."[9]

Officially, the USDA touted the new program as an improvement over the old one. "Total depopulation was costly, and adequate funding was not always available," stated USDA officials. "It was felt that the drastic measure of total depopulation drove the disease underground, and a number of cases were not reported. A portion of the research community argued against the significance of lateral transmission and stated that most cases of disease spread could be attributed to maternal transmission. After 31 years of a total depopulation approach, scrapie still existed in the United States."[10]

You didn't need a rocket scientist, however, to figure out that eliminating money for flock depopulation would make farmers even less likely to report the disease. Maynard Potter, a sheep rancher in California, experienced first-hand the consequences of the new policy when he became one of the few farmers who *did* report scrapie in his flock. According to a report by the state veterinarian, some 15-20 of Potter's 200 animals died between the years of 1985 to 1987, driving him finally to contact a veterinarian. Three more animals died before a diagnosis of scrapie was confirmed, and another six deaths occurred over the course of the subsequent two years.

At first, state and federal veterinarians followed advice from the USDA, telling Potter that scrapie was "strictly a bloodline transmitted disease." As the disease spread through his flock, they were forced to change their opinion. His sick animals only marked the beginning of his losses. After adding his name to the USDA's list of scrapie-diseased flocks, he found that he could no longer sell any of his sheep. "We have not sold any registered stock for close to three years and can no longer participate in registered sheep shows and sales, which . . . in essence, puts us right out of the livestock business," he stated in an imploring letter to the USDA. "The real problem is that the government has not only taken us out of the livestock business in practice, but they have left us in business until we become financially bankrupt! Basically, we still have the sheep; we still have to purchase feed; we still have to practice livestock health management under a very difficult situation; and we have ongoing labor costs. We have no outlet for these animals as no one else will purchase them, but I would not expect them to. You cannot justify and maintain a clear conscience taking them to a livestock sales yard and selling them at auction, which would spread the disease statewide, and at the same time open us up to unquestionable lawsuits. I could have done what some other breeders throughout the United States have done and not report the situation, kill off the infected animal, bury it, and say nothing!"[11]

Potter's friends included Jack Parnell, a deputy secretary at the USDA, and by early 1990 he managed to persuade the agency to make an exception in his case and provide funds for total flock depopulation. Even this, however, failed to solve his problem. After reading the scientific literature on scrapie, Potter realized that the disease agent could survive in soil even after the animals had been removed. "We do not feel comfortable re-entering the purebred sheep agency on the farm where we are presently located," he stated in another letter to the USDA. But the government's aid came with strings attached: a rule that the money could not be used to purchase uncontaminated land.[12]

A letter from Jack Parnell expressed sympathy for Potter's dilemma. "We certainly agree with you and all sheep producers on the need to determine whether the scrapie agent remains on a premises after diseased animals have been removed," Parnell stated. "Unfortunately, we do not yet have firm scientific evidence to support or oppose the theory of scrapie-caused contamination. I am sorry that I cannot provide you with the definitive information you need to resolve your situation." As consolation, Parnell added, "You may be pleased to learn that our Animal and Plant Health Inspection Service is cooperating with Utah State University in conducting applied research on the disease. The goal of one project is to determine whether premises can be contaminated with the scrapie agent. Hopefully, this research will provide us with more conclusive answers about scrapie contamination."[13]

Later that year, however, budget constraints led to the abandonment of the Utah study which could have provided the answers that Potter needed. "It is very unfortunate that this study could not be completed," stated researcher Warren Foote. "The infectivity of the contaminated premises remains a critical unanswered question in scrapie control and of special concern to the sheep industry. It is unlikely that the primary questions addressed in this study will ever be answered."[14]

Thanks for Nothing

Maynard Potter was not the only farmer to discover that reporting a case of scrapie had in practice become an offense punishable by bankruptcy. In South Carolina, farmers Pete McConnell and Bill Dees went through a similar ordeal. "We were quarantined the day each flock was diagnosed, which has completely stopped our incomes but certainly not our costs," they stated in a February 1991 letter to Senator Strom Thurmond.

After learning that his flock had the disease, McConnell contacted Dr. Linda Detwiler, the APHIS official in charge of scrapie. She told him that the federal allocation for scrapie indemnification had already been spent that year, so he waited until the federal budget was completed for the following year and contacted Detwiler again. "She was unsure at that point of what monies they would receive so she could give no appraisal of whether depopulation money would be available or not," McConnell and Dees stated in their letter. "For the whole month of December and the first weeks of January, we heard nothing. Therefore, McConnell contacted Dr. Detwiler again and found that $870,000 was appropriated but that only $70,000 would be available for producers (i.e., for the ones with the total financial burden of the problem!). She said we would have to wait for the end of the fiscal year and see how the $70,000 could best be split among the current 139 flocks with scrapie plus other flocks that would get it before October 1991."

McConnell and Dees told Thurmond that they were "frankly 'worn out' hassling with the system to get relief. . . . Less than 10% of the federal scrapie indemnity dollars go to farmers, which we feel is a disgrace." In addition to their financial losses, they were worried by recent reports suggesting that scrapie might be linked to human disease—"hence our legitimate fear of selling to a consumer"—but they had lost patience with efforts to get help from the government. "The disease is contagious and obviously reportable to federal authorities, although few producers report it," they wrote. "We now know why." [15]

The government's scrapie eradication program had been transformed, by accident or by design, into a program that effectively eradicated *reporting* of the disease, which in turn made it easier for the disease itself to spread. On May 10-11, 1988, the USDA met with representatives of the sheep industry. Minutes from the meeting reported that the U.S. "needs a workable program to address scrapie disease of sheep and goats. The existing program is not working." Unfortunately, the cost of an effective program was considerably more than anyone was willing to pay: "The USDA would probably need between $10 to $30 million for a full eradication program." [16]

By 1989, the disease had been diagnosed in 476 flocks throughout the United States, with 87 new cases in the first three months of 1989 alone. "There is great danger, in these days of interstate commerce, in letting a deadly, contagious disease such as scrapie invade our sheep flocks," warned Iowa Agriculture Secretary Dale Cochran in a letter to the USDA. On behalf of Iowa's Task Force on Scrapie, he urged the government to provide "funding for the eradication of scrapie." [17]

Rather than allocating such funding, the USDA was moving even further away from solutions to the problem. On November 2, 1988, APHIS published an advanced notice in the *Federal Register* of its proposed plan to discontinue the scrapie eradication program and to develop an alternative in its place.

In 1990, APHIS convened a "Scrapie Negotiated Rulemaking Committee," comprised of leading farm organizations, renderers and other representatives of the meat industry. By this time, concerns were coming from within the American Sheep Industry Association itself. In an October 1989 report, the association had stated, "The devastating disease known as scrapie is growing rapidly. A viable scrapie control program is urgently needed to bring the disease under control." [18] Within the sheep industry, however, producers of Suffolk sheep—whose flocks were the ones most contaminated with the disease—realized that they would have to absorb most of the cost of any control program. Their opposition effectively doomed the effort to negotiate a solution.

A "Voluntary" Solution

"Each of the sheep associations was represented," recalled Dick Marsh, who participated in the committee. "There were two separate Suffolk sheep associations at the table—the American Suffolk Society and the National Suffolk Association. . . . What happened at our first couple of meetings was that first of all Lonnie King from the USDA got up and said this had to be a consensus rule. We all had to agree to it. If we had even one dissenting vote, no one will go forward with the plan. The first two meetings were a waste of time, because the Suffolk associations were against any kind of regulation at all. Then a guy from the rendering industry got up and as much as told them, 'Look, if you people don't come to the table, we're going to stop rendering your blackface sheep.' "

This ultimatum from the renderers amounted to an economic gun pointed at the heads of the sheep producers. They had to agree to *something,* if only to save face. "As soon as this guy said, 'We're not going to render any of your sheep,' they came up with some kind of a proposal for a voluntary certification program," Marsh said. "All the time, of course, they knew that their members weren't going to participate in it, so it would not be effective." [19]

The final plan—adopted by consensus of both USDA and the meat industry's leading trade organizations—abolished altogether the indemnity to affected farmers and redirected funds toward research and education of farmers and veterinarians. The "voluntary certification program" was supposed to prevent spread of the disease by simply identifying scrapie-free flocks. Farmers who enrolled would be monitored by inspectors, and if they passed five years without a case of scrapie, APHIS would certify them "scrapie-free."

The voluntary certification program had the official support of the American Sheep Industry Association. Within the industry, however, a number of dissenting individuals questioned the direction that USDA was taking. Some criticized the certification program on grounds of cost and ineffectiveness, particularly since no test existed that was capable of identifying the disease in live animals.

"Lamb and wool prices are depressed and nearly a third of Iowa's sheep producers have recently been forced out of business," wrote Iowa farmer James Lein. "I have asked veterinarians about certification as a necessary expense. First they agree that a diagnostic test is the first step. Second they comment that sheep producers seldom call them because they cannot afford to do so and that additional expense will force them out of business. Certification has been ineffective in England. The proposal for the United States would be an equal farce." The absence of a live test, combined with the voluntary nature of the certification program, left an ample window of opportunity for farmers who wished to continue concealing the disease. "Those who created it did so to buy time for their purebred flocks," Lein stated. "A check of the labs will reveal that one to two flocks [with scrapie] are reported each week. How many more are not turned in?"[20]

Other people felt that the scrapie program was an attempt to shift the burden of concern for mad cow disease onto the shoulders of sheep producers, who were relatively weak players within the U.S. meat industry. "The program has been imposed by the cattle industry, rendering and packer industries of the United States because of fear of a tie between BSE and scrapie," stated Ohio Department of Agriculture Director Fred Dailey.[21]

"There is a definite need to not only continue but to expand the present scrapie eradication program," argued a letter to USDA from George Scott, a sheep producer and former sheep and wool specialist at Colorado State University. "If there is no indemnity many producers suspecting scrapie in their flocks will simply destroy the animals exhibiting symptoms of the disease and sell those that do not exhibit symptoms, thereby spreading the disease even more rapidly. . . . Total flock depopulation is necessary. . . . A scrapie-free certification program would be unreliable and should not be considered. Since there is no live animal test for scrapie, a flock could never be certified free of the disease." Noting the recent outbreak of mad cow disease in England, Scott summarized his concerns with a warning: "If, as suggested by many knowledgeable researchers that there is an association between scrapie in sheep and goats and bovine spongiform encephalopathy, any action that could increase the spread of the disease could have a long-lasting negative effect on the U.S. red meat industry."[22]

Others pointed to the inverse relationship between the size of the problem and the government's willingness to pay for the elimination of infected animals. "I am well aware of the budgetary restraints on USDA programs," stated U.S. Senator Tom Harkin in a March 10, 1989 letter to Agriculture Secretary Clayton Yeutter. "I believe it is noteworthy, however, that APHIS figures for 1982 show 18 flocks having been identified with scrapie with total federal indemnities for depopulation of $1,323,000. For 1988, over 50 flocks were identified as infected, but only $224,883 was paid in federal indemnities. Hence, despite a worsening scrapie problem, it appears that APHIS has markedly reduced its commitment to controlling the disease."[23]

"If the USDA does not continue the scrapie program, the magnitude of this problem will grow to an outrageous level," warned Sandra Cox, a member of the board of directors of the Cashmere Producers of America. "The government already allowed this problem to multiply by changing the program from total herd depopulation to a bloodline program in 1983. Since that time, affected herds have been on the upswing. One of the worst mistakes made was when an infected herd was released from quarantine because of insufficient funds. That herd went on to infect at least six other herds through the sale of exposed animals. Insufficient appropriated funds in the animal disease fund, and especially in the scrapie fund, will jeopardize our entire sheep and goat industry. . . . If it spreads to cattle, like it has in England, the entire red-meat industry could be lost, and U.S. exports will dramatically decrease."[24]

"I am reasonably certain that we now have more sheep scrapie in the United States than ever before in our history," stated veterinarian Vincent Marshall in the June 1, 1991 issue of the *Journal of the American Veterinary Medical Association.* "A disease that can increase 100-fold in the first few years of its existence in British cattle, and has the capability of infecting many other species, cannot continue to be ignored," Marshall wrote. "Forty years of ignoring scrapie has been ineffective and costly and leaves us with serious problems."[25]

Marshall's letter prompted a response from Linda Detwiler, the head of USDA's scrapie control program. In a letter signed by herself and three other USDA veterinarians, Detwiler challenged Marshall's conclusion that the number of scrapie cases had increased. "Since there is no preclinical screening test for scrapie in sheep, how does anyone know the true incidence of the disease or if the disease is increasing?" she wrote. "What we do know is the number of flocks *reported* to have scrapie. It is true that, during the 1980s, the number of newly reported infected flocks per year did increase." However, "In 1990, there were 38 newly reported flocks. This is more than a 25% decrease in the reported cases of scrapie from the preceding 2 years. Would anyone be willing to say that the program is finally beginning to work because the reported number of newly infected flocks has declined?"

Detwiler took exception to Marshall's charge that the USDA had "ignored" the disease, pointing out that efforts "to eradicate scrapie have been in effect since 1952." Moreover, scrapie "is a complex and often confusing disease to deal with. The causative agent has yet to be defined, the route of natural transmission is not fully understood, there is no prevention, there is no treatment, and there is no test for nonclinical or even clinically ill animals. Taking all of these unknowns, including a number of unproven scientific theories (some of which conflict) and many unscientific theories on these unknowns, and trying to make sound, effective public policy with a limited amount of funding, while not totally destroying the U.S. sheep industry, is the task with which we are charged."[26]

The truth of the matter is that Detwiler's hands were tied. Congress was simply unwilling to allocate enough funding to do the job properly. As scrapie spread, moreover, the gap between money available and money needed was bound to widen. The Voluntary Scrapie Flock Certification program began on October 1, 1992. In response to critics who insisted that the program needed funding to pay for the destruction of sick animals, the USDA threw in a six-month, one-time-only "limited indemnity" available to farmers who reported infected animals by July 7, 1993. After that, nothing—just "voluntary certification." Three years later, APHIS announced that it had reached a milestone when the "number of sheep flocks enrolled in the Scrapie Voluntary Flock Certification reached the 100 mark."[27] In the entire United States, with 92,000 sheep producers, only 100 had bothered to enroll. By August of 1996, only one flock in the entire country had actually made it through the monitoring process and attained scrapie-free certification.[28]

Measuring the Risk

At its worst, however, the scrapie problem in the United States was still an order of magnitude smaller than the problem in England. This fact offered some comfort to USDA analysts, who used it as the basis for their attempt to assess the likelihood that mad cow disease would emerge in the United States. Their analysis became the basis for two companion documents titled a *Qualitative Analysis of BSE Risk Factors in the United States* and a *Quantitative Risk Assessment.* Written in 1991, the two documents based their conclusions on two main factors: (1) the level of scrapie in the U.S. sheep population was lower than in England, and (2) the United States had fewer sheep.

"The United Kingdom has four times as many sheep and three times as many ewes on a land mass slightly smaller than that of Oregon," the *Qualitative Analysis* stated. "The ratio of all sheep to all cattle is 32 times greater in the United Kingdom. . . . Sheep in the United Kingdom account for 14 percent of raw rendering material versus 0.6 percent in the United States. This computes to 3.4 pounds per dairy cow in the United Kingdom versus 2.8 ounces per head in the United States." The report noted that "the United States produces 8 times more animal rendered product than the United Kingdom, but concluded that the "risk of introducing the BSE agent through sheep meat and bone meal is more acute in both relative and absolute terms in the United Kingdom."[29]

The *Qualitative Analysis* included 36 charts and tables: comparative inventories of cattle and sheep; age distributions of dairy cows; milk production statistics; graphs and flowcharts comparing rendering processes in the United States and England; pie charts showing the composition by content of animal feed mixtures; and breakdowns showing how much rendered protein was being fed respectively to pets, poultry, hogs and cattle. The *Quantitative Risk Assessment* added another 13 charts, focusing on regional variations in different parts of the United States, just in case states with larger sheep populations might be "at higher risk than states with large dairy populations." Taking all of these factors into consideration, the analysts concluded that "little evidence exists to support a broad risk for BSE among a large portion of the dairy population of the United States."[30]

Beneath all this impressive marshalling of facts and numbers, however, the risk assessment was seriously flawed. Where evidence was not available, it relied on unfounded assumptions. According to the *Qualitative Analysis,* for example, "An important difference between the two countries' feeding practices has been the inclusion . . . of meat and bone meal in calf starter and other calf feeds in the United Kingdom. . . . The feeding of meat and bone meal in calf starter in the United States is not believed to occur." [31] Feeding rendered material to calves was considered a risk factor because young animals would have more time to incubate the disease before slaughter. It may not have been "believed to occur" at the USDA, but in fact it was widespread in the United States.

The most fatal flaw was the USDA's assumption that sheep were the source of BSE—an assumption that was not only unproven but ran contrary to the evidence that Dick Marsh had collected with his studies of mink. And yet, as the *Quantitative Risk Assessment* stated in its conclusion, "the entire risk assessment considers scrapie infected sheep as the only source of the BSE agent." [32]

If sheep were *not* the source—if cattle *themselves* carried a rare spongiform encephalopathy, as Marsh believed—the conclusions of the USDA's analysis were not only invalid but inverted. The fact that the United States had 10 times as many cattle as England suddenly became an *increased* risk factor rather than cause for reasurrance. The assumption that the disease would never appear here suddenly lost its theoretical basis, giving new and ominous significance to the one risk factor that the USDA admitted was clearly higher in the United States: "The potential risk of amplification of the BSE agent through cattle meat and bone meal is much greater in the United States where it accounts for 59 percent of total product or almost 5 times more than the total amount of rendered product in the United Kingdom." [33]

A Makeshift Experiment

To their credit, U.S. scientists recognized the need to actually test whether scrapie could infect cattle, but this was easier said than done. To be meaningful, an experiment would have to test all of the different rendering processes being used in the United States. It would also have to take into account all of the different strains of scrapie that existed in both the United States and England. No one even knew how many strains existed, and even if they did, testing all the possible combinations of this many variables would cost more money and take more time than they could possibly hope to spend.

As a compromise, APHIS devised a shorter, less expensive experiment. In a document titled *Bovine Spongiform Encephalopathy: Rendering Research Priorities,* the Service proposed doing two tests. In one, they would render a group of sheep, all of whom were considered likely to be infected. In the other, they would render a batch of healthy sheep and throw in a single infected animal, hoping that this would approximate the percentage of sick sheep going into commercial rendering plants. Rather than *feed* the result to cows, they would inject it directly into their brains in order to speed up the experiment.

Unfortunately, injecting the material into brains wouldn't necessarily give a true reading of the danger from *eating* infected material, since intra-cerebral inoculation was considered to be approximately 10,000 times more effective at transmitting the disease than oral exposure. As a result, the APHIS proposal itself admitted, "The above experiment has several weaknesses, particularly its lack of real significance from a policy-making perspective of either a positive or a negative result. For example, even if infectivity is found in any of the samples using any of the bioassays inoculated via an intra-cerebral route, this says little about the risk to the cattle industry. . . . On the other hand, the failure to detect infectivity also indicates little about the risk to the cattle industry. . . . This experiment will use such small numbers of animals for bioassays that there will be little statistical significance to a negative result. It is unlikely that the experiment will be helpful in assessing the probability of BSE occurring in U.S. cattle via oral exposure to rendered products." [34]

The experiment also had other limitations. For one thing, no one knew whether feeding could induce a spongiform epidemic in animals *other* than cattle, such as pigs and chickens. "Research focused on the susceptibility of poultry to scrapie is particularly important. The poultry industry has several features that make it especially attractive as a market for feeds containing scrapie-contaminated rendered protein. . . . The inability of spongiform encephalopathy agents to reproduce in poultry, although frequently assumed, has not been proven."

These shortcomings notwithstanding, researchers decided to go ahead anyway with the experiment, which "represents a reasonable compromise between doing a large-scale statistically valid (and enormously expensive) experiment and doing nothing at all." Finding a rendering plant where they could get permission to perform the test proved to be a bit of a challenge, since the APHIS research proposal noted that rendering plants themselves could become contaminated with TSE disease agents: "If scrapie or BSE-infected animals are rendered, it may become necessary to disinfect the rendering facilities. Unfortunately, both the resistance of spongiform encephalopathy agents to many disinfectants and the need to avoid corrosive chemicals in rendering plants create major limitations on the choice of technology used for disinfection; indeed, it is not clear that there is any technology available." [35]

With the help of Fred Bisplinghoff from the National Renderers Association, APHIS made arrangements to conduct the experiment at a rendering plant in Minnesota. On June 29, 1990, however, word came back that the board of directors of the rendering plant was fearful of allowing an experiment that might result in permanent contamination of their facility. Before they could agree to the experiment, USDA would have to provide "a letter accepting full liability for any damages or loss of business that occurs as a result of the plant's participation in the rendering study." [36] USDA preferred not to accept this financial liability.

Bisplinghoff made some phone calls and lined up another rendering plant, this time in West Point, Nebraska, that agreed to allow the experiment. The actual rendering was carried out on July 9. Bisplinghoff flew in to observe, along with USDA scientists Randall Cutlip and Mark Robinson.

The Nebraska plant was using older equipment than most modern facilities—batch cookers rather than continuous rendering. In the old days, a typical rendering plant would have contained 10 or 15 individual batch cookers, all lined up in a row and cooking away. "This type of cooking has almost disappeared, I would say, in the United States," Bisplinghoff said. "Of the 280 rendering plants in the U.S. there are fewer than 15 batch plants left. Of those 15, only three are of any reasonable size. The other 12 are one- or two-cooker operations." [37]

From a scientific standpoint, the fact that the test would be performed on outmoded equipment added one more level of unreliability to the result—particularly since recent innovations in rendering technology were suspected to have contributed to the rise of BSE in England. From a practicality standpoint, however, batch cookers handled smaller quantities of material and made it easier to do the experiment. For the high-risk experiment, the scientists threw in about 6,000 pounds of scrapie-infected sheep, spiked with a few infectious brains from previous USDA scrapie research.

The scientists' presence seemed to have a disconcerting effect on the workers at the Nebraska plant. "Since we had so many people walking around in white coats, the poor employees got a little nervous and forgot to close the door of the first batch cooker," Bisplinghoff recalled during a 1996 presentation to a U.S. audience. "So Randall Cutlip, Mark Robinson and myself are standing in front of this cooker. It is boiling over into a boil tank. You put these 6,000 pounds into a boil tank and you blew it over by steam all at one time into the batch cooker. It went into the cooker, but it came out the front end.

"I want to tell you, I am living proof," Bisplinghoff said. "Not only did it go in the percolator pan, it went all over the front of the cooker and on us. And then we had to clean up, pick up that 6,000 pounds and put it in barrels and disinfect the area. But I am living proof that you can have scrapie brain sprayed all over you, in your eyes, in your mouth, your ears, and you can get in among it and you can clean it up with shovels, put it in barrels, bring it back around and do it all over again and, after five and a half years, only have a couple of twitches here and there."

In the end, the Nebraska adventure yielded some 20 barrels of meat and bone meal, which Cutlip hauled back to his lab in Ames, Iowa. Some of the material was injected into the brains of twelve test cattle. The remainder was fed to them orally over the course of the subsequent year. Cutlip sat back and waited to see what would happen to the animals. By May of 1996, one had died of a perforated gut, and another had gone down with a vague disease that the scientists were unable to identify, but none had shown signs of spongiform brain disease. The scientists who had been sprayed with the stuff also seemed healthy. "This is a very good research project going on," Bisplinghoff joked. "Who is going to die first, those cattle out there in Ames, Iowa . . . or Mark, Randall and myself?" [38]

Bent Proteins

In 1988, Carleton Gajdusek undertook a simple but dramatic experiment that underscored once again the remarkable indestructibility of the infectious agent responsible for spreading scrapie-like diseases. He took an infected hamster brain, mixed it with soil, and packed the mixture into pots that he buried in his back yard. Three years later he dug up the package and discovered that "between 2 and 3 log units of the input infectivity of nearly 5 log units survived this exposure, with little leaching of virus into deeper soil layers. These results have implications for environmental contamination by scrapie and similar agents, including those of bovine spongiform encephalopathy and Creutzfeldt-Jakob Disease."

"Log units" refer to the logarithmic scale commonly used by scientists to measure infectivity. Five log units equals 10 to the 5th power, or 100,000. A sample containing "input infectivity of 5 log units" was enough to kill 100,000 hamsters, and after burial for three years, it still retained enough infectivity to kill between 100 and 1,000. Gajdusek's experiment helped explain how the infectious agent could persist in soil and defeat even Iceland's severe scrapie eradication campaign.

Gajdusek undertook another experiment, in collaboration with Paul Brown and other researchers, which showed that the scrapie agent could even survive for an hour at 360 degrees centigrade (680 degrees fahrenheit)—a temperature adequate to melt lead and to reduce a good-sized slab of meat to fine ash. "From a practical standpoint, therefore, autoclaving has no laboratory value for the decontamination of formalin-fixed scrapie tissues, nor, by extension to the hospital setting, for neuropathologic processing of tissue from patients with CJD," they concluded. "Our finding that some infectivity in both crude brain tissue and fibril extracts survived a one-hour exposure to dry heat at 360°C raises the disturbing question of whether even incineration can be guaranteed to inactivate the agent."[2]

Scrapie researcher Gordon Hunter questioned the wisdom of the British government's strategy for disposing of the carcasses of infected cows. "The policy of the Ministry of Agriculture has been to dispose of them by burning," Hunter stated. "Initially, there was extensive burning on open ground, and this has continued from time to time when incinerator facilities have been overstretched. This procedure is, in my view, quite appallingly misconceived. The scrapie agent (and hence, presumably, the mad cow agent) is exceptionally resistant to heat, and a large proportion would simply depart intact with the smoke and gases generated by the fire. I can think of few better techniques for distributing it far and wide over the countryside. . . . What they should be doing is burying the bodies of the cattle in lime on the farms where the disease occurred. If the scrapie analogy holds, the soil surface on those farms will be heavily contaminated anyway, and there would be no danger of contaminating men and vehicles when transporting the carcasses away."[3]

In an article titled "Friendly Fire in Medicine," Paul Brown described the history of instances in which Creutzfeldt-Jakob disease had survived normal hospital sterilization procedures and managed to infect others. "When in the course of war the military unwittingly takes aim at its own men, the resulting casualties are sometimes euphemistically attributed to 'friendly fire,'" Brown observed. "Physicians have an almost equally picturesque term to describe the unexpected turn of events that harms rather than helps the patient: 'therapeutic misadventures.'" In one such case in 1977, "CJD was reported in two patients 16 and 20 months after they had had stereotactic electroencephalographic depth recordings for epileptic conditions. The same electrodes had previously been used for stereotactic exploration of a patient with CJD, . . . and they had then been sterilized with 70% alcohol and formaldehyde vapor. Although this sterilization procedure is effective for conventional pathogens, neither chemical inactivates the agents of spongiform encephalopathy, and one of the electrodes subsequently transmitted spongiform encephalopathy to a chimpanzee 18 months after implantation in the cerebral cortex."[4] Several medical personnel had also died of CJD, including a neurosurgeon, a neuropathologist, and two histopathology technicians. There was no way of proving whether they had gotten their disease through occupational exposure, but it seemed a good possibility.

Aside from medical accidents, however, Creutzfeldt-Jakob Disease seemed generally difficult to transmit. Kuru, the other known human spongiform encephalopathy, had spread fairly rapidly within a specific tribe, multiplying into a devastating epidemic within a contained geographic region. CJD, by contrast, spanned the globe but was considered so rare that it often went completely unrecognized until health authorities started looking for it. The first cases were observed in Germany in the 1920s, but the disease did not receive much attention until Gajdusek started taking it seriously in the 1960s, and it has never been made a reportable disease, so statistical estimates of its frequency can only be roughly charted. Under Gajdusek's leadership, though, surveillance began in a number of countries around the world, and the data that filtered back showed a fairly consistent pattern. Everywhere they looked, they found about one case per million people per year. It occurred in meat-eaters. It occurred in vegetarians. It occurred in England, where scrapie was endemic, and it occurred at similar rates of incidence in New Zealand, where scrapie had never been reported.

This pattern raised an obvious question: If CJD was this rare and difficult to transmit, where was it coming from, and how did it manage to maintain itself throughout the world? Its worldwide distribution resembled the pattern you might expect from a rare genetic disorder or sporadic mutation, and some characteristics of the disease supported this conclusion. In fact, about one in ten cases of CJD—10% to 15%—ran in families, following a pattern indicating that it was transmitted by a dominant gene. And yet Gajdusek and Gibbs had proven that it was transmissible. CJD and the other spongiform encephalopathies seemed to be both transmissible *and* inherited, a characteristic that made them unique among all known diseases.

A theory that promised to explain this paradox came from Stanley Prusiner, a neurologist at the University of California School of Medicine at San Francisco. Prusiner first became interested in the problem in 1972 after one of his patients died of CJD. He had a background in biochemistry research, and was fascinated when he started reading about the spongiform diseases. "It became clear that this was a wonderful problem for a chemist," he said. "It had been attacked by pathologists, physicians, veterinarians. Those who tried to unravel the chemistry of the disease hadn't taken a very careful approach. I spent much of my time thinking about how I was going to do this problem. When I finished, I set up a lab here." In collaboration with William Hadlow, the scientist who had first drawn Gajdusek's attention to the similarities between kuru and scrapie, Prusiner began sifting through brain tissues, hoping to isolate and identify the infectious agent. "The task was daunting," he recalled. "Many investigators had tried and failed in the past. But with the optimism of youth, I forged ahead."[5]

In order to accelerate the abominably slow pace of laboratory research, Prusiner took advantage of a breakthrough scored in 1975 by Dick Marsh and British scrapie researcher Richard Kimberlin. Marsh and Kimberlin had discovered that hamsters could incubate the disease even more rapidly than mice and that their brains accumulated higher levels of the disease agent than other experimental host animals. By using hamsters instead of mice and by modifying the testing procedure, Prusiner was able to complete experiments in 60 days that previously would have taken a full year.

Prusiner's initial research was aimed at purifying the disease agent. He spun samples in centrifuges and treated them with enzymes trying to break down other brain tissues while leaving the infectious agent intact. "We used at least five different techniques to show that a protein was necessary for infectivity," he said. "Then we used five different techniques to look for a nucleic acid. We couldn't find any."[6] Eventually he was able to achieve a 5,000-fold enrichment of his samples, and found that the infectious agent consisted largely of a single protein which showed unusual resistance to most proteases— enzymes that digest proteins. Further studies showed that it was a "glycoprotein"—a protein with sugars attached to the amino acid chain.

These discoveries slotted in neatly with research in England by a young Indian scientist named Harash Narang. Using an electron microscope, Narang had found rod-shaped particles in sections of scrapie-infected brain tissue and shown that the particles could be stained by substances that selectively bind to sugars. He called them "tubulofilamentous particles," and they looked at first like good candidates to be the long-sought scrapie virus. Other scientists had looked long and hard for so long with so little success that at first they doubted Narang's result. Gajdusek guessed that Narang was looking at a contamination accident, but when other scientists found that they could reproduce his result, the mood turned excited. Gajdusek wrote a personal letter to Narang's employers at the British Public Health Service Laboratories, congratulating them on the discovery of what Narang called a "nemavirus."[7]

Further research, however, showed that the particles only occur rarely in some spongiform brain diseases. It appeared that they were byproducts of scrapie rather than its cause. Prusiner studied Narang's particles and concluded that they were composed largely, if not entirely, of the protein he had been observing in his experiments. The same protein was also found in another type of deposit that appeared in some, but not all, spongiform-infected brains— "amyloid plaques." Similar plaques, involving different proteins, were also found in the brains of Alzheimer's patients and in the brains of elderly people with no signs of degenerative brain disease. Amyloid plaques looked like little waxy buildups in the brain, and for a long time they had been considered accumulations of waste material formed as byproducts of aging or some unknown disease process.

Prusiner was struck by the fact that the protein he was studying was sticky. Solutions of the protein tended to cluster together and to crystallize into rodlike structures resembling Narang's particles. Prusiner proposed a new theory— that both the particles and amyloid plaques were crystallized formations of a protein that, by itself, might constitute the disease agent. If this were the case, Prusiner suggested scrapping the term "slow virus" and replacing it with a new term coined to capture the concept of a protein that behaved infectiously *like* a virus. He called it a "prion" (pronounced PREE-on), combining the words "protein" and "infectious," and rearranging the vowels in order to give it a more distinctive sound. Prions, he said in a 1982 article in *Science* magazine, were "proteinaceous infectious particles which are resistant to inactivation by most procedures that modify nucleic acids." Writing in *Scientific American* in 1984, Prusiner argued that the prion protein (PrP for short) "may stand out as a remarkable exception to the rule that every organism carries nucleic acids defining its own identity. The prion is known to be capable of initiating the production of new prions, at least in certain mammalian cells. . . . One would expect to find a DNA or RNA template specifying the structure of the protein. The evidence gathered so far, however, indicates the prion has no nucleic acid at all."[8]

So far, Prusiner was simply elaborating on a "self-replicating protein" theory that had been proposed previously by British mathematician J.S. Griffith. He had found some evidence to support the theory, but it was circumstantial, highly speculative evidence. And as he himself acknowledged, his theory ran so contrary to existing scientific knowledge that it could rightly be considered a "heresy" against "the principle that genetic information invariably flows from nucleic acids to proteins," a principle so entrenched that it "has been called the central dogma of molecular biology."

Like any heretic, Prusiner was headed for a collision with the dogma's true believers. "Naming something before you discover it is a risky business," thundered science reporter Gary Taubes in a sarcastic critique of Prusiner's work that appeared in the December 1986 issue of *Discover* magazine. "Yet if you play your public relations right, the press will make you famous for discovering something you haven't yet found. . . . The prion remains a mystery in more ways than one—perhaps the most controversial being why the government gave $4 million to a scientist whose work is disputed by virtually every other researcher in his field save his immediate collaborators."[9]

Taubes portrayed Prusiner as a relentless self-publicist bent on reaping "laurels, money and headlines" while engaging in the type of research that "is often written off as quackery." He had no problem finding scientists willing to support the attack. They charged Prusiner with egotism, hogging the scientific spotlight, and medical McCarthyism aimed at suppressing research by his competitors. One of Prusiner's former post-doctoral research assistants accused him of flacking the word "prion" to the press: "He rammed that word down the throats of everybody in that laboratory and in the world." Another former collaborator, Dave Bolton, said Prusiner had coined the word in order to make his research sexy to potential funding sources. "Stan discussed this with us," Bolton said. "He said, 'Look, this whole area's getting lost in a muddle of slow virus this and unconventional that and a whole bunch of other things. If we coin a new term for it, and go out and tell people of the potential link to Alzheimer's, we're going to draw people's attention to this. And we're going to get money.' "

Taubes even quoted an "anonymous researcher" who satirized Prusiner in rhyming couplets:

> *There was a young turk named Stan*
> *Who embarked on a devious plan.*
> *"If I simply rename it,*
> *I'm sure I can claim it,"*
> *Said Stan as he pondered his scam.*
>
> *"Eureka!" cried Stan, "I have found it.*
> *Well . . . maybe not actually found it.*
> *But I talked to the press*
> *Of the slow virus mess*
> *And invented a name to confound it!"*

Criticisms with more substance came from scientists like Bob Rohwer and Richard Kimberlin. Rohwer reexamined previous research into the infectious agent and disagreed with researchers' conclusions regarding its size and seeming indestructibility. Maybe it *was* a virus after all. Kimberlin opposed the prion theory based on his work showing that there were dozens of different strains of the disease agent. According to Kimberlin, the existence of strains showed that the disease agent contained genetic information—a "genome" made of nucleic acid. Instead of Prusiner's prion, he proposed an alternative model. Maybe the protein part of the disease agent came from the host animal's DNA, but interacted with a small piece of nucleic acid derived from outside the host. The two pieces together might form what Kimberlin called a "virino"—an unconventional virus. "The biology of scrapie tells us the damn thing has a genome," Kimberlin said. "To try to create models of an infectious protein with which you can encode strain variation is damn difficult. And Stan Prusiner, bless his heart, never even tried—which is wise, because you can't do it." [10]

Laura Manuelidis, a neuropathologist at Yale, also vigorously attacked Prusiner's theory, insisting that prions could not be infectious. In New York, scientists at the Institute for Basic Research in Developmental Disabilities also formed a united front. IBR researchers Henry M. Wisniewski and Patricia Mertz had identified string-like structures in scrapie brains—somewhat more elaborate shapes than Narang's rod-shaped structures—which they called "scrapie associated fibrils." They believed that what they had found was a fiber-shaped virus causing scrapie, thereby disproving the prion theory.

In 1985, even Prusiner's own research seemed to undermine his theory. He engaged molecular biologists to help him clone the gene that makes the scrapie protein. They succeeded, and to Prusiner's surprise, discovered that the PrP gene was found in normal hamsters as well as sick ones. Not only did they find PrP in healthy hamsters, they found it in healthy mice, humans and every other mammalian species that they examined. If PrP existed equally in healthy animals and sick ones, it seemed impossible that it could be causing the disease.

"Prusiner's best evidence that the scrapie agent was an infectious protein had now been contradicted," Taubes crowed. "The infectious protein theory was teetering on the abyss." [11]

If Prusiner's research had stopped at this point, the prion might have remained a minor footnote in the already-full bestiary of strange theories surrounding the spongiform brain diseases. Fortunately for his career, his chemical analyses of the prion protein turned up an odd discovery: The PrP found in infected brains had the same chemical structure as the PrP in healthy animals, but it reacted differently. When exposed to protease enzymes, normal PrP broke down. Infectious PrP, however, resisted protease digestion.

To explain the paradox, Prusiner took up another aspect of the hypothesis proposed in 1967 by J.S. Griffith: Maybe the proteins were chemically identical, but *differently folded.*

Since the 1950s, scientists had regarded genetics as a sort of Morse code inscribed in nucleic acids. Deoxyribonucleic acid, or DNA, served as the coding mechanism. Chromosomes were made of DNA, organized into "alleles," each of which contained the coding necessary to produce a specific protein. The process of manufacturing a protein was carried out through a cellular mechanism known as "translation" which "transcribed" the message by manufacturing proteins—linked chains of amino acids. The original DNA allele contained a series of "codons," and the transcription process produced a corresponding chain of amino acids in the translated protein.

Based on this understanding, scientists had achieved remarkable breakthroughs. They had developed techniques for splicing genes from one species into another, creating new transgenic hybrids. You could put a pig's gene into a duck's DNA and create ducks that produced pig protein. You could create

E. coli bacteria that produced human insulin needed for treatment of diabetes. You could splice human genes into cows, and they would give milk containing the same proteins produced in the breasts of human mothers.

But biological organisms were more complicated than mere transcriptions of their DNA sequences. A protein wasn't simply a chain of amino acids laid out in sequence like a string of beads or a line of text waiting to be read. It went through a variety of "post-translational" transformations, some of which were still only dimly understood. The prion protein, for example, became a glycoprotein by conjugating with sugar molecules. More to the point for Prusiner's theory was the fact that proteins folded up into themselves. Weak attractions between the individual amino acids in a protein sequence pulled them into "conformational states" that made the protein look more like a tangled bit of yarn than a straight chain.

Maybe, Prusiner reasoned, there was more than one way to fold a protein—a normal way and a deadly way. The infectious form of PrP could have the exact same amino acid sequence as the healthy form, only folded differently in a way that gave it different chemical properties. And maybe infectious proteins had some way of making normal ones refold into the deadly conformation. This theory marked a modification of his previous idea that prions were "capable of initiating the production of new prions." Maybe they didn't *produce* proteins, but imply acted like missionaries, converting others to flip the same way they had flipped. It was the "one bad apple" theory of scrapie. One bad prion could spoil the whole bunch.

This was, of course, simply one more theory, and there was no way to test it directly. You couldn't exactly reach in with your hand and try to refold a protein. You couldn't take a picture of it either. Even electron microscopes were incapable of magnifying a single protein enough to let you see how it was folded.

Prusiner turned his attention to Gerstmann-Straussler-Scheinker syndrome, a genetically-induced form of spongiform encephalopathy that was even more rare than Creutzfeldt-Jakob Disease. Like CJD and kuru, GSS was a progressive, fatal dementia. Like kuru, it deposited large numbers of amyloid plaques in the brain. Unlike CJD and kuru, GSS had been clearly shown to be an inherited illness which ran in families—and yet in 1981, Carleton Gajdusek performed an experiment which successfully transmitted Gerstmann-Straussler-Scheinker disease to monkeys. Once again, it seemed to be both genetic *and* infectious.

In 1988, Prusiner's laboratory acquired clones of a PrP gene obtained from a man who had GSS in his family and was dying of it himself. They compared his gene with PrP genes obtained from healthy people. The PrP gene contained more than 750 codons, specifying more than 750 amino acids. In the dying man, they found a change in just one of those codons, representing the 102nd link in the amino-acid chain. In healthy people, codon 102 usually produced the amino acid *proline*. In the GSS victim, man, it produced *leucine*.

Researchers began looking at other people with GSS and found the same mutation. "In other words," Prusiner said, "we established genetic linkage between the mutation and the disease—a finding that strongly implies the mutation is the cause." Now they had strong evidence that the PrP protein was responsible for a spongiform disease, and that the disease could be caused by a simple mutation in that protein, without any evidence of an outside virus.

Dr. Laura Hsiao, a scientist in Prusiner's lab, took the research to its next stage by creating genetically-engineered mice. Using gene-splicing, she cut out the mouse PrP gene and replaced it with the mutated human gene. The mutation, by itself, was sufficient to induce disease in the transgenic mice. Moreover, the genetically-altered mice were infectious. Injecting their brains into other mice successfully transmitted the disease.

Over the course of the next several years, other scientists announced results that strengthened Prusiner's case. They found 18 different mutations in the prion protein that could be linked to inherited spongiform diseases. "Together the collected transmission studies persuasively argue that prions do, after all, represent an unprecedented class of infectious agents, composed only of a modified mammalian protein," Prusiner stated. "Many details remain to be worked out, but one aspect appears quite clear: the main difference between normal PrP and scrapie PrP is conformational. Evidently, the scrapie protein propagates itself by contacting normal PrP molecules and somehow causing them to unfold and flip from their usual conformation to the scrapie shape. This change initiates a cascade in which newly converted molecules change the shape of other normal PrP molecules, and so on." [12]

How did strange prions recruit normal one to change their folding habits? No one knew. Gajdusek had a theory that it might occur through something resembling the physical process of crystal formation. A single abnormal prion might serve as the "seed crystal," aggregating with healthy prions into rods, fibrils and amyloid plaque formations, and causing the normal prions to flip conformations in the process.

By the 1990s, scientific evidence was mounting in favor of Prusiner's prion theory. The charges of quackery faded and were replaced with accolades. He was honored with scientific laurels including the prestigious Albert Lasker Basic Medical Research Award and the Paul Ehrlich Award, and was considered a likely candidate for a Nobel Prize. Science reporter Gary Taubes was forced to recant the "sardonic tone" of his hatchet job in *Discover* magazine.

At a very minimum, Prusiner had proven beyond reasonable doubt that his prion protein was closely linked with the spongiform diseases, but some people still strongly disagreed with his other conclusions. England's Richard Kimberlin clung to his virino theory, pointing out that Prusiner still had not managed to explain why prion diseases came in so many different strains. In the United States, Bob Rohwer, Laura Manuelidis, Henry Wisniewski and Patricia Mertz also believed a nucleic acid had to be part of the scrapie equation, and they produced scientific evidence to support their positions.

Worst-Case Scenario

In the absence of known effective methods for deactivating the infectious agent, mad cow disease only needed to fulfill two conditions in order to threaten human health. First, it had to be capable of being transmitted from cows to humans. Second, parts of the animal which carried the agent had to contaminate humans through the food chain or some other route of infection.

Short of direct experimentation on humans, scientists could only guess at whether BSE would meet the first condition. In order to arrive at a crude estimate of the odds, they began a series of experimental inoculations of various nonhuman species. If it turned out that 25 percent of the species tested went down, the odds of human susceptibility might be very crudely guesstimated at roughly 25%. Seven species other than cattle were selected for the tests: pigs, marmoset monkeys, goats, sheep, mice, mink, and Syrian golden hamsters—Stanley Prusiner's favorite test animals, known for their rapid susceptibility to scrapie.

Regarding the second condition, no one knew *which* parts of the cow were infectious. It was clear that brains and spinal cord should not be eaten, but what about livers and kidneys? What about intestines, which were routinely used to make sausage? Lips, which went into taco filling? The cheeks, used in sausage and baloney? Even the parts that were not eaten, such as thyroid, pancreas and adrenal glands, were frequently used to produce medicines and over-the-counter nutritional supplements. Cow pituitary glands produced drugs prescribed to help human beings control their blood pressure and heart rate. Their lungs produced heparin, an anti-coagulant. Spleens were consumed for food and also used went into medicines used to induce blood clotting. Bovine ovaries produced medications used to regulate menstruation in women. And what about the meat itself? All meat is laced with microscopic nerve tissue needed to stimulate muscle actions. In fact, experiments on TSE-infected goats and mink had shown that their muscle tissue *was* infectious. If the infectious agent could be found in brain and spinal cord, how could anyone be sure that the nervous tissue inside a regular cut of beef wouldn't also carry low levels of infectivity? And, of course, what about milk?

The difficulty of answering these questions was acknowledged in 1989 by the British government's reconstituted scientific advisory committee on BSE, led now by Dr. David Tyrell. "Compared with almost all other infections, work on spongiform encephalopathies is severely handicapped by lack of laboratory tests for the presence of the agent in apparently normal tissue," stated a Tyrell committee report.[1]

Without laboratory tests, the only way to get accurate results would be to inoculate hundreds of healthy cows with various organ tissues from infected animals and see which cows developed the disease. Unfortunately, such experiments would be enormously expensive, and—given the slow incubation period of the disease—would take years to produce answers.

In response to these concerns, the government issued a rule known officially as the ban on "specified bovine offals" (SBOs for short). Offals—a word which literally means "garbage parts"—are the internal organs of an animal. The SBO ban excluded brain, spinal cord, spleen, tonsils and thymus from sale for human consumption. However, it did *not* exclude peripheral nerves (which had demonstrated TSE infectivity in sheep, goats and mice); eyes (which transmitted CJD in human beings); liver or lymph nodes (infectious in sheep, goats, mice and mink); kidney or lung (infectious in mice and mink).

"What do brain, spinal cord, spleen, thymus, tonsils, and the intestines of cattle have in common?" asked microbiology professor Richard Lacey. "They have little commercial value. They took those organs out, because they had to take something out that might be dangerous, so they selected only those organs that caused the minimal commercial loss. Could this be true? I'm afraid it could."[2]

Lacey was a portly, ruddy-complected man in his fifties whose affable demeanor made him at first glance an unlikely candidate to be the British meat industry's worst nightmare, a man whom some people considered a fearless crusader and others considered an "intellectual terrorist." His vocation as a scientist-activist began in the 1970s, when he opposed drug companies for selling antibiotics that he considered unnecessary and expensive, but his early concerns were mostly expressed in academic settings and did not particularly mark him as a troublemaker.

Like most medically-trained professionals of his generation, Lacey grew up thinking of vegetarians as misguided cranks. "My career took me from general medicine, to microbiology and bio-chemistry and then to food microbiology in the 1980s," he recalled. "All this time my consumption of meat was dropping. I have a vivid memory of visiting the U.S.A. and being appalled by greedy Americans guzzling huge steaks. I am not sure exactly why I was so appalled, but I must have been aware then of the sheer inefficiency of meat production from the point of wasted energy and basic nutrients. However, it was not until the 1980s that my professional work and knowledge began to impinge to any real extent on what I ate, and in retrospect, I cannot understand why it took so long. In defense, I can offer the excuse that I was trained as a doctor and doctors were themselves indoctrinated to preach the need for meat."[3]

In 1983 Lacey was appointed to head England's largest combined university and health service microbiology department at the University of Leeds. In 1986 he was appointed to the Veterinary Products Committee, a scientific panel that advises the British Minister of Agriculture on matters concerning the use of drugs in animals, birds and fish. He would later conclude that political criteria had influenced the government's decision to select him. "Prospective members are, to varying degrees, vetted—certainly inasmuch as their general views and philosophy of life, rather than their exact political leanings," he observed. "I was appointed because I had previously researched and stated that most antibiotic resistance in bacteria was selected as a result of antibiotic use in the human population, rather than in animals. My presence would therefore counteract the view that much antibiotic resistance was due to the use of antibiotics in animals . . . and so defend such use. I would not say that this is exactly my view today, but the appointment to this committee did let me see how the inside of the U.K. Ministry of Agriculture worked."[4]

The Great Egg Scare

Lacey was still a sitting member of the committee in 1988 when he vaulted to media prominence amid a controversy that served as a sort of trial run for the soon-to-explode food scare over mad cow disease. The controversy began when Edwina Currie, a junior health minister, made the mistake of mentioning publicly that eggs infected with salmonella had poisoned over 1,000 people that year. Currie was quickly humbled and forced to resign over her remarks, but Lacey took up her defense, insisting that England was indeed experiencing its worst-ever outbreak of salmonella, with 300 cases reported each week. Taking into account the fact that many cases passed as flu and went underreported, he estimated that 150,000 people per year were getting salmonella food poisoning from eggs. "One person a week is dying from salmonella in eggs and that is a conservative estimate," he said. "Mrs. Currie has been made a scapegoat by the egg producers, by the Ministry of Agriculture and by all those trying to find someone to blame. It won't work because it does not solve the problem—the salmonella is still there."[5]

Salmonella bacteria is harmless to chickens but in humans causes an intense flu-like illness which can occasionally be fatal. The type of salmonella appearing in eggs, moreover, was salmonella enteritidis phage type 4—an unusually virulent strain. Previously, officials had tallied about 1,000 cases per year of poisoning by the phage 4 strain, but in 1988 the number leapt to 14,000 cases. The reason, Lacey explained, was that the phage 4 strain had invaded the oviducts—the egg laying organs—of hens, enabling the infection to pass from one generation to the next. The root of the problem was the system of modern factory farming, which packed chickens together in overcrowded quarters and relied on antibiotics rather than good hygiene to control infection. In addition, chickens had been highly inbred and selected for their egg-laying characteristics. "The result is they are genetically uniform, which means that if the organism adapts to one chicken it can adapt to the lot," Lacey said. The practice of animal cannibalism was also part of the problem. Chickens were eating feed derived from the rendered remains of their own species, enabling salmonella to recycle and multiply in much the same way that cow cannibalism created the BSE epidemic.[6]

"The public debate on food poisoning took off in earnest and to many people the revelations were appalling," Lacey said. "For the first time people became aware of the terrible cruelty of intensive rearing and the effective cannibalism that results from refeeding a species its own remains after processing in the rendering plants. These facts were not news to me, but the more I looked into the causes of food contamination, the more revolted I became. . . . I soon began to write about general matters of food, using my basic medical and nutritional knowledge in addition to my microbiological training."[7]

A run of salmonella stories in the news triggered a nearly 50-percent drop in egg sales, and food industry officials implored shoppers to avoid panic. In an attempt to restore consumer confidence, the government hastily introduced a $45 million agricultural assistance package to subsidize the slaughter of four million at-risk chickens. The government also launched a PR offensive, taking out full-page newspaper ads claiming that the number of salmonella cases blamed on eggs "is very small by comparison with the huge numbers of eggs that are consumed," and spending $1.4 million on a glossy full-color brochure titled "Food Safety: A Guide from Her Majesty's Government." Supermarkets circulated millions of copies of the booklet, which focused on home cooking practices that would minimize the risk of salmonella exposure.[8]

Lacey lost no time denouncing the effort as an expensive public relations exercise, "a crafty way of diverting the blame from farmers and the food industry to the hapless consumer." The government also came under fire from Dr. Tim Lang of the London Food Commission, an independent food watchdog organization. "Highly professional leaflets are no substitute for a sane food policy," Lang said. "If the food that consumers buy from the shelf is already contaminated, just what are they supposed to do?"[9]

The salmonella controversy was still raging in January 1989 when Lacey launched a new salvo of warnings about high levels of listeria bacteria in "cook-chill meals"—a British term for precooked frozen foods. Lacey had purchased 24 samples of microwaveable dinners from grocery stores and found that six of them contained listeria, a bacteria that can cause fatal blood poisoning, meningitis, and miscarriages in pregnant women. Moreover, the microwaving instructions on the package were insufficient to heat the food adequately. Lacey cooked the meals according to instructions and found that in most cases the listeria survived. A week after he announced his findings, the story flared into a full-scale food scare focusing on the death of a baby girl who had acquired listeria in the womb when her mother ate a packet of chicken sandwiches and soft cheeses from a supermarket.[10]

After several months of official efforts to downplay or deny Lacey's warnings, the British government itself began reporting evidence that supported his conclusions. In February, the British Public Health Laboratory reported that it had discovered "disturbing" levels of listeria in cook-chill dinners and ready-to-eat chicken. In April, the head of food microbiology at Nottingham University noted that the number of cases of salmonella-related food poisoning in England had doubled since 1985 and warned that the number of cases could reach one million a year by the end of the century.[11]

By 1989 salmonella enteritidis phage type 4 had become "the predominant salmonella in broiler chickens" according to research published by Dr.

Bernard Rowe, director of the Public Health Laboratory Service. "The surprising thing is that this strain seems to have pushed out other salmonellas," said Dr. Anita Rampling, a consultant bacteriologist who participated in the research.[12] The researchers examined frozen broiler chickens in supermarkets and found that 40 percent were infected with phage 4 salmonella. According to the World Health Organization, Europe as a whole was probably already seeing at least a million cases of salmonella and several hundred deaths per year. WHO experts said up to half of poultry carcasses for sale in industrial countries were infected with salmonella, "a highly unacceptable situation."[13]

Concerns came also from Professor Bevan Moseley, head of the government's Institute for Food Research. "Figures for all types of food poisoning are going up and up," Moseley said. "They never go down and have not done so for 10 years. That suggests that we do not have the situation under control."[14] During the first half of 1989, England saw 23,500 reports of food poisoning, compared with 17,000 for the same period a year earlier.[15]

Conspiracy Theories

The food industry, however, remained unimpressed and hostile to criticism. Teresa Gorman, a Tory member of the British House of Commons, began to talk darkly of a left-wing conspiracy, with Lacey at the center of "a series of apparently-unconnected publicity campaigns against preservatives, additives, hormones, salmonella, listeria and cook-chill, which have left the food industry reeling." She described Lacey as "a cohort of the London Food Commission . . . little more than a team of left-wing activists." Gorman's views were supported by the industry-supported Food and Drink Federation, which denounced "scaremongering activities by individuals or groups." Similar red-baiting sentiments came from the Institute of Food Science and Technology, a professional association of food safety consultants: "There may well be some left-wing influence behind the food scares of late, but it is difficult to prove."[16]

During 1989, the salmonella and listeria controversies easily eclipsed BSE as public health concerns. Even scientists and MDs were generally unfamiliar with the unusual characteristics of the spongiform encephalopathies and therefore relied heavily on the government's analysis—an analysis which strained mightily to offer reassurance even at the expense of fudging the facts.

Lacey himself, in fact, continued to accept the government's interpretation. "Perhaps the most reassuring fact is that while scrapie has been occurring in sheep for many years, there is no proof that we can catch it," he wrote in a 1989 book titled *Safe Shopping, Safe Cooking, Safe Eating.* "BSE in cattle is too new for us to be certain that we cannot catch it from infected cows, although that is unlikely," he concluded.[17]

Lacey's concerns began to rise, however, in tandem with his growing unhappiness on the government's Veterinary Products Committee. "In addition to members being hand-picked, we were manipulated, controlled, influenced, and sometimes threatened by the large number of 'invisible' civil servants always present," he would write later. "By 'invisible' I mean that their presence was never formally admitted in published details of the membership of committees. There were always more civil servants than members."[18]

The issue that troubled him the most was the government's eagerness to approve the use of the Monsanto Company's genetically-engineered recombinant bovine growth hormone (rBGH). Injections of rBGH into specially-fed dairy cows induce an increase of up to 25 percent in milk production, and Monsanto was aggressively pushing the hormone in an attempt to claim leadership in the fledgling biotechnology industry. Critics, however, charged that the hormone was bad for animal health, suspect for human health, and potentially harmful to the environment. One activist characterized rBGH as "crack for cows." It forced cows to produce more milk at the price of increased stress on their overall health, exacerbating illnesses such as mastitis, and mining the calcium from their bones. In order to achieve the higher levels of milk production, moreover, cows needed to consume more energy-dense food, adding to the pressure for farmers to use protein and fat supplements derived from rendered animals—the feeding practice which had created the BSE epidemic in the first place.

In January 1990, the rBGH issue led Lacey finally to resign in protest from the Veterinary Products Committee. "The cow was not asking for it, nor was the consumer, nor was the farmer," he stated. "It was only of interest to the pharmaceutical company who produced it, and to a notion that the Ministry of Agriculture had about improving 'efficiency.' . . . In any case it was becoming increasingly difficult to criticize an organization that I had responsibility to advise." [19]

Mad Cow Hits the Headlines

Lacey's concerns were also beginning to mount regarding mad cow disease, and in February the British government's prediction that cattle would be a "dead end host" for BSE began to unravel, beginning with its announcement that the disease could be transmitted experimentally to mice. "The preliminary results show that in experimental laboratory conditions BSE can be transmitted to cattle and mice," reported the official news release. It could be transmitted "to cattle by inoculating infected brain tissues into their brain and blood stream, and to mice by feeding large quantities—over half their weight—of BSE-infected material. These results show that the disease can be transmitted using unnatural methods of infection, which can only be done experimentally in laboratory conditions and which would never happen in the field." [20]

Reading the announcement, Lacey was struck by the carefully-crafted, superficially reassuring wording. The claim that the disease had been transmitted using "unnatural methods of infection" was a misleading attempt to downplay the significance of the result. *All* laboratory experiments are unnatural, by definition. In this case, the mice had been fed large quantities of BSE-infected material as a necessary way of speeding up the outcome of the experiment, but the result was still bad news. If the exposure method was too unnatural to give meaningful results, why had they bothered with the experiment in the first place? Once you stripped away MAFF's rhetorical attempt at spin control, what you were left with was the fact that their own experiment had proven the disease could transmit to other species.

MAFF's final conclusion was an even more astonishing stretch of inter-pretation: "Similar results were obtained some years ago in relation to exper-imental transmission studies of sheep scrapie to sheep and mice. The BSE results therefore provide further evidence that BSE behaves like scrapie, a disease which has been in the sheep population for over two centuries with-out any evidence whatsoever of being a risk to human health." [21]

The obvious question, Lacey realized, was, "How do these experiments provide evidence of similarity with scrapie, except for establishing the trans-missibility of BSE? And I would have thought that it was precisely the transmis-sibility of BSE which did pose a potential risk to human health." [22] In fact, Creutzfeldt-Jakob Disease was *also* transmissible to mice in laboratory tests. Using the evidence at hand, MAFF could just as logically have concluded that BSE behaves like CJD, the human disease.

Lacey began to contemplate the worst-case scenario. The spongiform encephalopathies varied widely in their impact on susceptible populations. CJD occurred at the low rate of one case per million people per year. Scrapie, on the other hand, was endemic in sheep, and kuru had devastated the Fore tribes-people of New Guinea. With transmissible mink encephalopathy, there were well-documented cases in which almost 100% of all mink on a ranch suc-cumbed following exposure to contaminated feed. If you took TME as a model for predicting the human consequences of eating infected beef, England could literally lose *an entire generation* to the disease.

Other people were also reading between the lines and drawing worried conclusions from the new announcement. The European Community made BSE a notifiable disease and announced restrictions on the export of British cattle and various cattle organs used in the manufacture of pharmaceutical products.

In March 1990, more bad news came when the *Times* of London reported the previously unpublicized fact that five types of antelope had died in British zoos from spongiform encephalopathies. The first animal, a nyala, had died in 1986, the same year in which BSE was first identified in dairy cattle. A gems-bok had died a year later. In 1989 London Zoo lost a kudu and a rare Arabian oryx, and an eland went down in a zoo near the site of the first reported cases of BSE. Zoo officials confirmed that the affected animals had been fed com-mercial cattle feed. [23]

In April, worried local officials in the British county of Humberside banned the use of British beef in school meals.

In the first week of May, mad *cat* disease hit the headlines. The feline in question was a neutered five-year-old male Siamese named Max. He had become ill earlier in the year, and veterinarians spent several weeks testing him but could do nothing to help. No one had seen a case of spongiform encephalopathy in a cat before, so it came as a shock when a routine post-mortem examination spotted the characteristic microscope holes in Max's brain and spinal cord.

In all likelihood, other cats with the disease were going undetected, since most cat deaths did not undergo the level of scrutiny that Max had received. "Vets are presented with cats showing nervous disorders like this one every day," noted John Bower, president of the British Veterinary Association. "Some can be treated, some can't and have to be destroyed. But in 90 per cent of cases when they do have to be put to sleep the owners don't want us to carry out a post mortem." [24]

The cat's death was troubling for another reason. Cats had not succumbed when exposed to sheep scrapie, but experiments had shown that they were easily susceptible to Creutzfeldt-Jakob Disease. At a very minimum, therefore, Mad Max blew away the argument that BSE behaved the same as scrapie. If cats were not immune to BSE, there was no particular reason to expect that humans would be immune either. There was even reason to suspect the opposite. If they can get *ours,* why couldn't we get *theirs?*

"My involvement with the BSE issue began by chance," Lacey said. "On about May 10, I had a telephone call from a London radio station asking if I would give a telephone interview with a Mr. Andrew Neil who was rehearsing as a part-time radio presenter. I agreed, little realizing that the Andrew Neil in question was Andrew Neil, the editor of *The Sunday Times.* We talked about food matters in general including, of course, BSE. It was a relaxed discussion and I explained that the numbers of cattle confirmed as having BSE were still rising, implying that BSE must be spreading between cattle and that all the infected herds should be destroyed. Common sense, I thought. Next day, a journalist from *The Sunday Times* telephoned and I repeated these comments. On Sunday, May 13, the paper carried the front page lead headline, 'Leading Food Scientist Calls for Slaughter of Six Million Cows.' Put bluntly like this it does seem rather draconian. But the scale of the problem was not my making." [25]

The *Times* story quoted Lacey's call for "authoritative advice from medical doctors instead of all these ministers, vets and civil servants who are telling us that everything is safe. We now have two new mammals, cattle and cats, infected naturally for the first time by this agent. The likelihood is increased of the possibility of transmission to man from cattle." Lacey recommended destroying every herd that had seen even a single infected cow—which by that time represented half the herds in England. Until the cull was carried out, he recommended that people avoid eating beef, although people over the age of 50 might not need to worry in light of the fact that spongiform encephalopathies in humans seemed to take decades to incubate.

The government's response, quoted in the *Times,* was scathing:

> Keith Meldrum, the government's chief veterinary officer, accused Lacey of "pure supposition, over-reaction and scare-mongering." Beef was safe to eat, he said.
>
> "To suggest that the discovery of a spongiform encephalopathy in a cat increases the risk to man is absolute nonsense. The basis on which we are saying beef is safe is that the agent of scrapie has not been detected in the muscle of sheep affected with scrapie." . . .
>
> David Maclean, the food minister, said last night: "Professor Lacey is good at popping up in the media with scare stories. Let him send me his scientific evidence and we will look at it. Even the most elementary scientist knows that this disease cannot be passed from cow to cow like an infection. As far as telling

people not to eat beef if they are under 50, if anyone is daft enough to believe his doomsday scenario, then the age of 50 appears plucked out of thin air and is nonsensical." [26]

The controversy had an immediate and profound impact. An opinion poll found that 43 percent of the British public thought schools should not serve beef to children. Local government officials followed the example of Humberside county and removed beef from the menu at some 2,000 British schools, as did Magdalene College in Cambridge after taking "general medical opinion from our medical fellows." The *Independent,* a British daily newspaper, described the scene that Friday at "the beef-laden meat counter at Safeway's Barbican branch in the City of London. . . . By 7:15 P.M., there were only two packs of boneless chicken breasts left. But a few feet away, the fridge display shelves groaned with beef. Mounds of unsold fillet, rump and prime-diced braising steak lay above joints of topside and silverside. All declared themselves 'home produced.'" [27] By late May, the country as a whole had seen a 25-percent drop in beef consumption.

The main burden of placating the public fell on the shoulders of Agriculture Minister John Gummer, who entered the fray with the enthusiasm of one of beef's true believers. Gummer's personal intervention was credited for putting beef back on the menu in Westminster schools and for preventing other member nations in the European Union from banning British beef altogether. When appeals to science and common sense were insufficient to soothe fears, Gummer turned to personal testimonials. "My wife eats beef, my children eat beef, and I eat beef," he said. "That is everyone's absolute protection." [28] For proof of this "absolute protection," he arranged a publicity stunt with Cordelia, his youngest daughter, posing with her and a pair of hamburgers. At least, that was the way the day was supposed to go. Once they got in front of cameras, Cordelia decided she didn't want a burger that day and refused to eat. Gummer improvised by taking a bite out of her burger himself and posing it in front of her face as TV cameras rolled. "It's delicious," he said. It was a photo opportunity that would come back to haunt him in subsequent years, becoming a symbol of the government's shameless eagerness to flack for beef despite mounting evidence of human danger.

"One Siamese cat dies a nasty death in Bristol and suddenly the country is catapulted into another bout of 'mad cow disease' anxiety," commented the *Guardian.* "Is it mass hysteria or the deep rumblings of despair from people who deeply mistrust modern farming methods and government assurances that our food is fine? . . . The government is accusing Professor Lacey of scaremongering. Ministers didn't much like it either when he was first to back Edwina Currie on salmonella in eggs, and then highlighted the dangers from listeria in cook-chill products heated in microwaves. . . . All the other food scandals have had a measurable risk. The elderly and infirm could die from a really bad egg, and listeria could claim the life of an unborn baby in the womb. The rest of us were fairly safe. BSE is very different. Mr. Gummer may be right that there is no risk. And he may be wrong. If he is wrong, we have no idea how dreadful the slowly incubating epidemic may be." [29]

In an attempt to allay fears, Agriculture Minister John Gummer poses with his daughter and a pair of well-placed burgers. Note the extra hand helping Cordelia hold hers. (*photo ©Jim James, PA News Ltd. Used with permission.*)

The controversy could not have come at a worse time for the meat industry, which was on the brink of unveiling a million-pound advertising campaign to bolster sales of red meat. "The publicity campaign has been in preparation for some months and is not a response to the latest scare over BSE," insisted the Meat and Livestock Commission's Garry Dobbin. "It reflects our concern about the general pressure to eat less meat. Meat is the biggest and best source of proteins, minerals and vitamins and an invaluable part of the modern diet." [30]

In June 1990, the propaganda war culminated in hearings before the U.K. Parliamentary Agriculture Committee. By that time, government veterinarians had retrospectively examined the brains of 31 cats which had died from unexplained nervous symptoms, and found that four had a spongiform encephalopathy. The committee asked British chief veterinarian Keith Meldrum how likely it was that the cats had gotten the disease from their food. "That's a hypothesis, but I'm not sure it is the one I would support," Meldrum answered, repeating once again his opinion that the cat deaths posed no public health risks whatsoever. [31]

In preparation for his own testimony, Lacey submitted a written memorandum, co-authored with a colleague, Dr. Stephen Dealler.

The main line of reassurance that BSE in cows and cattle presents no danger to man comes from the claim that in effect BSE *is* cattle scrapie and that the evidence for sheep scrapie causing diseases such as Creutzfeldt-Jakob Disease

***Food Minister Nicholas
Soames said he ate British
beef "in large quantities,
whenever I can and with the
greatest pleasure."***
(*photo © Eric Roberts.
Used with permission*)

in man is either tenuous or nonexistent. The evidence that BSE is due to sheep scrapie is . . . virtually non-existent. . . . It is also possible that BSE arose in, say pigs, or even in bovines themselves. Indeed the latter seems the most plausible explanation for the high incidence of BSE. . . . Much of the hope that BSE in cattle will not pass to man has now evaporated. There is now a crisis of major magnitude. Once the host-range of the BSE agent was found to be beyond that of cattle, the Southwood Committee should have been immediately reconvened. Even after the cat deaths, the only official action seems to be the parrot-like claim from ministers that our beef is completely safe.[32]

At the hearing itself, the verbal cross-examination of Lacey was led by Christopher Gill, a Conservative member of parliament. Gill was also a cattle farmer himself as well as director of a private company engaged in slaughtering and the manufacture of meat products. "Professor Lacey," he began, "when the Chairman asked you whether beef was safe to go into the food chain you said that we simply do not know and yet on page four of your written evidence you say that: 'There is little reason to believe that the agents responsible for transmissible spongiform encephalopathy are found actually within or around muscle fibers.' I think the general perception amongst the people in this room would be that it is only the muscles of animals that we generally consume." [33]

"This, I am afraid, is not true," Lacey replied. "The muscles have to be associated with nerves. The muscle will not work unless it has a nerve supply. There must be nerves in meat and you cannot take the nerves out of all the meat. The reason I am concerned about the nerves is that for many years it has been known that the scrapie type agent can be transmitted from peripheral nerves. That was work done by Pattison in 1962 and other people. All right, theoretically if you go with a fine microscope and take out all nerve fibers it will be safe in my view, but you cannot do it in practice. . . . In practice you cannot get meat to be pure, it must contain some of these extra tissues."

"Professor Lacey, I am rather surprised that you have not actually produced that evidence for the Committee to study in advance of of this morning's meeting," Gill replied. "Given the fact that you are a scientist it is perhaps surprising that your written evidence is rather short of fact because, again, the popular perception of a scientist is one who actually works on the basis of facts and upon the findings of the evidence and research available to him."

"I find that quite extraordinary," Lacey retorted, his temper rising. "The point about nerves and muscles, I am sorry, I should have realized that there are Members of Parliament who are not aware that muscles have a nerve supply. If I had been aware of that I would have drawn diagrams from *Gray's Anatomy* and shown it to you. I regret that you did not know that. In future I will assume that you actually know nothing."

"I think, Professor Lacey, my criticism of what you have presented to the Committee for their consideration is that so much of it is speculation and supposition and conjecture," Gill said. "Before we go on to that, could I invite you to comment on another statement that you are reported to have made which is that 'We cannot rule out the possibility of the disease spreading to humans, particularly pregnant women and young children'? Now the point I am trying to make to you, Professor Lacey, is that this is hardly the language of a scientist basing his pronouncements on scientific evidence and research, and when you say 'particularly pregnant women and young children,' I think you are being sensationalist."

"This is absolutely wrong," Lacey replied. "This is being accurate. . . . If a pregnant woman gets an infectious virus, for example the BSE agent, you have two people to think about. The baby will have no immunity whatsoever if it spreads from the pregnant woman into the baby. As far as young children go, we are concerned about the young people particularly if we have a disease with an incubation period that may be anything from 20 years to 40 years or more. As I have said, if one is over 50 the risk of getting a serious infection 40 years hence does not matter very much but in young people it does matter. We are particularly worried about the eating habits of young people who eat a great deal of processed beef, burgers and sausages, and we do not know what is in them."

Another member of parliament, Alan Amos, weighed in: "Professor Lacey, it does seem to me, and I am not an expert in these matters at all, that you seem to be expecting the Government to give a degree of scientific certainty which no scientist could or would wish to give, yet in your submission it seems a cry vague when you talk about 'may,' 'could be,' 'possibly.' On the one hand you are demanding scientific certainty yet in your submission you accept that certainty is not available and it is not possible."

"The point about the difference between science and philosophy is not that I am demanding proof," Lacey said. "I am not. I am saying it is impossible to generate scientific proof because it will take too long. The possibility exists that there is a very substantial risk to man, and I am saying that we cannot wait to generate scientific proof. I am speaking in my main capacity as a person responsible for prevention of infection rather than as someone who is doing experiments with micro-organisms. . . . I cannot believe that a scientist will say: 'In order to find out how big the problem is we are going to see how many people die.' I cannot accept that." [34]

On July 10, 1990, the Agriculture Committee delivered its final report, giving chairman Jerry Wiggin the chance to take one final parting shot. "That not all scientists carry equal authority was amply borne out in our evidence," Wiggin said. "Professor Lacey, in particular, showed a tendency to extrapolate sensational conclusions from incomplete evidence in order to publicize his long-standing concerns about food safety. The result was a mixture of science and science fiction—a quite unsuitable basis for public policy. When he told us that, 'If our worst fears are realized, we could lose a whole generation of people,' he seemed to lose touch completely with the real world. We do not doubt the sincerity of Professor Lacey's concerns, but we must question the judgment of television producers and newspaper editors who beat a path to his door as an authority on all aspects of food safety." [35]

Two months later, the Ministry of Agriculture issued a carefully-worded news release reporting that a pig had died after experimental exposure to mad cow disease. "This result is the first evidence of the susceptibility of pigs to any form of transmissible spongiform encephalopathy," the statement said. "It does not indicate the degree of susceptibility, or provide any evidence that pigs might be susceptible under natural conditions or show whether there might be any difference in susceptibility between breeds of pigs. It does demonstrate that pigs are capable of succumbing to the disease under extreme laboratory conditions. So far only one of the ten animals that were subject to identical exposure has succumbed to the clinical disease. There are no cases of the disease occurring in natural conditions. The experiment's results were immediately referred to the Tyrell Committee. It concluded that there were no new implications for human health as a result of this experiment." [36]

Of course, there *were* implications. The practice of feeding rendered pigs back to pigs was even older and more common than the practice of feeding cows to cows. If pigs could contract a TSE, this practice might not be as safe as authorities thought. The health and economic implications of this possibility were too enormous to contemplate—which might explain why, seven years later, the head of USDA's Food Safety and Inspection Service would falsely claim that pigs had never been shown to contract a TSE.

An experiment is being carried out to see if humans can catch BSE.

These are the guinea pigs.

Everybody who eats beef is taking part in an horrific long term experiment. Because no other research is being carried out in order to discover the effects of BSE on humans.

If BSE can be transmitted to humans, the disease would take a form similar to Creutzfeldt-Jacob Disease, an incurable degenerative disease of the brain. This led the Tyrrell Committee to conclude that "the best way" to find out if BSE can pass to humans is to "monitor all the UK cases of CJD over

the next two decades". In other words, wait and see.

There is no evidence that beef is safe. If it isn't, it will be too late to save thousands of people by the time we know. Fortunately, this is an experiment nobody has to be part of. We can stop eating beef. If you'd like the truth about BSE, contact us on 0161 928 0793 for a free information pack.

THE VEGETARIAN SOCIETY Ⴅ
F E E D I N G   Y O U   T H E   F A C T S

This poster, published by England's Vegetarian Society, ridiculed the government's statement that "the best way" to find out if BSE could transmit to humans would be to "monitor all the UK cases of CJD over the next two decades."

One Bad Apple

The United States, meanwhile, was experiencing its own round of food scares and scandals. As public concerns mounted, the food industry launched a massive counterattack—an attempt to shift the debate in its favor by literally making it a criminal offense for journalists and food safety activists to discuss and debate their concerns.

In Washington, some industries and their lobbyists are recognized as relatively "enlightened" capitalists, while others are regarded as hardball players unwilling to give an inch. The agribusiness industry is one of the "hardball" players. Agribusiness leaders have no use for consumer concerns about the way their food is produced. Consumers worry about the pesticide residues that routinely contaminate fruits and vegetables. Surveys indicate strong opposition to food irradiation. Most people are unhappy that dairy products come from cows injected with hormones and antibiotics, and become alarmed when they learn that sewage sludge is increasingly used as fertilizer for food crops. They also have ethical concerns about the inhumane treatment of livestock. From the point of view of the large companies dominating the food and agriculture business, however, these concerns are merely "irrational" attitudes which need to be "managed" through expensive and clever public relations campaigns.

In 1989, this gap between consumer concerns and industry insensitivity became a chasm when the so-called "Alar scare" hit the United States food industry in the one place it *did* notice—the pocketbook. Symbolically, at least, Alar marked a watershed in industry thinking. According to the industry's own carefully manufactured mythology, the Alar scare was an unscrupulous and unfair attack by environmentalists against apple growers, which destroyed farmers' livelihoods by stirring up unfounded fears about a chemical which later turned out to be harmless. The facts, however, are somewhat different from that myth.

Alar was a chemical, first marketed in 1968, that growers sprayed on trees to make their apples ripen longer before falling off. In use, Alar breaks down to a byproduct called "unsymmetrical dimethyl hydrazine" or UDMH. The first study showing that UDMH can cause cancer was published in 1973. Further studies published in 1977 and 1978 confirmed that Alar and UDMH caused tumors in laboratory animals. The U.S. Environmental Protection Agency (EPA) opened an investigation of Alar's hazards in 1980, but shelved the investigation after a closed meeting with Alar's manufacturer. In 1984, the EPA re-opened its investigation, concluding in 1985 that both Alar and UDMH were "probable human carcinogens," capable of causing as many as 100 cancers per million people exposed to it in their diet for a lifetime—in other words, 100 times the human health hazard considered "acceptable" by EPA standards. Under pressure from the manufacturer, however, the EPA allowed Alar to stay on the market. Its use continued, even after tests by the National Food Processors Association and Gerber Baby Foods repeatedly detected Alar in samples of apple sauce and apple juice, including formulations for infants.

By 1989, the states of Massachusetts and New York had banned the chemical, and the American Academy of Pediatrics was urging a similar ban at the federal level. "Risk estimates based on the best available information at this time raise serious concern about the safety of continued, long-term exposure," stated an EPA letter to apple growers which estimated that 50 out of every million adults would get cancer from long-term exposure to Alar and that the danger to children was even greater. Aside from these urgings, however, federal agencies continued to avoid regulatory action.

On February 26, 1989, the public at large first heard about Alar's dangers when CBS-TV's *60 Minutes* aired an exposé titled "A is for Apple," which became the opening salvo in a carefully-planned publicity campaign developed for the Natural Resources Defense Council (NRDC) by the Fenton Communications PR firm. Fenton helped NRDC distribute public service announcements featuring actress Meryl Streep, who warned that Alar had been detected in apple juice bottled for children. Streep's movie-star status guaranteed a large audience for the message, and public outcry ensued, as mothers poured apple juice down sink drains and school lunchrooms removed apples from the menu. The industry, its back to the wall, hastily abandoned its use of Alar, and the market for apples quickly rebounded. Within five years, in fact, apple industry profits were 50 percent higher than they had been at the time of the *60 Minutes* broadcast.[1]

At first blush, NRDC's PR campaign produced what looked like a victory for environmentalists and public safety. Over time, however, the episode began to look like a winning battle in a losing war, as the food industry fought back with its own infinitely better-financed PR campaign. The EPA, USDA and FDA began the counter-attack with a face-saving joint statement claiming that NRDC's warning lacked scientific validity. "Available data show overwhelmingly that apples carry very small amounts of Alar," the agencies argued. "It should also be noted that risk estimates for Alar and other pesticides based on animal testing are rough and are not precise predictions of human disease. Because of conservative assumptions used by EPA, actual risks may be lower or even zero."[2]

Apple growers claimed that the scare had cost them $100 million and sent dozens of family-owned orchards into bankruptcy. On November 28, 1990, apple growers in Washington state filed a libel lawsuit against CBS, NRDC and Fenton Communications. The food industry's publicity machine began cranking out propaganda. Porter/Novelli, a leading agribusiness PR firm, helped an industry group called the "Center for Produce Quality" distribute more than 20,000 "resource kits" to food retailers which scoffed at the scientific data presented on *60 Minutes*.[3] Industry-funded organizations such as the Advancement of Sound Science Coalition and the American Council on Science and Health hammered home the argument that the "Alar scare" was an irrational episode of public hysteria produced by unscrupulous manipulators of media sensationalism.

In court, the apple industry lost its lawsuit. The growers were able to show that the scientific evidence of Alar's dangers was *inconclusive,* but they were not able to prove that it was *wrong.* In dismissing the lawsuit, the presiding judge pointed to failures in the federal government's own food safety policies, noting that "governmental methodology fails to take into consideration the distinct hazards faced by preschoolers. The government is in grievous error when allowable exposures are calculated . . . without regard for the age at which exposure occurs."[4] Notwithstanding years of industry efforts to disprove the merits of NRDC's warning, the National Academy of Sciences (NAS) in 1993 confirmed the central message of the Alar case, which is that infants and young children need greater protection from pesticides. NAS called for an overhaul of regulatory procedures specifically to protect kids, finding that federal calculations for allowable levels of chemicals do not account for increased childhood consumption of fruit, for children's lower body weight, or for their heightened sensitivity.

SLAPPing Back

A victory in court, however, was only part of the objective behind the apple growers' lawsuit. As authors George Pring and Penelope Canan observed, the Alar case was part of a growing trend by corporations to intimidate their critics using "strategic lawsuits against public participation" (known in the legal trade as "SLAPP suits"). "Thousands of SLAPPs have been filed in the last two decades, tens of thousands of Americans have been SLAPPed, and still more have been muted or silenced by the threat," Pring and Canan stated. "We found that filers of SLAPPs rarely win in court yet often 'win' in the real world, achieving their political agendas. We found that SLAPP targets who fight back seldom lose in court yet are frequently devastated and depoliticized and discourage others from speaking out—'chilled' in the parlance of First Amendment commentary."[5]

SLAPP suits achieve their objectives by forcing defendants to spend huge amounts of time and money defending themselves in court. "The longer the litigation can be stretched out . . . the closer the SLAPP filer moves to success," observed New York Supreme Court Judge J. Nicholas Colabella. "Those who lack the financial resources and emotional stamina to play out the 'game' face the difficult choice of defaulting despite meritorious defenses or being brought to their knees to settle. . . . Short of a gun to the head, a greater threat to First Amendment expression can scarcely be imagined."[6]

"Initially we saw such suits as attacks on traditional 'free speech' and regarded them as just 'intimidation lawsuits,' " stated Pring and Canan. "As we studied them further, an even more significant linkage emerged: the

defendants had been speaking out in government hearings, to government officials, or about government actions. . . . This was not just free speech under
attack. It was that other and older and even more central part of our Consti-
tution: the right to petition government for a redress of grievances, the 'Petition
Clause' of the First Amendment."

Pring and Canan warned that SLAPP suits threaten the very foundation of
citizen involvement and public participation in democracy: "Americans by the
thousands are being sued, simply for exercising one of our most cherished
rights: the right to communicate our views to our government officials, to 'speak
out' on public issues. Today, you and your friends, neighbors, co-workers, community leaders, and clients can be sued for millions of dollars just for telling
the government what you think, want, or believe in. Both individuals and
groups are now being routinely sued in multimillion-dollar damage actions for
such 'all-American' political activities as circulating a petition, writing a letter
to the editor, testifying at a public hearing, reporting violations of law, lobbying for legislation, peaceful demonstrating, or otherwise attempting to influence government action."[7]

SLAPP suits reflected collaborative efforts between government and industry aimed at suppressing the views of people with complaints against the
system. In Washington, ironically enough, SLAPP-happy bureaucrats and industry mavens eagerly hyped the lawsuits as populist *solutions* to the problem of
too much government.

The contradictions and hypocrisy inherent in this position were embodied in Tom Holt, a Washington policy wonk whose career reflected in micro-
cosm the pattern of collusion that unites government and industry interests.
Holt's training in journalism came from the Morton Blackwell Leadership Institute, a corporate-funded school that teaches conservative college students how
to start their own campus newspapers to compete against perceived liberal
bias in schools' official newspapers.[8] Following a brief stint with the Richmond,
Virginia *Times-Dispatch*, he became "research director" for the Commonwealth
Foundation, helping churn out a study which argued that lawsuits against the
tobacco industry did more harm than good by creating a "litigation super-
highway where lawyers are the ones who will make the most money."[9] After
serving as a speechwriter for two U.S. secretaries of transportation, Holt went
to work as a public-relations staffer for the far-right Heritage Foundation before
signing on at another right-wing Washington think-tank called the Capital
Research Center. As a CRC "visiting fellow," he authored a book titled *The Rise
of the Nanny State: How Consumer Advocates Try to Run Our Lives,* which
accused the consumer movement of "capitalizing on the public's ignorance of
science and the media's eagerness for calamity." Holt called for reforms that
would make make it harder to sue corporations because "the consumer movement has imposed significant costs on industry—costs ultimately passed on to
consumers—and has violated individual freedoms in a futile effort to protect
us from our own actions and judgment."[10]

In order to restore those freedoms, Holt called for new laws so that corporations could use the nanny state more effectively to sue, chastise and punish

their enemies. "Could lawsuits be the cure for junk science?" he asked in Priorities, the monthly publication of Elizabeth Whelan's corporate-funded advocacy group, the American Council on Science and Health. Holt complained bitterly that current libel law "has been a major stumbling block to the progress of a lawsuit brought by the Washington Apple Growers against the Natural Resources Defense Council, perpetrators of the Alar scare. The growers initially filed suit in Yakima County (WA) Superior Court; but . . . the growers lost their case." Fortunately, "agribusiness is now fighting back, shepherding what are known as 'agricultural product disparagement laws' through state legislatures. . . . On the national level, the National Association of State Departments of Agriculture wants similar provisions to be included in the 1995 farm bill." [11]

Silence is Golden

Nicknamed "banana laws" or "broccoli bills," agricultural product disparagement laws were designed to give even more power to SLAPP suits by rewriting the rules of evidence so that the food industry would have a better chance of winning in court. In the eight years since Alar hit the headlines, cries of "never again" from the food industry prompted legislatures to pass product disparagement laws in 13 states—Alabama, Arizona, Colorado, Florida, Georgia, Idaho, Louisiana, Mississippi, North Dakota, Ohio, Oklahoma, South Dakota, and Texas. Other states were in the process of considering similar measures.

The new legislation was designed specifically and expressly for the purpose of protecting industry profits by preventing people from expressing opinions that might discourage consumers from buying particular foods. "An anti-disparagement law is needed because of incidents such as the Alar scare several years ago," argued the Ohio Farm Bureau in lobbying for the new law. "Apple producers suffered substantial financial losses when people stopped eating apples because of reports that Alar, a pesticide which can lawfully be used on apples, would cause serious heath problems. These reports were later proven to be false, but the damage had been done." [12]

The penalties for broccoli bashing varied from state to state. In Idaho, defendants could be required to pay a penalty equal to the plaintiff's claimed financial damages. In Texas, the penalty was *three* times the damages. In Colorado, the legislation included provisions for actual jail time of up to a year. According to Holt, the new laws placed "the onus on the disparaging activist, rather than under liability law, which would place the onus on the grower or manufacturer of the disparaged product." [13] Shifting the onus meant that instead of corporations being forced to prove their critics were *wrong*, food critics could be judged guilty unless they could prove what they had said was *correct*. "That type of speech, I don't feel needs to be protected," argued Kansas cattle rancher Jim Sartwelle. "It's important to have some sort of backstop in place to penalize people for making unsubstantiated comments." [14]

The problem, of course, is that no one except God can consistently and correctly distinguish between "correct" and "incorrect" views. "Who knows what the hell that is?" asked Tom Newton of the California Newspaper

Publishers Association. "Scientists say there is no such thing as reliable scientific fact, that science is based on hypothesis and conclusions, and is ever-changing." [15]

"If I say that hogs kept in confinement are being cruelly treated, am I making a mistake of fact?" asked farmer and Illinois law professor Eric Frey-fogle, explaining his opposition to the legislation. "Indeed, I am not. What I'm talking about is a matter of ethics. I may view as unethical behavior that which someone else finds entirely reasonable. But that's the great benefit of a democracy based on free speech—we can air our differences in public, without worrying about the speech-police coming to arrest us. . . . Take the case of bovine growth hormone. . . . Am I wrong if I assert that its use is unsafe? The answer depends, I submit, entirely on how we define safe, which has less to do with facts than with our standard of evaluation. Do we know whether it is fully safe for humans to drink milk for 40 years from a cow given such hormones? The answer, plainly is that we do not, no one knows, because no one has ever done it. . . . The underlying issue is this: Should we assume that a product is safe until we have proven otherwise, or should we assume it is unsafe until its safety has been fully demonstrated? Some people, of course, advocate one burden of proof; others use another; and many people end up somewhere in the middle. The point here is that debates about safety deal only in part with issues of fact. There are important questions of value here, and they need to be publicly debated, without the danger of being thrown in jail or having one's savings drained through litigation." [16]

"Agricultural disparagement statutes represent a legislative attempt to insulate an economic sector from criticism, and they may be strikingly successful in chilling the speech of anyone concerned about the food we eat," observed David Bederman, Associate Professor of Law at Emory University Law School. "The freedom of speech, always precious, becomes ever more so as the agricultural industries use previously untried methods such as exotic pesticides, growth hormones, radiation, and genetic engineering of our food supply. Scientists and consumer advocates must be able to express their legitimate concerns. The agricultural disparagement statutes quell just that type of speech. Any restriction on speech about the quality and safety of our food is dangerous, undemocratic, and unconstitutional." [17]

Similar concerns came from a news media coalition that included the ABC, NBC and CBS television networks, along with CNN, PBS, the *Los Angeles Times*, the *New York Times* and the *Washington Post*. During the alar case, media attorneys argued as follows:

> The exalted American tradition of the "muckraker," of course, began with pioneering investigations of the heath risks posed by the industries of the day. In *The Jungle*, Upton Sinclair revealed the risks posed to the food supply by the meat packing industry: "There was never the least attention paid to what was cut up for sausage; there would come all the way back from Europe old sausage that had been rejected, and that was mouldy and white—it would be dosed with borax and glycerine, and dumped into the hoppers, and made over again for home consumption. . . . It was too dark in these storage places to

see well, but a man could run his hand over these piles of meat and sweep off handfuls of the dried dung of rats." . . . More recently, Rachel Carson's *Silent Spring* . . . first warned against the hazards posed by the then-prevalent consumer use of insecticides: "A common insecticide for household use, including assorted uses in the kitchen, is chlordane. Yet the Food and Drug Administration's chief pharmacologist has declared the hazard of living in a house sprayed with chlordane to be very great." . . .

The importance of journalism about health and safety issues to our system of self-government cannot be overstated. Neither can the threat to the efficacy of such reporting. . . . A cause of action for "product disparagement" would apparently have been available to the tobacco industry in 1950, and again in 1954, when the *New York Times* first reported . . . tobacco-related risks to the public health well before the government took final action to estimate and to regulate that risk. . . . Like the producers and distributor of tobacco products, the manufacturers of products containing asbestos would presumably have also had a cause of action for "product disparagement" based on early news media reports describing the dangers of their products. . . .

Today, news reporting about studies identifying a link between the consumption of red meat and certain types of cancer could apparently serve . . . as the basis of product disparagement claims brought by cattle farmers, meat producers, meatpackers and butchers. . . . Books, articles and broadcasts about irradiation, the subject of an ongoing public policy debate, could be charged with disparaging lettuce, cucumbers or broccoli. . . . Likewise, news media coverage or reports discussing contaminants such as mercury, PCBs and lead found in tuna, salmon, clams and other seafood could be alleged by a host of potential plaintiffs to have disparaged the fish they catch, sell and serve. . . . Journalism exploring the environmental impact to whole classes of products would apparently also be the proper subject of disparagement claims. . . . The law of product disparagement . . . would render actionable news reporting about the health risks to humans of any product—from tobacco, to asbestos, to Alar. . . . The product disparagement claim . . . provides those with an economic incentive to continue producing and selling products that may nevertheless pose an "unreasonable risk" to public health a powerful weapon with which to stifle public debate about those risks.[18]

These objections notwithstanding, the news media found it hard to devote much coverage to the debate over product disparagement laws, which lacked the visceral entertainment value of simple morality tales such as the O.J. Simpson murder case. Reporters who did cover the topic felt compelled to punch up their stories with wisecracks about "veggie hate crimes" or humorous wordplay. "Mind how you disparage asparagus or berate broccoli," advised the headline in the *Los Angeles Times*. "Don't bad-mouth that Brussel sprout. It could cost you," quipped *USA Today*.

Apparently vegetable jokes were more amusing than jokes about meat. Reporters ignored the fact that much of the leadership behind the campaign against food disparagement was actually coming from the animal products industry. The drive was spearheaded by the Animal Industry Foundation (AIF), which calls itself "animal agriculture's collective voice on food animal production, its effect on diet and environment, and its contributions to our quality of life." AIF's trustees include a who's-who list of meat industry lobby and trade associations: the American Farm Bureau Federation, American Feed Industry Association, American Sheep Industry Association, American Society of Animal Science, American Veal Association, National Broiler Council, National Cattlemen's Beef Association, National Milk Producers Federation, National Pork Producers Council, National Turkey Federation, Southeastern Poultry & Egg Association and United Egg Producers.

"The model for these statutes was developed by the American Feed Industry Association," boasted an AIF newsletter. "If you'd like a copy of the model state legislation, please contact in writing Steve Kopperud at AFIA."[19] AIF in fact shared the same address, phone and staff as AFIA—the American Feed Industry Association, a "national trade association representing the manufacturers of more than 70 percent of the primary formula livestock and poultry feed sold annually."

In a letter to *Consumer Reports,* Kopperud defended the industry's rationale behind food disparagement laws, claiming that they "do not repress free speech, but rather compel a speaker to think twice about opportunistic or false statements and the damage such rhetoric can do. . . . Food disparagement laws, as tools to make more honest our national discussion of food safety, are the ultimate consumer protection."

The AIF spoke more bluntly in literature aimed at farmers: "Animal rights activists . . . threaten the survival of today's farmers and ranchers. . . . It's time to fight back! . . . through advertising, elementary school programs, publications and videos, news media outreach and public opinion research."[20]

Real Fears

Beneath the surface of this feisty attitude, the meat industry was itself uneasy about the dangers associated with its products. In 1990, the Food and Nutrition Board of the National Academy of Sciences published a report on cattle inspection. "In the United States, foodborne diseases appear to be steadily increasing," the report stated. "An estimated 5 million cases of foodborne disease and approximately 5,000 related deaths occur annually. This apparent increase is variously attributed to automated food processing, increased reliance on fast foods, greater use of prepackaged foods and microwave ovens, urbanization, public naïvete about food production and slaughter methods, and lack of knowledge about the hygienic precautions required at all stages of food handling."[21]

If anything, this was a conservative estimate of the human toll, as James Reagan of the National Cattlemen's Beef Association admitted in 1994. "Today, foodborne illness is a major problem for the industry, and it's a major cost for our country," Reagan told the American Meat Science Association. "If you look at some estimates, there are about 12.6 million cases of foodborne illness a year. The cost is estimated to be about $8.4 billion, including lost time at work, health care cost, etc."[22] The U.S. government's General Accounting Office estimated that the true incidence of foodborne illness could be even higher—as many as 81 million cases per year.[23] By 1997, 9,000 U.S. deaths a year was the accepted figure.

As in England, salmonella and listeria were at the top of the list of common infections. In addition, a new, virulent form of E. coli bacteria was making the rounds—*Escherichia coli* O157:H7. "It's a critical problem for us and it's a major problem, since it occurs most of the time in children who are somewhere between one and eight years of age," Reagan said. First identified in 1982, E. coli O157:H7 can induce abdominal cramping so severe that it is sometimes described as mimicking labor pains or appendicitis, followed within 24 hours by watery diarrhea which later became grossly bloody, described in some cases as "all blood and no stool." In one out of twenty patients, especially children, these symptoms progress to a more severe condition known as hemolytic uremic syndrome (HUS), marked by clotting of the red blood cells which in turn can cause kidney and heart failure, disorders of the central nervous system, seizures, coma and death.

Undercooked ground beef was the most common vehicle of E. coli infection, which was popping up increasingly in day-care centers, nursing homes, restaurants and other institutional settings. The most notorious single outbreak was a highly-publicized case involving contaminated hamburgers at Jack-in-the-Box restaurants, which sickened more than 700 people, causing 55 cases of HUS and four deaths. The media reaction from that case prompted James Reagan to ponder "how today's headlines compare with those at the turn of the century when Upton Sinclair wrote *The Jungle*. We know how revolutionary that was and how devastating it was for the meat industry," he said. "I think back over the number of discussions I've had during the last six months with regulatory agencies, meat packers and others. I left some of those conversations thinking that this outbreak in January may be as revolutionary as what happened around the turn of the century." [24]

Outwardly, the cattle industry was bullish. Inwardly, a siege mentality was intensifying. This attitude was spelled out explicitly in a 1991 speech to the National Cattlemen's Association by public relations executive Ronald Duchin of the Mongoven, Biscoe and Duchin PR firm. He warned that a "plethora of public interest groups including churches, the animal rights people, consumer advocates, small dairy farmers and environmental activists" were among the "great many forces and pressures that play against the cattle industry." [25]

These were the worries that weighed heavily on the U.S. beef industry as the mad cow controversy blossomed in England. No cases of BSE had been detected in the United States, and few Americans had even heard of the new disease. Meat industry executives were determined to do everything possible to make sure things stayed that way. If the controversy ever *did* emerge here, they knew they needed contingency plans in place and laws on the books that would help drown out the voices of this menacing "plethora of public interest groups."

We See Nothing

USDA's mad cow task force, renamed the "Scrapie/BSE Consultants Group," met for the second time on April 30, 1990. In the year since the first meeting, key representatives from the agribusiness industry had been added to the committee: John Adams of the National Milk Producers Federation, Tom Cook of the National Cattlemen's Association, and Paul Rodgers of the American Sheep Industry Association. Dr. Linda Detwiler, the USDA official in charge of the government's scrapie program at the Animal and Plant Health Inspection Service (APHIS), was another new member, and Don Franco of the National Renderers Association would soon join the list. The group's membership was now industry-dominated, without even token representation by a consumer organization. None of the meetings were publicized, and for all practical purposes took place in secret.

According to the meeting minutes, committee members recognized that they were still lacking important information about the disease. William Hadlow "emphasized that some very basic questions concerning transmission, extraneural and neural involvement, genetic resistance, symptomless carriers, etc., must be answered in order to formulate a rational control strategy."

Mark Robinson, a researcher from Seattle, had just returned from a visit to Great Britain and reported that the number of cases there continued to climb: "England is currently experiencing approximately 1,400 cases per month, a dramatic increase over the 600 cases per month reported in the latter part of 1989." The increase was raising serious fears that cattle might indeed be passing the disease to each other in addition to getting it through their feed. "While cow-to-cow or cow-to-calf transmission has not been documented, Dr. Robinson indicated that the currently accepted theory that infection occurs exclusively through the ingestion of contaminated feedstuffs is only one of several epidemiological hypotheses being considered by the Ministry of Agriculture." Most disturbing of all, "He also stated that the rendering processes employed by the United Kingdom and the United States are virtually the same."[1] If this were the case, maybe nothing but blind luck had kept BSE from emerging first in the United States instead of England—and as long as the U.S. continued feeding rendered cows back to cows, there was nothing to prevent the disease from emerging in the future.

Whatever concerns they expressed in committees, however, scientists and agricultural officials were expected to behave properly in public. No one wanted to be responsible for stirring up "the next Alar scare," and scientists who talked to the press either couched their concerns in hedged language or offered soothing bromides that stopped just short of outright falsehoods.

Al Strating, USDA's director of science and technology at APHIS, demonstrated the proper tone of reassurance in an August 1990 interview with *Agri-View,* Wisconsin's largest farm newspaper. Strating told editor Joel McNair that BSE "is certainly not an immediate cause for concern. . . . We feel a good bit more comfortable with the U.S. situation than we did three weeks ago. There are not so many unknowns." By that date, APHIS had begun testing rabies-negative cattle brains in the United States to see if they carried a spongiform disease. Only 13 brains had been tested so far, but Strating exuded confidence: "I think there's been no problem here and there is no reason to believe there is going to be a problem. I feel very good that we are on top of this." Following Strating's lead, McNair headlined his story, "Bypass Protein Still Safe," and advised: "What with mad cows running around England, might it be wise to avoid feeding bypass protein supplements to your dairy herd? Relax, say veterinarians. Don't bypass the protein just because all of England is in an uproar about BSE."[2]

Officials were acutely aware of the volatility of consumer eating habits and the consequences in the event that mad cow disease should become an issue of public concern in the United States. "The mere perception that BSE might exist in the United States could have devastating effects on our domestic markets for beef and dairy products," stated a 1991 APHIS report which grappled with the public relations problems posed by the disease.[3]

The report began by analyzing 240 articles that had appeared in the British press: "Three-fourths of these articles appeared in May and June 1990. Before 1990, only 15 articles had appeared in the British press. After a May 1990 article announcing the death of a cat with BSE-like lesions, 81 additional articles speculated on the relationship between the cat's death and its food, and on possible links to human health. These articles were followed by a large number of stories about the economic and political impact of bans on beef in British schools and of import bans by France, West Germany, and other countries."

According to APHIS, a major factor affecting the media's portrayal of the BSE issue was the absence of clear knowledge about the disease. "The causative agent has not been identified, the means of transmission is not understood, and the susceptibility of humans to the disease controversial. These unknowns, especially with regard to human safety, make BSE a topic for which it is easy to obtain contradictory opinions from 'experts.' The press thrives on differences between individuals. . . . Another significant factor was that [the British Ministry of Agriculture, Fisheries and Food (MAFF)] initially de-emphasized the importance of the disease and denied any possibility of human health risk. . . . The Ministry assured the public that there was no danger from eating beef when, in fact, absolute safety cannot be proven, and the safety of British beef cannot be demonstrated for 20 or more years. . . . The MAFF lost public confidence by repeatedly making statements that could not be supported; regaining public trust will be very difficult."

"A Conservative Policy With Regard to Human Safety"

To avoid a similar debacle in the United States, APHIS recommended a strategy of "complete honesty and forthrightness, especially to industry leaders and the press. . . . The positive feature about this approach is that we appear confident and show that we have nothing to hide. The goal is to provide completely truthful information, gain public trust and alleviate fears. . . . The advantages of this approach outweigh its disadvantages. It anticipates a program encompassing (1) total honesty with regard to unknowns; (2) a conservative policy with regard to human health and safety; (3) relaxation of restrictions as the safety of products becomes known, rather than placing more restrictions as hazards become more apparent."

Unfortunately, these honorable sentiments clashed with the agency's own predisposition to discount the seriousness of the human risk associated with BSE. As an example of that bias, the report fretted over a story in *The Economist* which "could potentially create alarm among U.S. consumers" because it reported that "many veterinarians and medical experts have come around to the belief that humans could catch the mystery brain infection." As an example of "more objective coverage," APHIS approvingly quoted a June 26, 1990 *Washington Post* article in which Clarence Gibbs stated, "I don't think there is any danger in consuming British beef."[4]

Beyond the question of bias, there was the problem of *defining* "a conservative policy with regard to human health and safety." The British had already banned cannibalistic feeding practices, but no such policy existed yet in the United States, and APHIS was internally divided over what policy it should recommend. In a 1991 report, titled "Bovine Spongiform Encephalopathy: Rendering Policy," the agency used data supplied by the National Renderers Association to assess the scale of the practice. "The U.S. beef and dairy industries have fed meat and bone meal for at least 10 years," the report stated. "Most is fed in the dairy industry to [calves] and lactating animals (up to 4 percent of the ration). Feeding of meat and bone meal to U.S. dairy cattle became significant after 1987, and reached its highest level in 1989 and 1990. . . . There were approximately 7.9 billion pounds of meat and bone meal, blood meal, and feather meal produced in 1989." Of that amount, 34% went to pet food; 34% to feed poultry; 20% for swine feed, and 10%—i.e, 790 million pounds— to the beef and dairy industry.[5]

The authors of the APHIS report outlined a variety of policy options, ranging from the status quo ("voluntary industry guidelines"), to "non-binding federal guidelines," to actual mandatory regulations. The advantage to "voluntary industry guidelines" would be that "it has no federal cost." At the other end of the spectrum, mandatory regulations would cost money and would be "likely to encounter considerable industry opposition," the report noted. "Nevertheless, some APHIS staff members prefer this option. They argue that because there is evidence that pigs, cats, mink, deer, and a wide variety of experimental animals may be susceptible to transmissible spongiform encephalopathies, the only prudent policy is to not feed products that may contain these agents to any species of animal."

The report admitted that a more cautious policy would be "to prohibit the feeding of sheep and cattle-origin protein products to all ruminants, regardless of age. The advantage of this option is that it minimizes the risk of BSE. The disadvantage is that *the cost to the livestock and rendering industries would be substantial*" (emphasis added).[6]

At first glance, it might seem that the feed industry could simply revert to the practice of restricting meat-and-bone meal to poultry and swine feeds, which had been the norm "for decades before it was extensively promoted for use in cattle in the early to mid-1980s." In practice, however, APHIS noted "two reasons why ruminant-origin meat-and-bone meal may not be absorbed by these alternative feed markets. First, the swine and poultry market for meat-and-bone meal has greatly diminished due to fears of salmonella that surfaced in the 1970s and early 1980s. Second, the cattle industry and the swine and poultry industries in the U.S. are sufficiently separated geographically so that transportation costs could be a significant factor."[7]

A *mandatory* ban on animal cannibalism would have met USDA's stated intention to carry out "a conservative policy with regard to human health and safety," but USDA behaved with characteristic deference to the imperatives of the food industry and stuck instead to the status quo—a so-called "voluntary ban" on feeding rendered adult sheep—just sheep—to cattle and other ruminant animals. The "voluntary ban" had been announced by the rendering industry in 1989, but no means of enforcement existed. In 1992, the U.S. Food and Drug Administration carried out a survey of 19 rendering plants and found that 15 of them were continuing to render sheep. "These 15 plants processed more than 85 percent of the adult sheep rendered in the United States," the FDA reported. Six of the 15, moreover, were continuing to sell the rendered protein for use in cattle feeds.[8]

In November 1992, BSE concerns prompted the FDA to issue a letter to manufacturers of dietary supplements, "Some supplements contain brain, nervous tissue, or glandular materials from a variety of animal species," noted Fred Shank of FDA's Agency for Food Safety and Applied Nutrition. "We are concerned that some amount of these materials may have come from countries experiencing Bovine Spongiform Encephalopathy. . . . The possibility of transmission of animal spongiform encephalopathy agents to humans from consumption of animal brains from a variety of species, such as squirrel, goat, sheep, and hogs, and from consumption of sheep's eyeballs has been examined in the past. Although proof of such dietary transmission is lacking, some suspicions remain. The rarity of the disease, coupled with what is believed to be a long onset time (median—13 years), make more precise epidemiological studies extremely difficult."

Moreover, Shank added, "FDA has recently been involved in investigating a consumer complaint involving a confirmed case of CJD. It is standard procedure for FDA to follow up on all consumer complaints involving death or serious injury. In the course of this investigation, FDA learned that the woman had taken a bovine tissue-containing dietary supplement. Although at the present there is no basis to conclude that this supplement played any role in

A "voluntary ban" in action: This advertisement, published in Render magazine in April 1991, touted lamb byproducts as "the ideal protein ingredient for all animal feeds," especially pet food.

causing this disease, FDA and NIH have decided that it is prudent to further investigate this matter. Therefore, both agencies have begun to conduct cooperative studies to determine whether nutritional supplements containing brain, nervous tissue or glandular materials from bovine and ovine species might be linked to human spongiform encephalopathies."

In the absence of clear scientific knowledge, FDA requested that manufacturers of food supplements "reformulate your products using neural or glandular tissues that you are assured are BSE or scrapie free. . . . We fully recognize that there is no proven link between BSE or scrapie, and human disease, but given the devastating consequences of human spongiform encephalopathies such as CJD, we believe that our request is a prudent step at this time."[9]

In subsequent letters, FDA officials extended similar advice to manufacturers of drugs and medical devices, to producers of FDA-regulated animal feed supplements, and even to cosmetics companies, noting that "extracts of listed tissues . . . are used in cosmetics. Additionally, FDA is unaware of data demonstrating that processing techniques used in the manufacture of cosmetics will inactivate TSE agents. Further, little is known about the human risk of transmission from topical application of cosmetics containing TSE agents to intact, broken or abraded skin."[10]

Once again, however, this advice remained nothing more than wishful thinking, strictly voluntary in nature. No penalty for noncompliance was imposed, nor were measures taken to monitor compliance.

✳ ✳ ✳

Richard Marsh, meanwhile, was becoming increasingly concerned. In 1989, he was one of the participants in the NIH international roundtable on BSE and had shared the consensus opinion of other roundtable participants, arguing that the "possibility of infection with BSE in the United States . . . is judged to be low, on the basis of the following: (1) meat and bonemeals imported into the United States from Great Britain between 1980 and 1988 were used mainly in poultry, not ruminant feed; (2) the Scrapie Eradication Program had reduced the prevalence of scrapie in the United States compared with that in Great Britain; and (3) little, if any, rendered animal products are used for protein supplements in cattle feed in the United States." [11]

"I was really naive at the beginning," Marsh would recall later. "The fact is, we simply didn't have any idea how many rendered cattle were being fed to cows here in the United States. Not even as a veterinarian would you think that it was happening. It's not something the beef industry likes to talk about. Eventually I caught on. I think the first time I had an inkling was at a meeting on BSE with Don Franco of the National Renderers Association, when I heard him say, 'Well, we've been feeding cows to cows for 100 years. Why haven't we seen a problem up to now?' " [12]

By the time the roundtable proceedings were published in the May 1990 *Journal of the American Veterinary Medicine Association*, Marsh's thinking had already changed considerably. In a published retraction, he warned that his initial reassurances had been "incorrect, because of the recent trend of using less assimilated 'by-pass' proteins in cattle feed. A large amount of meat-and-bone meal is being fed to American cattle, and this change in feeding practice has greatly increased the risk of bovine spongiform encephalopathy (BSE) developing in the United States. . . . As emphasized in my article, there is some evidence that a BSE-like infection may already exist in American cattle. The current practice of feeding meat-and-bone meal to cattle solidifies the most important means to perpetuate and amplify the disease cycle. . . . The practice of using animal protein in cattle feed should be discontinued as soon as possible. Waiting until the first case of BSE is diagnosed in the United States will certainly be 'closing the barn door after the horse is gone.' With a disease having a 3- to 8-year incubation period, thousands of animals would be exposed before we recognize the problem and, if that happens, we would be in for a decade of turmoil." [13]

This statement—hardly a revolutionary manifesto—began what for Marsh would often feel like a lonely crusade. Over the course of the next six years, he would sometimes stand alone and sometimes stand with others in calling for an end to the practice of feeding cows to other cows. Among the U.S. scientists working in the field of spongiform encephalopathies, Marsh would emerge as the most consistent and outspoken critic of beef industry feeding practices, drawing heat and outright harassment from industry and government officials determined to characterize his warnings as "speculative" and "based on anecdotal evidence."

Shortly after the first cats began dying in England, Marsh was quoted in the British press in a story headlined: "Type of 'Mad Cow Disease May Exist in U.S. Cattle.'" The London *Independent* reported that "one of America's leading experts in this field believes . . . that BSE, or something very similar, may have been missed in the United States." The story continued:

His best evidence comes from studies of spongiform encephalopathy (SE) in mink. There have been 23 outbreaks around the world, several on U.S. mink farms.

The agent causing the disease almost certainly entered the mink through their feed mixtures—in the 1985 case studied by Professor Marsh they were fed raw cattle carcasses. . . .

The British BSE outbreak is thought to have been caused by cattle eating feed containing sheep protein that had not been heated for long enough. However, it has never been shown conclusively that the affected mink had any scrapie-contaminated sheep protein in their feed mixtures.

Professor Marsh believes that the U.S. should stop the widespread practice of feeding its cattle on feed mixtures containing cattle protein because of the risks of an outbreak. Britain has already had to introduce such a ban because of BSE. "If we don't stop feeding our cattle on this animal protein we're setting ourselves up for the same thing as happened to the British," he said.[14]

Marsh was not alone in these views. Before the advent of BSE in England, in fact, his controversial hypothesis had been aired by others for decades. "For 15 years, I had been convinced by our research colleagues in the U.S. Department of Agriculture that there must be this class of disease present in the North American cattle population, the reason being outbreaks of transmissible mink encephalopathy (TME)," scrapie researcher Alan Dickinson would say in 1996. "The reason for my conviction was that TME had been established as arising from exposure to infected materials which were exclusively cattle and did not involve sheep."[15]

Indeed, a close reading of the history of mink outbreaks pointed more to cattle than to sheep as the source. The first known outbreak of TME, in 1947, had occurred in mink that ate dead and downer cattle along with packing plant byproducts, fish, liver and cereal. The second outbreak occurred in animals that had eaten a ready-mix feed ration. It was impossible to determine what animals had gone into the feed, but since the outbreak occurred in Wisconsin, it was reasonable to conclude that cattle were a good part of the mix. The two ranches that saw outbreaks in Wisconsin in 1963 shared a common feed source that was limited to dead and downer cattle. A separate outbreak in Canada that same year occurred in mink eating some horsemeat along with slaughterhouse byproducts consisting of cattle parts deemed unfit for human consumption. No information was available on feed sources for the outbreak that year in Idaho, or on the outbreaks in Finland and Russia. Then there was the 1985 Stetsonville outbreak that Marsh investigated personally, where the owner had kept detailed feeding records and swore that he hadn't used sheep or sheep byproducts. His feed consisted mainly of downer cattle with a few horses thrown in.[16]

Downer Cows

The common denominator in all of these outbreaks was either "cattle" or "unknown." It was possible, of course, to imagine other scenarios, but Marsh believed he had at least strong circumstantial evidence that a TSE similar to mad cow disease already existed in U.S. cattle. "You can trace it back to feed real easy in mink," Marsh said. "And then you're left with the question, what was it in the feed that affected them? And what we find is it's these downer cows that are the common link. You don't have to be a genius to figure it out." [17]

Within the field of veterinary medicine, "downer cow syndrome" was a "garbage can" category, used indiscriminately as the official diagnosis for any animal that died or had to be put down after failing to stand on its own legs for 24 hours or more. These included cows suffering from paralysis, arthritis, grass tetany, ketosis, bone fractures, and a form of calcium deficiency known as "milk fever." Most downer cows died from causes unrelated to the spongiform encephalopathies, but it was possible that the generic nature of the classification enabled some TSE-infected cows to slip into the mix.

It was impossible in practice to absolutely *prove* the link between downer cows and transmissible mink encephalopathy. By the time the disease appeared in mink, any cow that might have been the source would be long gone, its tissues unavailable for testing. To test his theory, therefore, Marsh did the next best thing—a series of experiments using brain matter from one of the mink that had died in the Stetsonville outbreak. He puréed the brain in a blender and used hypodermic syringes to inject the homogenized liquid into test animals: fourteen healthy mink, eight ferrets, two squirrel monkeys, twelve hamsters, forty-five mice and two Holstein bull calves.

The mice, remarkably, all stayed healthy, but every other species proved susceptible. The mink went down first, four months after inoculation. The two monkeys were the next to show neurological signs, at months nine and thirteen respectively. Two of the twelve hamsters survived, but the other ten succumbed in the fifteenth and sixteenth months. The two calves went down in months eighteen and nineteen. The ferrets lasted longest, but eventually the disease emerged in all but one of them, with incubation periods ranging between twenty-eight and thirty-eight months. These species barrier effects corresponded closely to the results from experiments with previous mink outbreaks. [18]

Cattle are expensive test animals, and Marsh's experiments marked the first time that cattle had been tested for susceptibility to transmissible mink encephalopathy. His results proved that cattle *could* get the mink disease, and in turn led to unexpected new questions. "The real surprise of this experiment is that the clinical signs were quite different from what we've seen in Great Britain," he said. "This is what's changed our perspective on a surveillance of BSE in the United States. We thought BSE in the U.S. would look like BSE in Great Britain—a mad cow type of disease where the animal would have behavioral changes, become aggressive and look very much like a rabies infection does in cows." [19]

Marsh's bull calves showed none of the unusual "mad" behavior that emerged as early warning signs in British cattle. "Eighteen months after inoculation, one animal simply collapsed in its holding room and could not be returned to a standing position," he reported. "This animal had shown no previous signs of behavioral change or loss of body condition. . . . The second animal was normal until nineteen months after inoculation when it too suddenly collapsed."[20]

Indeed, the test bulls behaved exactly like downer cows—the type of animals which the Stetsonville rancher had been feeding to his mink. "The most disturbing finding of all is that they have very minimal spongiform lesions in their brains," Marsh said.[21] In previous experiments with mink, he had shown that the spongy holes in brains were a secondary effect of the disease which did not always appear in noticeable quantities. Some mink breeds infected with TME would develop all of the usual clinical symptoms, but upon autopsy their brains showed a marked lack of spongiform degeneration. Now it appeared that cattle could also develop a form of TSE without the telltale lesions to aid in diagnosis. Their symptoms would look like downer cow syndrome, and even a brain autopsy might find nothing out of the ordinary.

"Without the brain lesions, the best way to diagnose the infection is a protein in the brain," Marsh said. "But there are only a few labs in the country that can look for this protein. This is not something that can be done by the local veterinarian or even most state diagnostic laboratories. You need to have pretty sophisticated means of testing. This is going to complicate our efforts at surveillance and testing for BSE in this country."[22]

Histopathology and immunohistochemistry tests confirmed that Marsh's bulls had died of a spongiform encephalopathy, but it was a different strain of spongiform encephalopathy than the one that was killing cows in England. Its behavior in test animals showed significant differences also. In England, mice succumbed when exposed to brain tissue from mad cows, but hamsters seemed immune. In Marsh's experiments with the Stetsonville isolate of TME, the pattern was exactly the opposite: mice lived, but hamsters died. To test whether passage through cattle altered the characteristics of the Stetsonville isolate, Marsh injected another 45 mice with brain tissue from his two test bulls. They also stayed healthy, just like the mice he had previously injected with mink brains.

By itself, the fact that mink encephalopathy could infect cows was not terribly significant or surprising. After all, scientists had previously shown that TME could be transmitted to a wide variety of other test animals. What *was* significant was the result when Marsh took the brains of the dead bulls and used them on further tests with healthy mink. When backpassaged into mink, the bull brains behaved exactly the way *mink* brains behaved, causing symptoms of TME to emerge within four months after exposure by inoculation, or within seven months after oral exposure. "There was no evidence for any deadaptation of the bovine agent for mink compared to . . . non-bovine-passaged mink brain," Marsh observed. "This suggests that there are no species barrier effects between mink and cattle in relation to the Stetsonville source of TME"—more evidence pointing to cattle as the source of the infection.[23]

"If mink on the Stetsonville ranch were exposed to TME by feeding them infected cattle, there must be an unrecognized scrapie-like disease of cattle in the United States," Marsh concluded. "If this is true, the disease is rare. The low incidence rate of TME and the fact that the Stetsonville mink rancher had fed products from fallen or sick cattle to his animals for the past 35 years suggests a very low prevalence of this disease."[24]

The rarity of the disease, however, did not mean that it posed no danger. In fact, it could mean the very opposite. Mad cow disease had also been rare once in England. The very fact that it *was* rare, combined with its slow incubation period, were the factors that prevented the British from recognizing its dangers until it had already infected tens of thousands of animals. Moreover, the British had an advantage that U.S. farmers might not enjoy. *Their* strain of bovine spongiform encephalopathy was picked up fairly soon once cattle started behaving strangely. If a *different* strain of BSE existed in U.S. cattle— a strain where the animals didn't act deranged but simply fell over, like the cows in Marsh's tests—the disease could conceivably go unrecognized for a long time, invisible within the larger population of U.S. downer cows.

Every year, some 100,000 U.S. cows get classified as downers. Marsh was not suggesting that all 100,000 were carriers of a spongiform encephalopathy. What concerned him was the possibility that downer cow syndrome could mask the emergence of a TSE in the cattle population, allowing the disease to invisibly spread until it reached dangerous levels. It could multiply the same way it had multiplied in England, as rendering plants recycled the infection by converting sick animals into meat and bone meal which was then fed back to other cattle. The only certain way to prevent a cattle epidemic, therefore, would be to adopt the same policy that the British had already been forced to adopt: ban the practice of feeding rendered cows and other ruminant animals back to members of their own species.

In England, meanwhile, the consequences of failing to take action sooner were becoming painfully evident. By the end of 1991, nearly 50,000 cases of mad cow disease had been confirmed—more than twice the total predicted by the Southwood Committee. And the end was nowhere in sight.

In December 1991, the British Medical Research Council announced interim results of an experiment in which MRC researchers had injected two marmoset monkeys with scrapie and two others with BSE. The ones injected with scrapie had died, but the ones injected with BSE remained healthy. Given the closeness of monkeys to human beings, the result seemed encouraging, prompting a story in the *Meat Trades Journal* headlined "Meat Given Clean Bill of Health."

By the summer of 1992, however, the BSE monkeys had also died of spongiform brain disease. Dr. Rosalind Ridley, who had overseen the experiment, struggled to put a positive spin on the result by pointing out that the BSE monkeys had lived longer than monkeys exposed to scrapie. "Everything we know tells us that scrapie is not a risk to humans," Ridley said. "Now we have this encouraging evidence that BSE is even less of a risk."[25] Her statement was absurd, lacking any scientific basis whatsoever, but at least it *sounded* reassuring.

Counting Sheep

"Within the next year we will see the start of a rapid decline in the number of confirmed BSE cases," predicted British chief veterinary officer Keith Meldrum in September 1991.[1] By early 1993, however, the number of new cases each week had surpassed 800. More than 80,000 British cows had been confirmed with BSE, and cases were popping up elsewhere including Guernsey, Ireland, Jersey, the Isle of Man, Switzerland, Portugal, France, Oman and the Falkland Islands.

Disturbing results were also emerging from the experiments in which scientists had injected test animals with material from infected cattle. Six out of seven of the species tested—goats, sheep, mice, marmoset monkeys, pigs and minks—had gone down with TSEs. The only animals that seemed immune, oddly, were Syrian golden hamsters, known for their ready susceptibility to sheep scrapie.

On March 12, 1993, the British medical journal *Lancet* reported the death from Creutzfeldt-Jakob Disease of Peter Warhurst, a 61-year-old dairy farmer. Warhurst's herd of BSE-infected cattle had been destroyed in 1989, and he had been drinking milk from the herd for at least seven years. It was only natural that speculation would arise surrounding his death, which marked the first known CJD fatality in someone who had experienced occupational contact with mad cow disease. The population of dairy and beef farmers in England totalled 110,000. People reasoned therefore that one farmer would normally be expected to die of CJD every decade, assuming the disease was occurring at its expected rate of one case per million people per year. In July, therefore, concerns peaked significantly at the news that a *second* dairy farmer had died—Mark Duncan Templeman, age 65.

It was difficult to assess the statistical significance of a mere two cases. Government scientists warned against the dangers of overinterpreting something that could simply be an odd coincidence. For many, however, the deaths added one more reason to worry about possible infection from animals to humans.

Although no cases of BSE had yet been found in the United States, consumer groups were beginning to pay attention to the issue and express concern. One of the first warnings came from Michael Hansen, a scientific advisor to the Consumer Policy Institute (an arm of Consumer's Union, publisher of *Consumer Reports* magazine). Hansen worried that the use of Monsanto's genetically-engineered recombinant bovine growth hormone, then being considered for FDA approval, might increase the dangers of a spongiform disease outbreak. On March 31, 1993, Hansen testified before FDA Commissioner David Kessler and a Veterinary Medicine Advisory Committee:

> A potential adverse animal and human health hazard that has not been yet considered by the FDA concerns the change in diet associated with rBGH use. Cows receiving rBGH require more energy-dense food than control cows. One major source of energy- dense food are the protein and energy supplements that come from rendering animals. (Indeed, as a CVM official states in a 1991 memo: "There is a growing trend in the use of meat and bone meal for calf rations. . . . Most is used as a protein source for high production dairy cattle and for feed lot cattle.") . . . Use of rBGH will increase the amount of rendered protein fed to dairy cows. We are concerned that some of the rendered animals may be contaminated with bovine spongiform encephalopathy (BSE) or a BSE-like disease, and that rBGH will accelerate the spread of this disease. . . .
>
> Although U.S. officials have said that there are no cases of BSE in this country and that the disease is unlikely to occur here, there are some disturbing developments here. . . . The government has set up a BSE surveillance plan and has looked at some 459 cases of cows that died; none of them were confirmed BSE cases. This is not completely reassuring, however, because the surveillance program has a potential flaw; the only two risk categories of cows sampled are rabies-suspect cattle that are rabies negative, and cattle over two years of age that have been given protein supplements for a good part of their diet and have developed signs of neurological disease. Given Marsh's work and the work in Texas, it is possible that the USDA is looking at the wrong population of cows; they need to be sampling "downer cows." Since rendering does not appear to destroy the transmissible agent, and given the fact that authorities are only on the lookout for cows exhibiting "mad cow"-like behavior, the agent causing the spongiform encephalopathy may be spreading through the use of rendered ruminant protein.
>
> In conclusion, at a minimum, we believe the feeding of cows to cows should be discontinued, not expanded. We urge the Committee to recommend that rBGH not be approved on the grounds that it may promote dissemination of BSE, or a BSE-like disease, because cows given rBGH require high-protein feed.[2]

In June 1993, attorneys for Jeremy Rifkin's Foundation on Economic Trends formally petitioned the FDA for an immediate ban on the feeding of rendered cattle and sheep protein to cattle and other ruminant animals. Rifkin, a vegetarian activist, was the author of *Beyond Beef,* a critical exposé of the global cattle industry. Other signers of the legal petition included several dairy farmers and Virgil Hulse, a family physician and surgeon from Oregon.

"The health and safety of ruminant animals, primarily cows and sheep, are at grave risk because of the relatively recent and increasing practice of feeding ruminant animal protein—the otherwise unmarketable remains of rendered cows and sheep—to cows and other ruminants in the form of commercial animal feed products," the petition stated. It called for the FDA and

USDA to "(1) order a permanent halt to all feeding of ruminant animal protein to ruminants, especially cows and sheep; (2) develop a significant epidemiological investigation to determine the incidence of transmissible spongiform encephalopathies . . . among ruminant animals in the United States; (3) develop a separate, significant epidemiological study to determine the incidences of TSEs in 'downer' cattle; (4) establish a bovine brain bank for the ongoing study of TSEs; (5) develop a significant epidemiological investigation to determine the incidence of transmissible spongiform encephalopathies among the human population of the United States; and (6) develop an ongoing national monitoring and registry program utilizing autopsy examinations to determine any changes in the incidence of CJD-like diseases among the human population of the United States."[3]

Spokespersons for the U.S. cattle and rendering industries were quick to label the demands "unscientific" and exaggerated. Gary Wilson of the National Cattlemen's Association ridiculed the idea that BSE could pose a risk to humans, calling it a "very creative stretch of scientific research and evidence."[4] Wilson admitted that "his industry could find economically feasible alternatives to . . . [rendered] animal protein," reported the *Food Chemical News* in July 1993. "However, the association does not want to set a precedent of being ruled by 'activists.'"[5]

A Proposed Rule

The USDA response to Rifkin's petition amounted at best to a polite brushoff. After six months of silence, the agency sent back a letter stating that it was already engaged in "intensive epidemiological investigations for BSE-like diseases in cattle."[6] A somewhat better response came from Richard Teske of the FDA's Center for Veterinary Medicine. "FDA agrees with the petitioners that the recent BSE epidemic in the United Kingdom . . . warrant increased vigilance and precautionary practices to ensure that BSE is not introduced and spread among cattle herds in this country," Teske stated. "To this end, FDA is preparing a notice of proposed rulemaking that will address the issue of BSE and the feeding of certain materials to ruminants."[7]

Inside the Washington beltway, "advance notices of proposed rulemaking" are almost as common as rats or lobbyists—so common that policymakers refer to them simply as ANPRs. When an agency publishes an ANPR, it typically stipulates a comment period during which members of the industry and public may comment on the rule and suggest modifications before it is written into law.

The FDA's ANPR on "feeding of certain materials," however, was virtually stillborn from the day it was announced. The proposed regulation was not published until August 1994, and by then it had already been scaled back considerably. Both Rifkin and Hansen were calling for a ban on the practice of feeding rendered cows back to cows. Their call merely echoed the recommendations of the international roundtable on BSE sponsored in 1989 by the National Institutes of Health. Participants at the roundtable, including longtime TSE experts Clarence Gibbs and William Hadlow, had insisted then that the only way to prevent future outbreaks of transmissible spongiform encephalo-pathy would be a complete ban on feeding of rendered animal byproducts to all *ruminant* animals—cattle, deer and antelope as well as sheep—all of which were naturally vegetarian animals and seemed unusually susceptible to TSEs. The FDA's regulation simply proposed to stop the practice of rendering *sheep* into ruminant feed.

What about Dick Marsh's evidence that a TSE in cattle was already the source for U.S. outbreaks of transmissible mink encephalopathy? "The devel-opment of TME on a mink farm that reportedly fed only cattle byproducts has led some to believe that BSE exists at a low level in the United States," acknowledged a report accompanying the FDA's ANPR, before proceeding to summarily dismiss the Marsh hypothesis: "Based on available evidence, the U.S. Department of Agriculture (USDA) has concluded that the byproducts from United States cattle are unlikely to have caused the TME outbreak on the mink farm."[8]

Instead, the FDA stuck to the unsubstantiated British claim "that a disease agent contained in sheep may have survived the rendering process to cause BSE in cattle. . . . The agency recognizes that the processed slaughter byprod-ucts and 4-D [dead, dying, diseased, and disabled] adult sheep and goats have a long history of use in animal feeds without known adverse effects. How-ever, the evidence for the development of a new pattern of disease transmis-sion now indicates that these ingredients can no longer be categorically regarded as safe. . . . FDA cannot determine what level of feed ingredients from processed adult sheep and goat products, if any, is safe in ruminant feed."

Actually, though, the ANPR wasn't intended to *categorically* exclude these ingredients from the rendering mix. In order to lessen the financial blow to ren-derers and sheep ranchers, the FDA proposed to exempt young animals, "based on the observation that sheep less than 12 months old rarely exhibit clinical symptoms of scrapie, although a few cases have been reported in sheep as young as 7 months." For that matter, FDA wasn't planning to ban *whole* sheep—just the "specified offals" known to contain the highest concentrations of infec-tion, which FDA defined as "any tissue from the brain, spinal cord, spleen, thymus, tonsil, lymph nodes, or intestines (duodenum to anus, inclusive)."[9]

FDA estimated that its regulation would cost the meat industry somewhere between $2 to $2.9 million—and therefore "will not have a significant eco-nomic impact." This opinion was not shared by the sheep industry, which would be expected to shoulder most of the cost—as much as $2.4 million. Sheep producers could see themselves being offered up as sacrificial lambs and reacted accordingly. FDA might not see $2.4 million as significant, said the American Sheep Industry Association, but that amount was "very signifi-cant to the U.S. sheep industry and the farm and ranch families who are already facing severe financial hardships."[10]

The German politician Otto Von Bismarck once commented that "those who love sausage and the law should never watch either being made." This was a case in which *both* were being made, and the picture was not pretty. For all their moaning about the need for "sound science" as a guide to public policy, affected industries responded to the FDA proposal in an absolutely predictable fashion, offering scientific interpretations that varied from industry to industry in precise and slavish conformance to their particular economic interests:

- *The sheep industry* was the one whose ox would be most deeply gored. It therefore disagreed with the regulation and most of the underlying reasoning behind it. The American Sheep Industry Association (ASIA) stated that FDA was "in error to focus regulatory efforts on the hypothesized epidemiological link between sheep scrapie and BSE." Besides, it said, scrapie in the U.S. "is measured at a very low level." As for human risk, ASIA insisted that "a careful analysis of the large body of literature on the subject is practically conclusive that no causal relationship exists between the animal and human TSE." The group chastised FDA for its failure to absolutely rule out the possibility of animal-to-human transmission, characterizing the agency's language as "inflammatory and deceptive to the public." [11]

- *The rendering industry* was second in line to feel the sting: "Based on current information, there must be other options than a formal rule," said a joint statement from the Animal Protein Producers Industry and the National Renderers Association. The statement described adult sheep as "a micro factor" in the total production of rendering in the U.S. "We concur with the analysis of the Animal and Plant Health Inspection Service epidemiologists who have maintained that the BSE risk to cattle in the United States is remote," it concluded.[12]

- *The feed industry,* closely allied with the renderers, admitted that feed producers should *consider* "restricting/eliminating sheep offal," but decried FDA's ban as "unnecessary," arguing that there was "no scientific evidence" of risk to human health and that the "proportionally smaller" sheep population in the U.S., combined with the industry's voluntary ban, had already "substantially reduced" the amount of adult sheep byproduct being fed back to farm animals. Moreover, the association added, the rule was unenforceable, because "AFIA members are not aware of any method for detecting sheep offal in rendered protein or finished feed. . . . Feed manufacturers will be unable to comply . . . due to the lack of an analytical method for determining the presence (or absence) of sheep offal in delivered animal protein products." [13]

- *The American Veterinary Medical Association* (AVMA), traditionally allied to the livestock industry, also weighed in against the proposal with arguments that sounded similar to the Marsh hypothesis. "The very fact that byproducts from cattle are not prohibited makes the potential for BSE to be transmitted through cattle byproducts more realistic than its being transmitted by sheep byproducts," wrote AVMA vice president A. Roland Dommert. "This is especially probable considering that some 300 British-origin cattle are in the U.S., . . . to say nothing of their offspring and the cattle to which they have been exposed." Dommert noted that the 1989 international roundtable on BSE "makes it clear that if the danger of BSE being transmitted to cattle is real, then all ruminant byproducts, not just those from sheep and goats, must be eliminated from ruminant feeds." He stopped short, however, of personally calling for such a ban.[14]

- The *USDA's Animal and Plant Health Inspection Service* supported the FDA regulation, but urged the agency to soften the measure even further by exempting sheep flocks enrolled in the APHIS Voluntary Scrapie Flock Certification Program. APHIS deputy administrator Donald Luchsinger also recommended exempting goats, and repeated USDA's position that "the risks of BSE occurring in U.S.-origin cattle are minimal."[15]

- The *California Department of Food and Agriculture's* comments were shaped by the fact that California exports many of its mature ewes to Mexico for mutton production. The department's Kenneth Thomazin worried that the Mexican market could be lost "if an attack is mounted by animal rights advocates claiming the industry exists on the backs of unsuspecting Mexican consumers unaware that mutton is not eaten in the United States due to fear of human disease. This scenario may also develop when the inevitable question is asked about the safety of nerve tissue in the balance of the carcass when the brain and cord is suspect. Certainly it cannot be imagined that a dangerous agent exists in a three-year-old sheep due to infection acquired in utero or as a neonate, that does not exist in the animal at one year of age. This anomaly will not escape the attention of those dedicated to destroying the food-animal industry if this rulemaking proceeds." Thomazin also argued that "it has not been shown that inclusion of sheep offal was determinative" in Britain's BSE outbreak, stating that FDA's proposal "ignores the more likely explanation that some previously present but very rare bovine infection has been amplified in the feeding of rendered product to susceptible cattle. . . . It would be more rational to counsel against the feeding of any product derived from a given species back to that species." Of course, Thomazin did not advise FDA to actually *ban* same-species feeding.[16]

- The *American Meat Institute,* in which sheep growers were minor players, supported the FDA proposal, acknowledging that while the economic burden "may be unfairly placed on the sheep industry, we believe the proposed action is reasonable." It focused the bulk of its concern on the FDA's statement that the ban was meant to protect the health of humans. "We regard such a statement as not in the best interest of the public or the industry," wrote AMI's Jerome Breiter. "No good is accomplished by unduly alarming the public and prejudicing segments of society against the meat industry. . . . There are also persons in other parts of the world who are consumers of our products, but who look for any excuse to disrupt trade on allegations such as appear in the notice." Citing predictions that "sooner or later a case of BSE will be found in the U.S.," Breiter said, "We must be aware that if this were to occur, it would be an incident, not an outbreak. To use an incident to institute a broader feeding ban would cause severe disruption of the entire livestock industry which may not be justified." He urged FDA "to use caution in this area."[17]

- *Pharmaceuticals companies,* on the other hand, used animal tissues in the manufacture of their products. They had nothing to lose if the regulation was implemented, but a great deal to lose if their products became contaminated with TSE. Accordingly, AutoImmune Inc., a Massachusetts biopharmaceutical firm, urged the FDA not only to implement the regulation, but to follow England's example and ban cattle offal along with sheep. In addition, AutoImmune urged the FDA and USDA to develop an emergency plan to be implemented in the event that BSE should be detected in the U.S. "Any delay in the reevaluation of the agency's current position may prove too late to protect those industries and individuals which will be immediately affected," the company stated. The Pharmaceutical Research and Manufacturers of America, the industry's trade association, weighed in with similar views, calling on FDA to "take specific action to break the ruminant-to-feed-to-ruminant cycle . . . prohibiting the feeding of specified offal from all ruminants." [18]

- *U.S. consumers,* for the most part, had not even heard of mad cow disease, and their voices barely appeared in the official transcript. A few comments did trickle in, however, from individuals such as Gerald Reuter of Plattsburgh, New York, who urged FDA to guarantee a safe food supply by eliminating all meat and bone products from feed for animals intended for human consumption.[19]

Dick Marsh, in a joint statement with fellow Wisconsin researchers Doris Olander, Debbie McKenzie and Judd Aiken, also commented on the proposed regulation in a diplomatically-worded statement that described the FDA proposal as an "excellent first step." At the same time, they strongly disagreed with FDA's failure to propose a broader ruminant-to-ruminant ban. "Based on the scientific research carried out at this and other institutions, we believe that there is a high likelihood of cattle-to-cattle cycle of a transmissible spongiform encephalopathy in the United States today," they stated. "Waiting until 'BSE is documented in the United States' for 'reevaluation' of the ruminant-to-ruminant feed ban will place the United States' livestock and pharmaceutical industries at a severe disadvantage to those in the member countries of the European Union that have already instituted such a ban." [20]

In the end, FDA's proposal stirred discussion but no action whatsoever. Faced by overwhelming opposition from the industries most affected by its extremely timid proposed rule, FDA quietly backed down—and of course, no action was taken to establish a broader ruminant-to-ruminant feed ban. The agency might have believed that "these ingredients can no longer be categorically regarded as safe," but for the time being it preferred to continue gambling with that risk. The FDA would not begin again to consider regulatory action until after human deaths had already been documented in England— and even then its actions would be slow, tentative, and riddled with loopholes.

MELTDOWN

Apocalypse Cow

No one doubted that Harash Narang was an angry man. Beyond that simple point of agreement, however, most of the other allegations regarding Dr. Narang and his scientific career remained topics of considerable public debate.

According to his supporters—notably reporter Peter Martin of the *Daily Express*—Narang was a courageous researcher whose "once brilliant career, based on much original work on spongiform disease over 25 years, has been all but destroyed" by the British government in an effort to suppress early warnings about the human dangers posed by BSE.[1] His critics, on the other hand—who seemed to include virtually every scientist working in the field of the spongiform encephalopathies—regarded him as an inept and possibly unethical scientific pretender whose methodology and claims were highly suspect.

Early in his career, Narang won recognition for his discovery that tubulo-filamentous particles could be found in the brains of many animals infected with spongiform brain diseases. That discovery in turn led to a stint in the United States. Working with Carleton Gajdusek's research lab at the National Institutes of Health, Narang developed what he called a "touch impression technique" using electron microscopy to diagnose infected brains. According to his critics, however, Narang's discovery was merely a rehash of a technique that had been tried and found ineffective back in the 1960s.[2]

The main controversy surrounding Narang began in 1989, when the British Ministry of Agriculture rejected his application for funding to develop his procedure into a quick diagnosis technique for identifying cattle infected with BSE. According to his superiors at MAFF and the Public Health Laboratory Service, the grant was turned down because Narang's technique lacked scientific merit. According to Narang and his admirers, the rejection reflected a government cover-up aimed at concealing the fact that large numbers of BSE-infected animals were entering the human food supply.

In the absence of government funding, Narang turned to Ken Bell, a businessman and philanthropist whose brother, a butcher, had died of a dementia that Bell suspected was Creutzfeldt-Jakob Disease. Under Bell's sponsorship, Narang claimed a series of additional discoveries, including a urine test that he described as the first known method capable of detecting spongiform brain disease in preclinical live animals. Such a technique, if it existed, would have marked a major breakthrough for efforts to control the mad cow epidemic, but other researchers drew blanks when they attempted to replicate Narang's results. After several attempts, no one had been able to confirm either the effectiveness of his diagnostic technique or his broader theory that the TSEs were caused by a new form of spiral-shaped virus which Narang called a "nemavirus." Worse yet, he came under fire from colleagues who charged that his research had violated safety protocols. In 1994, following an inconclusive inquiry, the government rather gracelessly eased him out of his job by declaring his position "redundant." By 1995, Narang had begun to sound a bit mad himself, charging the government not only with wrecking his career but with sending goons to burglarize his apartment and slash the tires of his car.

However bizarre this story seemed, it took on a certain air of credibility in the politically polarized atmosphere surrounding mad cow disease. Narang's charges included the unsubstantiated claim that he had begun noticing unusual cases of Creutzfeldt-Jakob Disease linked to BSE as early as 1989. By 1994, the deaths of farmers had begun to raise new questions, and newspapers were reporting that Vicky Rimmer had become the country's youngest ever victim of CJD. Other unusually young victims were also beginning to appear, sometimes with Narang at their bedsides. Sober scientific minds pointed out that Narang's findings had not been published, let alone verified in independent scientific trials. Narang adamantly refused to publish the details of his "test," claiming that he feared it would be stolen by others. Some observers found this a rather fishy argument. If his test was valid, there was something obviously unethical about withholding information that might help fight a killer disease. If his science was *not* valid, on the other hand, Narang had become the worst imaginable sort of ambulance-chaser, misleading the relatives of sick victims by pretending that he and he alone held the key to understanding their tragedy.

The BSE rate in British herds had leveled off in 1992 and begun to decline in 1993. By 1994, the number of new cases was dropping dramatically, confirming the analysis of government scientists who had predicted that a ban on cannibalistic feeding practices would eventually eliminate the epidemic. By then, however, the government's other predictions about BSE had been proven wrong so many times that even wild-sounding allegations like Narang's seemed plausible. And somehow Narang was managing to find the right victims.

❋ ❋ ❋

The government's CJD Surveillance Unit required an autopsy after death in order to verify a diagnosis of CJD, so Vicky Rimmer's case remained officially unconfirmed. Stephen Churchill, the 19-year-old son of a fire inspector, therefore became the first officially acknowledged victim of what would soon be labeled a "*new variant* strain of Creutzfeldt-Jakob Disease" (nvCJD). Like most people, Stephen ate beef, and he had visited his aunt's farm every year for eight years, coming into contact with cows and drinking unpasteurized milk. However, no cases of BSE had been reported in his aunt's herd.

The first hints of illness came in 1994 when Stephen's college grades were worse than expected. He became depressed and dizzy, and his parents, David and Dorothy, watched him deteriorate into a living nightmare of madness and terrifying hallucinations. As his condition grew worse, he lost coordination and balance. Sometimes when he reached for a cup he missed it, but carried on with the movement that would have taken it to his lips.

"About four months before he died, he started to stagger," recalled Dorothy. "It brought back memories of seeing the cows we had seen on the news. I mentioned it to somebody, and then I dismissed it because it seemed a ridiculous idea."[3]

No one had ever heard of a teenager contracting CJD before, and Stephen's neurologist felt certain that some other disease must be responsible for his symptoms. David and Dorothy began a quest in search of clear answers.

The first report of Stephen's case appeared in the news shortly after his death in May of 1995. Without giving his name, the report claimed that the body of a dead 19-year-old was being specially tested for a link to mad cow disease. Five months later the *Lancet,* England's leading medical journal, reported his name and said another teenager had died—an anonymous sixteen-year-old girl of Turkish-Cypriot extraction who had been born and raised in England.

❀ ❀ ❀

Michelle Bowen, a dark-haired, 29-year-old housewife, had worked as a teenager at a butcher's shop. Her husband Anthony had worked in a slaughterhouse before becoming an engineer. They had two daughters, Natalie and Jacqueline, and she was in the early stages of her third pregnancy when she began suffering mood swings and memory loss.

"When Michelle started to change I thought it was a prenatal depression," Anthony said. "Then things began to get worse and worse. She became aggressive towards the children and quite often she didn't know what she was doing. One minute she'd be fine and the next she would be screaming and shouting." Her depression continued to deepen, and "at one point she said she wanted to kill herself. I didn't know at the time it was a symptom of the illness."

Other bizarre behaviors continued to emerge. "She'd run into the street and collapse. It was terrifying to see her so out of control," Anthony said. "On more than one occasion . . . I had to lock her in the house so she wouldn't just run off and forget where she was."[4]

Eventually, Anthony had to quit his job to take care of Michelle and their two girls. Michelle was seen by a psychologist, then admitted to Manchester Royal Infirmary, six months before she was due to give birth. "It was then that they first mentioned CJD," Anthony said. "As soon as they said it, I knew."[5]

Michelle's aggressive behavior forced the hospital staff to move her to a side ward. Her son, Tony, was delivered prematurely by emergency caesarean section, shortly before she lapsed into a permanent coma. She passed away in November of 1995, three weeks after his birth. Doctors were unable to determine whether she had passed the disease on to her child.[6]

Jean Wake, a housewife and mother of a teenage girl, had also held a job that required her to handle beef, chopping up meat in a pie factory. She was 38 years old when she started losing her balance. Like the others, she suffering a lingering, painful decline until her death in November of 1995.

"No one should have to watch a loved one go through that," said her 75-year-old mother, Nora Greenhalgh. "First her balance was affected and she couldn't walk. Then her memory started to fade, and it reached the point where she was staring at us and didn't know who we were."

"People ask me if she went peacefully," said Albert Henderson, her brother-in-law. "'No, she bloody didn't die peacefully. She went deaf. She went blind. She lost four stone in weight. . . . They die a horrible death. I couldn't see bloody Satan turn round and say: 'Here, look, I've invented this one.' "[7]

In October, Jean's family agreed to let Harash Narang take a urine sample for testing. The hospital agreed to provide the sample but refused to let him use their on-site facilities to do the testing. "They asked me why I couldn't go and do it in my garage," Narang claimed.[8]

Angry, Jean's mother sent a letter to British Prime Minister John Major demanding answers and asking him to intervene on Narang's behalf. Shortly after Jean's death, a reply came from Rachel Reynolds, Major's private secretary:

> The Prime Minister has asked me to thank you for your recent letter about your daughter. I have been asked to reply on the Prime Minister's behalf. The Prime Minister is sorry to hear of your daughter's illness and the distress which you are suffering as a result. I understand that the cause of your daughter's illness has not been established, but I should make it clear that humans do not get 'mad cow disease,' although there are similar diseases which occur in humans and have been known about for very many years. . . . I quite understand your concerns about the cause of your daughter's illness, but I must reassure you that there is no evidence to suggest that eating meat causes this sort of illness in people. The Government's Chief Medical Officer stated quite clearly that he is satisfied that meat does not pass on the disease to people and that the public is properly protected.

Regarding Nora's request on behalf of Harash Narang, Reynolds expressed sympathy but offered no assistance:

> These diseases are very difficult to diagnose and, unfortunately, there is no reliable way of confirming the diagnosis in patients while they are alive. You say that the hospital caring for your daughter seems to be trying to stop a scientist investigating the cause of her illness. However, I understand from the hospital concerned that they are content for the scientist to have the samples that he has requested in order to carry out his tests but, as he is not employed by the hospital, he will have to perform the tests elsewhere.[9]

Narang turned once again for help to businessman Ken Bell, who bought him a plane ticket to the United States, where Gajdusek had arranged for him to use facilities at the Bethesda Hospital of the National Institutes of Health's. The test, Narang claimed, came back positive for CJD.

Jean Wake, pictured at left, was one of the first victims of "new variant Creutzfeldt-Jakob Disease." At right, her mother displays the letter she received from Prime Minister John Major, denying any link between BSE and Jean's death. (photos © North News & Pictures. Used with permission.)

The end of 1995 was a difficult period for the government, as the names of other CJD victims began to appear in the press, most of them unusually young, and some of whom had died as much as a year and a half earlier:

- Fonnie Van Es, a 44-year-old Dutch woman, had died in Banbury, home to Europe's largest cattle market. Her death occurred on June 4, 1994, almost a year prior to Stephen Churchill's, but it was recorded as a normal case of "spontaneous CJD," not as a variant case. "What the doctors are telling me— and this makes me so angry—is that Mum's symptoms were different from the new strain," said her daughter, 23-year-old Ilja. "From what I've read they are just the same: the jerks, the loss of control, the blindness." After her death, a doctor from the CJD Surveillance Unit in Edinburgh asked about Fonnie's diet. Her favorite dish was mince, Ilja said, and since she was divorced and living on a low budget, she "did occasionally buy cheap meat."[10]

- Christine Hay, age 46, had been married for only one year when she started to experience memory loss in May 1994. She had lived in Australia for 12 years, but doctors said she almost certainly contracted the disease in England. By October, her condition was so bad that her mother, Muriel Jones, flew out to Australia to help nurse her for the last six months of her life. "She was like a little waif when I saw her at the airport and lost her speech three weeks later," Muriel said. "At the end she was like a little baby. My heart goes out to any family who is going through what we went through. . . . It is the most devastating disease." [11]

• In Belfast, Ireland, Maurice Callaghan died at age 30 on November 4, 1995. At his funeral, gravediggers were issued protective clothing and surgical gloves and his grave was dug to a depth of nine feet instead of the usual six. [12]

• In February 1996, CJD claimed Anna Pearson, a 29-year-old lawyer from Kent. "Anna lived in halls of residence as a student in London and you can imagine the sort of foods students eat—burgers from cheap places, from the rubbish end of the food market," said her mother. [13]

• Ann Richardson, a 41-year-old health care assistant and mother of one son, started showing symptoms and was diagnosed with depression in 1994. The disease took two years to run its course, ending with her death in January 1996. "She was diagnosed with CJD on December 9 and we were all very shocked," said her sister-in-law, Cathy Hilton. "We knew there was something seriously wrong because Ann was a strong person who was not the type to be very highly strung or nervous. Ann didn't eat a lot of meat, but she did eat it occasionally. Now all the family will not touch any beef products. It was a horrible death. Her nervous system completely closed down, she couldn't walk, talk or swallow, and at the end she was not aware of us." [14]

• Ken Sharpe, a 42-year-old businessman from Liverpool, died after first showing symptoms in April 1995.

• Ann Harness, a 53-year-old mother of two from Lowestoft, Suffolk, died in April 1995, ten weeks after contracting CJD.

• Gwendoline Lawrence, the 64-year-old wife of a dairy farmer, died in Wrexham, Clwyd, the same county where Vicky Rimmer lived. [15]

In October 1995, a report from the government's CJD Surveillance Unit showed that 54 people in England had died during 1994 from the disease, a record number of cases and twice the number recorded in 1985. Dr. Robert Will of Western General Hospital in Edinburgh, who chaired the surveillance unit, warned against jumping to conclusions, noting that other countries in Europe had also recorded more cases than usual during 1994. It was possible, he suggested, that more cases were being discovered due simply to increased surveillance rather than an actual increase in the disease.

Will admitted that the age of the victims was "obviously a very unusual occurrence in Britain but it is important to put it in context." He noted that three cases of CJD had been found in patients under the age of 30 in Warsaw within a period of only a few years. "These cases were found when the Polish authorities were monitoring a quite different brain disease," he said. "If you set out to monitor rare diseases, you will identify all sorts of oddities, but it's impossible to be sure there's a common cause." [16]

Will pointed out also that four teenage deaths from CJD had been observed outside England. "There have been two in America, one in France and one in Poland," he said. "So there is a precedent for teenagers getting CJD." [17]

Writing in the *Mail on Sunday,* reporter Peter Martin responded that these statistics were hardly reassuring. "Some might argue that two teenagers in Britain getting CJD as opposed to four in the whole of the rest of the world was a disturbing precedent all of its own," Martin observed. For that matter, Vicky Rimmer was still alive, so Will's numbers didn't include her case. And no one was talking yet about the *fourth* teenager.

❋ ❋ ❋

As late as Christmas of 1994, Peter Hall had never suffered a serious illness and had rarely missed school. He was a promising student in his first year of college, majoring in environmental studies at Sunderland University. In his spare time, he performed with a heavy metal band. Ironically, he had turned vegetarian not long before the first symptoms appeared. His mother, Frances, had also given up beef when the first alarming news stories appeared. "I expected something like this might develop," she said. "But not in my wildest nightmares did I think it would strike down someone in our own family."

Peter had long hair but was meticulous about his grooming. According to his father, Derek, the family first realized something was wrong when he started showing "an unusual self-neglect setting in around January 1995. Peter was looking scruffy, not eating, losing weight, becoming withdrawn and dark." At first the family doctor thought he was experiencing classic student depression. "But three kinds of anti- depressant tablets proved of no use whatsoever. Finally, the psychologist ruled out depression and Peter underwent a whole battery of tests—a CAT scan, EEG, bone marrow, lumbar puncture, chest X-rays, an endoscopy, and pints and pints in blood tests. All showed nothing."

Loss of coordination followed. Peter's hands trembled, he lost his footing coming down stairs and swayed unsteadily when he walked. By May, he had lost his short-term memory, and by July he was in a wheelchair. "He was completely apathetic," said Frances, "not talking except in a whisper, and even when the television was on, just sitting in his wheelchair staring at the wall." By August, he was no longer able to feed himself or control his bladder and bowels.[18]

The family had him admitted to a local hospital, and when traditional treatments failed, they tried alternative medicines: acupuncture, faith healers, reflexology, prayers on the internet, and an 82-year-old Chinese herbalist from New York. "We'd have done anything to save him," Derek said. "If we'd thought it would have helped, we'd have had a witch doctor dance on his bed." [19]

Frances gave up her job as a waitress so she could visit the hospital daily to nurse Peter herself, carrying him to the toilet and helping him shower. "I thought it was less undignified for a young man if his mum was doing it," she explained. "It was the cruelest thing to witness, like babyhood developing in reverse." [20]

"The most frightening thing was the similarity between his condition and disease we have seen cows suffering from," Derek said. "It included shaking, nervousness and what appeared to be hallucinations."[21]

Doctors at the hospital pronounced themselves baffled at the nature of Peter's illness. Frances and Derek asked if it could be Creutzfeldt-Jakob Disease, but the neurologist insisted it was highly improbable in someone his age. He was shown to a panel of 50 doctors, none of whom suggested CJD. The Halls were frustrated by the handling of Peter's case. The neurologist visited once a week, but the hospital was unable to offer any diagnosis or treatment. "If Peter's condition was unique and devastating, as we'd been told it was, why is it that no one bothered to study what he was suffering from?" Derek asked.[22]

By December 1995, Peter was emaciated and suffering from dementia. At about the same time, the story about Stephen Churchill's death broke in the British press. The Halls read that another teenager had died from CJD and about Harash Narang's claim that he had developed a test for the disease. They contacted Narang to have Peter tested, and in January of 1996 Narang reported that Peter had tested positive. "We must keep an open mind," said the neurologist when Derek Hall informed him of Narang's result. "Hand on heart, I can't honestly say it *isn't* CJD."

Death came finally at 4:30 in the afternoon on Thursday, February 8, 1996, a few days before Peter's 21st birthday. The death certificate listed his condition as "chronic neurological illness," with bronchial pneumonia as the immediate cause of death. In the space where the examiner was supposed to fill in the underlying cause of death, the doctor simply drew a question mark. He was buried at the cemetery in his home town. On advice from the hospital, no viewing of his body was allowed and the coffin was kept closed.[23]

In the absence of support or acknowledgment from the government, the survivors were beginning to organize themselves. The Halls joined with the families of Stephen Churchill, Maurice Callaghan, Jean Wake and Fonnie Van Es to form the "Northern CJD Support Group," with the goal of supporting other victims and pressuring the government to take action. They wanted CJD to be classified as a notifiable disease, which would ensure that every suspected case was centrally reported and collated. They wanted trials conducted to assess Harash Narang's claim that his test could diagnose the disease while patients were still alive. They also wanted the government to publish not just the annual number of CJD deaths but breakdowns by age, symptoms and the area of the brain affected. "Then we'll have a clearer idea of what's happening to us," Derek Hall said.

"Someone standing up in parliament saying we believe that beef is safe to eat is not good enough," Frances said in a television interview. "My son is dead now and we can't bring him back. I hope his death can do something to help other people."[24]

Who Will Tell
the People?

In September 1995, the British government announced that a third farmer had died of CJD. The following month, news of a fourth farmer's death reached the public after a member of the government's Spongiform Encephalopathy Advisory Committee (SEAC) accidentally sent a worried fax to a wrong number. "It is difficult to explain this simply as a chance phenomenon," the fax stated.[1]

In November, reporter Gillian Bowditch conducted a reassuring interview with Robert Will, "the medical detective who is looking for clues to a bizarre brain disorder. . . . No one can be better qualified than Dr. Will, who began studying CJD more than ten years ago and examined every known case that occurred between 1980 and 1984," Bowditch enthused. "His team of 12 have gathered statistics going back to 1970, and examined 600 cases. A member of his team visits each victim's relatives with a 44-page questionnaire. Information is elicited on a quite extraordinary range of activities, from whether the deceased had ever been in contact with ferrets to whether he or she had pierced ears."

None of this surveillance, Will said, had turned up any evidence of a link between CJD and mad cow disease. "My expectation is that we will not find any definite link," he said. "I still believe that very firmly, but I do think it will be years before we can be sure. Proving a definite association is a very difficult thing to do with a rare disease unless there is a major change. We have not had a major change."

Will admitted that the recent cases in farmers and teenagers were cause for some concern, and interviews with the families of victims had implicated some meats, including veal and venison. He pointed out, however, that several cases of CJD had occurred among lifelong vegetarians, and cautioned that information about the diet of victims was likely to be unreliable, due to the slowness of the disease and the extended time period that would separate exposure from onset of symptoms. In addition, relatives' memories could be subconsciously biased by scare stories about meat. "I still enjoy beef," Will offered by way of the obligatory personal testimonial.[2]

Back in 1994, when only two cases of CJD were known among farmers, Will had offered similar warnings against "over-interpretation," pointing out that CJD had not been reported among veterinarians or slaughterhouse workers.

In December 1995, his words came back to haunt him when Len Franklin, a 52-year-old former slaughterhouse worker, was admitted to York District Hospital with a diagnosis of CJD. His ex-wife, Olga Franklin, told reporters he had frequently been splattered with cows' blood and brains at work and sometimes had cuts on his hands that could have come into contact with the infection. Initially he had been diagnosed with Alzheimer's Disease. During a visit in September, Olga recalled, "his hands were shaking and he had difficulty holding a cup of tea. He complained of a pain in the back of his head and his mind was swimming all the time. At the time we thought it might be the disease but doctors didn't consider it until this month. Now he is more like a man of 70 or 80, can hardly move and has virtually lost his eyesight." [3]

By mid-December, stories about Franklin, combined with the deaths of teenagers and farmers, were circulating widely in the British media. Other reports indicated that a number of slaughterhouses were failing to comply with government regulations requiring them to discard the brain and other body parts considered most likely to carry the infection. Additional disturbing information surfaced regarding the case of Stephen and John Thompson, a father-and-son farming operation in Yorkshire which had recorded an astounding 1,200 cases of mad cow on their farm alone. "The only way in which so many BSE cases could be collected is by the farm representing a massive offloading station for other farmers who can continue to claim that their herds are BSE-free," charged David Hinchliffe, a member of parliament's Labour opposition. [4]

A Major Defection

The worst food scare to date erupted when Sir Bernard Tomlinson, the country's leading neurologist, appeared on a BBC radio program and announced that he feared a link between mad cow disease and CJD. "I would not eat beefburgers or meat pies under any circumstances because of the unknown effects on humans," Tomlinson said. He had already warned his children and grandchildren not to eat hamburgers, and said he'd like to see all beef offal banned, as well as liver. [5]

Previously, government officials had dismissed warnings from scientists such as Dr. Helen Grant, a retired neuropathologist and expert on brain diseases. Grant, they said, was "out of date." Richard Lacey was a "bogus professor," as was his colleague, Stephen Dealler, after Dealler published statistical work suggesting that more than 1.5 million infected cattle could have gone undiagnosed into the human food supply. Harash Narang was a lunatic or an opportunist. Marja Hovi, a government veterinarian, had been fired from her job as a slaughterhouse inspector after refusing to certify carcasses as BSE-free. She was described as "a difficult woman."

"Now Sir Bernard'll be getting it in the neck, of course," predicted Helen Grant. "Oh, they make me spit!" [6]

Tomlinson, however, had a reputation that made his opinions harder to dismiss. He was well-known, not just among scientists but among the general public, for his role in years past as the head of an inquiry into London hospitals. "A lot of people are going to listen to him," said Gavin Strang, the Labour

Party's Shadow Agriculture Minister. "Up to now the Government has been saying that any possible link between the two diseases is remote. I don't think that description can be justified any more."

Other scientists supported Tomlinson's position, such as Sheila M. Gore, an epidemiologist with the government's Medical Research Council. Writing in the *British Medical Journal,* Gore said the farmers' deaths were "more than happenstance." All four farmers were men who had worked full-time on British farms with cattle throughout their lives. Analyzing the number of farmers in England and the normal rate of occurrence of CJD, Gore concluded that "the probability of observing four or more confirmed cases in such men is less than one in 10,000." Combined with the recent deaths of teenagers, she said, they amounted to "an epidemiological alert."[7] The *Times* of London surveyed 50 scientists with expertise in spongiform encephalopathies, and only three said they could rule out the risk of BSE passing to humans.

Beef sales in Britain dropped dramatically, as pressure from concerned parents drove hundreds of schools to remove beef from their menus. The Four Seasons, a top London hotel, also stopped serving beef, and hospitals expressed unease about feeding it to their patients. Research in mid-December by the Nielsen marketing firm showed a steady decline in beef buying since the beginning of November, with sales down more than 25% compared to the same time in 1994. The survey estimated that 1.4 million British households were avoiding beef. Hamburgers were especially affected, falling more than 40%. "Parents have taken the threat of BSE very seriously and have cut home spending on beef burgers," stated a Nielsen spokesperson. "The possible implications of this for fast-food vendors cannot be ignored." The Federation of Fresh Meat Wholesalers confirmed Nielsen's statistics, but the Meat and Livestock Commission, a separate industry-funded agency, said it had only seen a 15.8 percent decline in sales, thanks to increased exports to other countries. Then exports came under the gun. Germany's upper house of parliament unanimously demanded a complete ban on British beef imports, notwithstanding objections from the European Union that such a ban was illegal. When the federal government of Germany failed to act, the German regional state of Rhineland-Palatinate imposed its own unilateral ban.

"All this has really frightened me. Who's to say mad cow disease can't jump to humans?" said Jo Morgan, a London housewife, summing up the popular mood: "When in doubt, cut it out."[8]

The government and beef industry fought back with a futile barrage of public relations and testimonials. "There is no scientific evidence that BSE can be transmitted to humans," Prime Minister John Major told the British House of Commons. The safety of beef, he said, was "not in question." In Ireland, the beef industry ran full-page newspaper advertisements claiming "BSE in cattle has nothing to do with the incidence of Creutzfeldt-Jakob Disease in humans." The Institute of Food Science and Technology, a U.K.-based association of food industry advisors, issued what it called an "independent, objective" statement decrying "experts and perceived experts" responsible for alarming the public. "Despite speculation, there appears to be no scientifically valid evidence to suggest that it is unsafe to eat British beef or that BSE can be transmitted from cows to humans," the statement insisted. "Such fears were exacerbated by alarmist publicity in the media, by bans on U.K. beef applied from overseas and by a dearth of easily assimilated and verified information. . . . The evidence available to date still indicates that within the normal environment cattle will prove a dead end host, and that if the control measures are strictly adhered to the disease will eventually become extinct."[9]

"Complete Confidence"

"I am an enthusiastic eater of British beef," said Agriculture Minister Douglas Hogg for the umpteenth time. He released figures showing a 40% drop since the previous year in the number of new mad cows. "We do not believe that BSE in cattle can be transmitted to humans," Hogg said. "The scientific evidence is reassuring on that point, though it doesn't enable us yet to prove that it cannot be transmitted. Against the possibility that we might be wrong, we have in place very rigorous regulations to prevent [specified bovine offals], that is the material capable of carrying the infective agency, getting into the food chain." Hogg said the government was "acting on the advice of an extremely distinguished committee chaired by Professor Pattison, the Dean of University College of the London Medical School, and has at the same time on it people of national and international reputation in these fields. So people can be certain that the Government is receiving the best possible professional and technical advice. . . . I think it is that which enables us to say with complete confidence that British beef is safe."[10]

To bolster his position, Hogg brought out Chief Medical Officer Kenneth Calman, Chief Veterinary Officer Keith Meldrum, Food Minister Angela Browning and Professor John Pattison. Browning said the government's handling of the situation was "ultra precautionary" and accused the media of an "unprincipled" effort to "whip this up to a frenzy of public alarm when there is simply nothing there."[11]

The government's experts insisted with uniformity that beef was "perfectly safe" and carried no conceivable risk. "It is understandable why the public are concerned. That is not unreasonable," Calman said. "What we need to do is reassure them, as much as we can, that beef is safe." SEAC members Pattison and Will stated that "if there was any risk to human health from BSE — and there may be none — there is no doubt that the risk is very much less now than it has ever been." Pattison attempted gently to undermine the impact of Professor Tomlinson's announcement, stating that he had received a letter from Sir Bernard and was hoping to meet with him to discuss the issue. "I personally believe that when all the evidence is made available . . . he will come to a different view," Pattison said.[12]

The flurry of testimonials failed to sway Diane McCrea, head of food and health at the British Consumers' Association. "This does nothing to reassure consumers who are confused about the potential risks of BSE and worried about what they are eating," she said. "Consumers must know exactly what is in the meat products they are buying and in the food they already have at home."[13]

The government got a brief reprieve when *Nature,* a prestigious British scientific journal, published preliminary results from an experiment conducted by John Collinge, a professor of biology and molecular genetics at the Imperial College School of Medicine in London. Collinge, one of England's leading proponents of Stanley Prusiner's prion theory, served on the government's Spongiform Encephalopathy Advisory Committee. In an experiment funded partly by the Ministry of Agriculture, Fisheries and Food (MAFF), Collinge had tried to test whether mad cow disease could be transmitted to humans. His experiments used "transgenic" mice—mice whose DNA had been genetically altered so that they produced a human rather than a mouse version of the prion protein. In theory, the modified mice would mimic human response to the BSE agent. Collinge injected one group of the mice with CJD, and then tested another group with BSE. The mice exposed to CJD had died, but the mice exposed to BSE were still healthy 264 days after exposure. True, these were interim results, and in fact the mice exposed to CJD had also lasted more than 264 days, but British Chief Veterinary Officer Keith Meldrum seized the opportunity to announce that "in some recent mouse experiments, the results are reassuring." [14]

Unfortunately, Collinge himself didn't find his results very encouraging. Prion experiments with genetically altered mice were complicated, based on an unproven theory, and had produced perplexing results in the past. In one experiment, for example, a scientist had created transgenic mice carrying a "hybrid PrP gene" that consisted of human codes mixed with mouse codes. When exposed to human spongiform brain tissue, the hybrid-gene mice became ill much more frequently and faster than mice carrying full human PrP.

As early as October 1995, Collinge had referred to the teenage deaths as "very concerning," adding, "There is no way of determining whether these cases have any direct connection with BSE." [15] And in December, he publicly disputed Will's suggestion that the recent reports were simply the result of improved surveillance. "Given the rarity of CJD in teenagers," he said, "it's unlikely that such cases would have been previously missed." [16]

What Collinge *wasn't* saying was even *more* "concerning." Researchers were privy to unpublished information, and what they were seeing was profoundly disturbing.

Flower-like Clusters

The first evidence of a BSE-CJD link appeared as early as September 1995—before the deaths of Jean Wake or Michelle Bowen or Jean Hays or Anna Pearson or Ann Richardson or Peter Hall. At the Neuropathogenesis Group in Edinburgh, Dr. James Ironside was assigned the task of examining the brain of England's first suspected teenage death from CJD. An experienced neuropathologist, Ironside had examined hundreds of spongy brains, but this time the microscope showed him something he had never seen before. Inside the cerebellum of the teenager's brain, a large, circular cluster of flower-like structures had formed—a striking accumulation of amyloid plaques. Typical cases of CJD attacked the brain primarily in the cerebral cortex. In this case, the disease had struck heavily at the cerebellum and the central gray matter, and to a lesser degree in the basal ganglia, thalamus and hypothalamus. The pattern looked more like kuru than CJD. For that matter, it was disturbingly reminiscent of BSE, which also hits hardest at the base of the brain.[17]

The victim had also shown unusual symptoms. In typical cases of CJD, the first symptoms are usually forgetfulness and out-of-character behavior. In this case, the victim had first begun to show signs of anxiety and depression, then ataxia—trembling and loss of coordination—before descending into dementia. The disease had also taken longer than usual to run its course. Again, the symptoms looked more like kuru than conventional CJD—and they were reminiscent, also, of BSE.

Taken together, these peculiarities could have been written off as a one-time aberration, but when the second teenager's brain arrived for examination, Ironside found the same pattern. The awful possibility emerged that he might be observing the first cases of a new strain of spongiform brain disease in humans, and mad cow disease was the obvious prime suspect to be its source.

Ironside informed Pattison of his discovery and began a review of brain samples taken over the previous two years. Within the space of a few weeks, he had confirmed six more cases, all with the striking, consistent pattern of flowerlike amyloid plaques. The pattern was so consistent that brain samples from the victims were virtually indistinguishable. Their average age was 27 years, and they had taken an average of 13 months to die, compared to nine months for typical Creutzfeldt-Jakob Disease. Electroencephalograms taken while they were still alive had failed to show the brainwave pattern changes normally associated with sporadic CJD.

Ironside also notified Robert Will, his boss at the National CJD Surveillance Unit. Even as Will continued publicly to issue reassurances against "over-interpreting" the significance of the recent CJD cases, his unit was frantically scouring the data in its 44-page questionnaires, looking for common lifestyle factors among the atypical CJD cases that might explain how they had gotten the disease. They only found one factor in common: All eight victims had eaten beef.[18]

By the end of February 1996, Will was convinced that it was necessary to inform the government's Spongiform Encephalopathy Advisory Committee (SEAC) of his finding. An urgent briefing was held on March 8 in London. The participants were acutely aware that their deliberations held enormous consequences. For the beef and dairy industry, billions of dollars were at stake. For the population of England, literally millions of lives might hang in the balance.

Will informed the committee about the eight young patients, and Ironside presented a series of slides showing the brain tissues he had examined under his microscope. The committee watched in stunned silence.

"When he showed us the slides and before he said anything, we could see what it was," Pattison said. "It was dramatically different."[19]

Eight days later the committee met again, hoping to hear that Will and Ironside had come up with evidence that could prevent them from drawing the obvious and horrible conclusion. The news was not good. In fact, a ninth case had been confirmed, and three days later a tenth name would be added to the list. Pattison realized that he could wait no longer. He had to inform Sir Kenneth Calman, the chief medical officer, and Keith Meldrum, the chief vet. Two days later, on March 18, they notified their respective ministers, Stephen Dorrell and Douglas Hogg, who immediately contacted Michael Heseltine, the government's chief political troubleshooter. The news was too big for Heseltine, and he in turn contacted Prime Minister John Major, who ordered a crisis meeting in the cabinet room the following morning, March 19.

In addition to Major's senior ministers, participants at the meeting included Calman and Pattison, summoned to brief the cabinet on the latest developments. The ministers listened, rapt with horror. The question that lurked beneath the surface was whether they would have to finally order the destruction of England's entire cattle herd—all 12 million animals. A slaughter on that scale would cost $15 to $30 billion, with devastating consequences for the economy and their own chances of reelection. Pattison was ordered to poll his committee and report back the following day with advice from the scientists.

The next question, equally terrifying, was who should release the news. Heseltine insisted that Hogg, with his imperious, arrogant manner, would be a disaster. Instead, he nominated Dorrell.

The announcement was planned for the following day, March 20, 1996. Pattison spent the morning with Meldrum giving another cabinet briefing. The ministers knew that their credibility would be nonexistent in the face of a reversal of this magnitude. If SEAC ordered them to destroy the country's entire cattle herd, they would have to do it. They breathed a collective sigh of relief when Pattison reported that this was not among the committee's recommendations for the moment. "The government had pinned its colors to the scientists' mast," said one source. "The policy was simple: we do what the scientists tell us." [20]

Dorrell was scheduled to give his announcement before the House of Commons at 3:30 that afternoon. As the hours ticked away, the word was already leaking out. The *Daily Mirror* printed a story claiming that the government was "about to do a U-turn about the killer disease," combined with a "major advertising campaign . . . aimed at reassuring people." [21] Contacted for comment, a spokesman at the Ministry of Health denied everything: "I know of no plans for Stephen Dorrell to make a statement on BSE or CJD." As for the rumored advertising campaign, "That rings no bells either. . . . We know of no advertising campaign being launched. Both the scientific bodies who would advise the Government if a change of policy is necessary have not said anything which would bring about such a change." [22]

A little later, Major's office confirmed, without elaborating, that both Dorrell and Hogg would appear before the House of Commons to deliver a Government statement "on beef matters." The Health Ministry abruptly conceded that Dorrell *would* make a statement, and that the Ministry was "considering a report from the CJD surveillance unit. The Government is committed to keeping the public informed of developments," the spokesman said. "Ministers have repeatedly made it clear that they will always act on the best possible scientific advice to protect public health." [23]

Somehow, Professors Stephen Dealler and Richard Lacey seemed to know already what was in the wind, and gave statements denouncing the government. Dealler not only had heard that a new strain of CJD had been detected, he described it correctly as attacking the base of the brain. He estimated that 100,000 Britons might already have eaten infected beef. "What this implies is that there is a good possibility that these people have caught the disease from eating beef infected with BSE," Dealler said. "Until there is evidence to the contrary we must assume that to be true. It is very worrying." [24]

Lacey told the press he suspected that the flurry of rumors followed new results from one of the government's research programs, and took the opportunity to issue an angry jeremiad. "This is one of the most disgraceful episodes in this country's history and I want a full and independent inquiry into the conduct of the Government and the way it has used and misused scientific advisors," Lacey said. "My feeling is that the Government has been deliberately risking the health of the population for a decade. The reason it didn't take action was that it would be expensive and damaging politically, particularly to the farming community who are their supporters. . . . I think we are seeing the beginning of a very large number of people acquiring the disease in the next century. The estimate of numbers is very, very broad. The maximum could be anything from 5,000 a year to 500,000 a year. It could be even more than that." [25]

By contrast, the Meat and Livestock Commission, a promotional agency for British meat, seemed to be caught flat-footed. A spokeswoman said the Commission was "astonished" by the rumored news. "We feel a bit let down by the Ministry as we had no prior warning of any announcement," she said. [26]

Almost lost within the general uproar, England's Mental Health Foundation happened to choose March 20 as the date to announce its own new research findings. The Foundation had conducted a study at four research centers, examining the brains of more than 1,000 people who had died of dementia. Nineteen of the brains they studied turned out to show the telltale signs of CJD when examined under a microscope, and only half of the CJD brains had been correctly diagnosed. The others had been misdiagnosed as Alzheimer's Disease or some other dementia. "It's clear that a significant number of CJD cases are slipping through the diagnostic net," said Foundation director June McKerrow. "We're concerned that public health information is currently being based on data which may be misleading or inaccurate." [27]

Prince Charles and Lady Diana were in the middle of their messy divorce, and Charles had just high-handedly refused to pay a $30,000 bill submitted by Diana's attorney. On some other day, the royal tantrum might have topped the news, but on this date Charles and Di were eclipsed when Dorrell stepped before a stunned House of Commons and began to speak:

I would like to make a statement about the latest advice which the Government has received from the Spongiform Encephalopathy Advisory Committee.
The House will be aware that this committee, which is chaired by Professor John Pattison, was established in 1990 to bring together leading experts in neurology, epidemiology and microbiology to provide scientifically based

advice on the implications for animal and human health of different forms of spongiform encephalopathy.

The committee provides independent advice to Government. Its members are not Government scientists; they are leading practitioners in their field and the purpose of the committee is to provide advice not simply to Government, but to the whole community on the scientific questions which arise in its field.

The Government has always made it clear that it is our policy to base our decisions on the scientific advice provided by the advisory committee. The committee has today agreed on new advice about the implications for animal and human health of the latest scientific evidence. . . .

The committee has considered the work being done by the Government Surveillance Unit in Edinburgh which specializes in Creutzfeldt-Jakob Disease. This work, which relates to the 10 cases of CJD which have been identified in people aged under 42, has led the committee to conclude that the unit has identified a previously unrecognized and consistent disease pattern.

A review of patients' medical histories, genetic analysis and consideration of other possible causes have failed to explain these cases adequately. There remains no scientific proof that BSE can be transmitted to man by beef, but the committee has concluded that the most likely explanation at present is that these cases are linked to exposure to BSE before the introduction of the specified bovine offal ban in 1989.

Against the background of this new finding the committee has today agreed to the series of recommendations which the Government is making public this afternoon.

The committee's recommendations fall into two parts.

Firstly, they recommend a series of measures to further reduce the risk to human and animal health associated with BSE. Agriculture Minister Douglas Hogg will be making a statement about those measures which fall within his department's responsibilities immediately after questions on this statement have been concluded.

In addition the committee recommended that there should be urgent consideration of what further research is needed in this area and that the Health and Safety Executive and the Advisory Committee on Dangerous Pathogens should urgently review their advice. The Government intends to accept all the recommendations of the Advisory Committee in full; they will be put into affect as soon as possible.

The second group of recommendations from the committee offers advice about food safety on the assumption that the further measures recommended by the committee are implemented. On that basis the committee has concluded that the risk from eating beef is now likely to be extremely small and there is no need for it to revise its advice on the safety of milk.

The Chief Medical Officer will be writing today to all doctors to ensure that the latest scientific evidence is drawn to their attention. In the statement by the Chief Medical Officer which we have placed in the Vote Office, Sir Kenneth Calman poses to himself the question whether he will continue to eat beef. I quote his answer: 'I will do so as part of a varied and balanced diet. The new measures and effective enforcement of existing measures will continue to ensure that the likely risk of developing CJD is extremely small.'

A particular question has arisen about the possibility that children are more at risk of contracting CJD. There is at present no evidence for age sensitivity and the scientific evidence for the risks of developing CJD in those eating meat in childhood has not changed as a result of these new findings.

However parents will be concerned about implications for their children and I have asked the Advisory Committee to provide specific advice on this issue following its next meeting.

Any further measures that the committee recommend will be given the most urgent consideration. As the Government has repeatedly made clear, new scientific evidence will be communicated to the public as soon as it becomes available. [28]

When Dorrell had finished speaking, Douglas Hogg stepped forward to make his statement:

The House will wish to know the action I propose to take to ensure the risk to the public is minimized.

The additional recommendations just made by the Spongiform Encephalopathy Advisory Committee that most immediately affect agriculture departments are that carcasses from cattle aged over 30 months must be deboned in specially licensed plants supervised by the Meat Hygiene Service and the trimmings kept out of any food chain; and that the use of mammalian meat and bonemeal in feed for all farm animals be banned.

The committee goes on to state that if these and their other recommendations are carried out the risk from eating beef is now likely to be extremely small.

The Government has accepted these recommendations and I will put them into effect as soon as possible. Any further measures that SEAC may recommend will be given the most urgent consideration.

Also, and with immediate effect, I have instructed that existing controls in slaughterhouses and other meat plants and in feed mills should be even more vigorously enforced.

I do not believe that this information should damage consumer confidence and thus the beef market. But I should say that support mechanisms exist in the Common Agricultural Policy and the Government will monitor the situation closely. I will naturally report developments to the House.

I recognize that there will be public concern, but the Government's Chief Medical Officer advises us that there is no scientific evidence that BSE can be transmitted to man by beef. Indeed he has stated that he will continue to eat beef as part of a varied and balanced diet as indeed shall I. In view of what I have announced, we believe that British beef can be eaten with confidence. [29]

Feeding Frenzy

The announcement broke on a Wednesday afternoon. That evening, Health Minister Stephen Dorrell got his first taste of public reaction during an appearance on BBC-TV's *Newsnight,* where he faced off against the mother of "new variant" CJD victim Peter Hall. "Pleased to meet you," he said as they were introduced in the moments before airtime.

"I wish I could say the same," Frances Hall replied before proceeding to shred him verbally on live TV.[1]

"Thursday was human victims day, with the blurred family snaps of those who had succumbed to CJD staring out from the front pages," observed Tony Delamonte in the *British Medical Journal.* "The speed with which the government decided to go public with its news precluded the setting of the usual firebreaks—the off-the-record briefings, the reassurances from authoritative 'neutral' spokespeople, the spin doctoring by special interest groups." The *Guardian* complained that the government "appears to have absolutely no contingency plans for dealing with an issue that has been threatening to explode for five years."[2]

The victims' families, meanwhile, showed no signs of similar paralysis. "Our first reaction was one of anger," said Stephen Churchill's father, David. "Anger because it could have been beef that killed our son. Anger because it may have been possible for the government to have acted sooner."[3]

"Why weren't we told there might be a link? If the government had been up front we would have stopped eating beef," said Ann Richardson's husband, Ronny. "They kept it under wraps to protect the beef industry. I am livid. I feel like I have been misinformed and patronized and both my wife and I have been put through a lot of unnecessary suffering as a result. We meant nothing to the government. It is a disgrace."[4]

"I think it is awful that they can now say that maybe there is a link and that over the last few years they have been denying it," said Helen Rimmer. "Surely they must have had doubts in the back of their minds. You have to ask why they have suddenly announced this now. It makes me wonder if more cases have emerged that we don't know about."[5]

Jean Wake's mother, Nora Greenhalgh, angrily displayed the letter she had received a few months previously from John Major's secretary denying any link between beef and CJD. "I didn't believe him then. I don't believe him

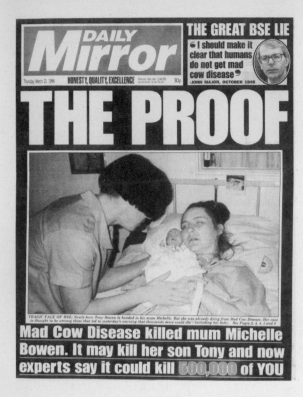

THE GREAT BSE LIE

DAILY Mirror

Thursday March 21 1996   HONESTY, QUALITY, EXCELLENCE   30p

❛I should make it clear that humans do not get mad cow disease❜
-JOHN MAJOR, OCTOBER 1995

THE PROOF

TRAGIC FACE OF BSE: Newly-born Tony Bowen is handed to his mum Michelle. But she was already dying from Mad Cow Disease. Her case is thought to be among those that led to yesterday's warning that thousands more could die - including her baby.   See Pages 2, 4, 6, 5 and 6

Mad Cow Disease killed mum Michelle Bowen. It may kill her son Tony and now experts say it could kill 500,000 of YOU

British tabloid newspaper coverage featured victims like Michelle Bowen on the day following the bombshell announcement of a link between BSE and human deaths from "new variant Creutzfeldt-Jakob Disease."

now," she told newspapers. "This was a deliberate cover-up to avoid tarnishing the reputation of British beef."

Media voices clamored simultaneously for panic and for calm. Exposés detailed the inadequacies of inspection procedures at meat processing facilities and offered gory descriptions of chicken manure being processed into cattle feed and farm fields being fertilized with bloody organs from diseased cows. "Beef is one of the great unifying symbols of our culture," observed the *Guardian*. "The Roast Beef of Old England is a fetish, a household god, which has suddenly been revealed as a Trojan horse for our destruction." The *Daily Telegraph* philosophized that "Life is a hazardous business. But among all the hazards we face, eating beef must rank as minor, even after yesterday's news." The *Evening Standard* called for a "calm and rational assessment of risks . . . All our lives bear some measure of risk, even when we cross the roads."[6]

The government struggled desperately to develop a plan that would restore the public's confidence, offering to subsidize the destruction of millions of animals from BSE-infected herds. In a moment of weakness or self-pity, Health Minister Stephen Dorrell made the mistake of complaining about the public uproar. "It isn't the cows who are mad, it's people who are going mad," he said. "What all of us have to do is step back from the hysteria and believe the facts."

"Dorrell is such a swine. He can't have any feelings," responded Beryl Rimmer, fighting back tears. "I only wish he could see my Vicky lying helpless in the hospital. One look at her would change his mind."

"The whole government should resign over this terrible cover-up," added Nora Greenhalgh. "I wouldn't touch British beef, and I think that companies banning it are very sensible."

"The Government should be trying to sort this infection out, not insulting people with such crass insensitivity," chimed in Richard Lacey. "If ministers think we're mad then it's probably because they made us mad by making us eat beef."

Appearing on a phone-in radio show, Dorrell faced further hostility from the public at large. "There isn't a government minister who has any credibility with me—and I'm sure I speak for others," said one caller. Another asked Dorrell whether he had ever heard of the saying, "better safe than sorry."[7]

Pigs and Chickens

"It now appears that I was wrong," admitted Paul Brown, medical director for the U.S. Public Health Service. Brown, a colleague of Gibbs and Gajdusek at the National Institutes of Health, had penned an editorial four months earlier for the *British Medical Journal* arguing that "there does not seem to be any need for new governmental hearings, committee meetings, or parliamentary debates about what more might be done because the precautions taken some years ago to eliminate potentially infectious products from commercial distribution were both logical and thorough." Following the March 20 announcement, Brown declared himself "still astonished . . . that human infection might be occurring from the ingestion of beef (or, even more improbably, from milk). . . . However, it must also be emphasized that the link to cattle products is itself only a presumption; how ironic, for example, if eleven million British cattle should be slaughtered in a preemptive strike . . . only to find belatedly that the true villains were pigs or chickens which were also fed contaminated nutritional supplements but were brought to market at such a young age that the disease had not had time to become manifest."

Brown concluded that "a good deal of work remains to be done in order to establish the link between bovine spongiform encephalopathy and Creutzfeldt-Jakob Disease, much of which has already been initiated. None of it will be of any help to those who may have been exposed to the infectious agent in the 1980s before precautionary measures were put in place to minimize the risk of human disease. Nor will it remedy the possible failure of the scientific pundits (including me) to foresee a potential medical catastrophe."[8]

Not everyone was ready yet to concede the link between beef and "new variant CJD." Government officials, perhaps from sheer force of habit, continued to treat the BSE crisis as a "food scare." British newspapers editorialized that the scare was some sort of plot by the French or Germans, or highlighted the irrationality of people who had given up beef but continued to smoke cigarettes. According to Emily Green, a food reviewer with the Conservative *Daily Telegraph,* the scare reflected "a curious, tortured, modern logic that turns an admission of uncertainty into the certainty that there is a threat. . . . My horror is that unnecessary, wantonly whipped-up panic will destroy the small farmers, abattoirs and butchers who most deserve nurturing."[9]

Scoffing at what he called "Mad Headline Writers' Disease," food industry consultant Ralph Blanchfield accused the government's Spongiform Encephalopathy Advisory Committee of a rush to judgment, suggesting that the new human disease might have come from sources that SEAC failed to consider: "One might look at possible shared exposure to a whole range of chemical substances, in recreational drugs, medical drugs, domestic preparations, garden preparations," Blanchfield suggested. "Before relatives of victims or anyone else indignantly react against any implication or mention of recreational drugs, how many parents really know or even suspect whether their offspring are using them? There have been well documented cases of deaths of teenagers where the parents had not the slightest idea."[10]

Blanchfield, who earned his living advising food companies and serving as a courtroom "expert witness," devoted himself to issuing and re-issuing frequent revisions of a "Policy Statement" on behalf of the Institute of Food Science and Technology, a professional association representing the food industry's safety advisors. "There is at present no scientific evidence that BSE can be transmitted to humans," the statement claimed. "It has now become apparent that SEAC's conjecture, and the statements based thereon, had little if any substance behind them."[11] Blanchfield described the government's conclusions as "merely a very weakly based speculation by the CJD Unit, echoed by SEAC and the U.K. Government. . . . It *might* be explained by a variety of as yet unknown and unexplored causes totally unrelated to BSE, or even by Martians having brought variant CJD when they landed at Stonehenge, There is no evidence whatsoever that nvCJD is BSE-related. . . . The so-called circumstantial evidence in this instance is ludicrously flimsy and may only be represented as being otherwise by exaggeration, misstatements, and selectivity by ignoring facts that don't fit the case being made."[12]

This assessment won a hearty endorsement in the United States from Dave Harlan of Taylor Byproducts, a rendering firm whose products are marketed primarily to the pet food and dairy industries. Harlan decried the "overreaction of industry and scientific associations in the U.S.A. which have been further supported by federal regulatory agencies. Of course their overreaction has been done in the name of 'Proactive moves to prevent consumer perception issues.' By not sticking to a scientific basis we (U.S.A.) have opened a can of worms in a country where no BSE exists. . . . This overreaction in the U.S. has given credibility to radical activist groups who preach the evilness of the cattle complex and fantasize about our future as a vegetarian society. It is a shame that a very, very small group of activists has us at their mercy."[13]

Outside the meat industry, the British government's announcement on March 20, 1996 marked the first time that most people in the United States had even heard of something called "mad cow disease." The news, however tragic, came packaged in such a silly name that people could not refrain from treating it humorously. "Have you heard about the two British cows standing out in a field?" went one joke. "The first one says to the other, 'I hear they're planning to slaughter all the cows in England because of mad cow disease.' The second cow says to the first, 'What do I care? I'm a *refrigerator!*' " Another joke had a feminist punchline. "Do you know why men can't get mad cow disease? Because all men are *pigs*." An internet jokester offered his own brand of humor, with a World Wide Web page listing "ways to tell if your cow has mad cow disease." Among the signs:

- Your cow appears on Oprah, claiming to be a horse trapped in a cow's body.

- She starts giving you Milk of Amnesia.

- Your cow spends half the day sitting in the Lotus Position chanting "MOO" backwards.

- Your cow asks you to brand her again but only if you'll wear something sexy this time.

The *Phoenix Gazette* took the British announcement as a pretext to editorialize against "America's present passion for political correctness." According to the *Gazette,* "There would have been no mad cow disease had it broken out on this side of the Atlantic. While the cattle might have reacted the same way, we believe Americans, especially those liberal Democrats in the Department of Agriculture, would have been more concerned with their plight—and dubbed the ailment something more sensitive, such as Neurologically Challenged Cattle Syndrome." [14]

Actually, the campaign for linguistic correctness came from the Republican-leaning National Cattlemen's Beef Association (NCBA). Fearing that the phrase "mad cow" would evoke images of rabies, the Cattlemen posted a statement on *their* web page advising the public that "bovine spongiform encephalopathy" was the "correct" name for the disease.

A "Voluntary Ban"

Unlike the people telling silly jokes, the Cattlemen understood immediately and clearly that this was no laughing matter. This was their livelihood at stake. Their reaction, aimed at dampening public concern in the United States, was a swift and deceptive public relations maneuver. Nine days after the British announcement, NCBA joined other animal industry organizations in issuing the following statement:

> National livestock organizations and professional animal health organizations today announced that they will immediately establish an aggressive voluntary program to assure that ruminant-derived protein is not used in ruminant feed products as an additional safeguard to ensure that the U. S. cattle population remains free of bovine spongiform encephalopathy (BSE).
>
> Today's announcement is an extra preventative measure. BSE is not in the U.S. cattle herd, according to a 10-year testing and surveillance program conducted by the U.S. Department of Agriculture.
>
> These groups, the National Cattlemen's Beef Association, the American Sheep Industry Association, the National Milk Producers Federation, the American Veterinary Medical Association, the American Association of Bovine Practitioners and the American Association of Veterinary Medical Colleges, support the following government action:

- The Food and Drug Administration's Center for Veterinary Medicine to expedite regulations prohibiting ruminant protein in ruminant feeds.

- USDA's Animal and Plant Health Inspection Service (APHIS) and Food Safety and Inspection Service (FSIS) to work with producers and private veterinary practitioners in augmenting U.S. surveillance efforts to ensure that BSE never enters the U.S. cattle population.

- USDA's Cooperative State Research, Education, and Extension Service to work with APHIS, producers, feed manufacturers and veterinary professional organizations to enhance the education of producers, veterinarians, and feed nutritionists about BSE.

- USDA's Agricultural Research Service to lead a cooperative research effort to gather more scientific information about BSE.

- Within 30 days, establish a working group from the public and private sectors to develop the necessary steps leading to full implementation of these safeguards.[15]

In theory, the "aggressive voluntary ban" on feeding cows to cows sounded like a great idea. The USDA immediately announced its support for the voluntary ban, stating that "the measures announced today will provide an additional level of assurance that the United States remains free of BSE." The Food and Drug Administration promised in addition that it would "expedite regulations"— meaning a *mandatory* ban—"prohibiting ruminant protein in ruminant feeds."

In reality, the "voluntary ban" was nothing but a news release. To ensure that it received minimal scrutiny, the announcement was released late on a Friday night in Washington, DC—the traditional time when most reporters are gone for the weekend. And in fact, none of the journalists who reported the announcement bothered to notice that *the feed and rendering industries were declining to sign on.* Opponents of the voluntary ban included the American Feed Industry Association, the National Renderers Association and the Livestock Conservation Institute, whose members included six major national agricultural associations and 46 producer organizations.[16]

Without the support of the feed industry, farmers alone could not be expected to observe a voluntary ban on ruminant feeding. Many farmers themselves were unaware of what the industry was putting into their feed and were genuinely shocked to find out. "We try to raise our animals as organically as possible," stated farmer Joan Spiczka. "I guess I am wondering what kinds of feed supplements are being used that are possibly passing along this disease. I may be ignorant, but I was unaware that cattle were fed animal byproducts at all. After all, they are vegetarian in nature. . . . I have looked at some of the labels that accompany feed supplements and such things from the places that we purchase them from, and unfortunately, most of them are all these large scientific words that I do not understand too well, and so it is a lot like trying to figure out what the foods at the grocery stores have in them as well. They label things in such a way that you have to have gone to college to understand what exactly you are buying."[17]

The USDA had spent the previous six years advising farmers that it was safe to continue feeding U.S. rendered animal byproducts to cattle. The National

Cattlemen and other meat producers had spent the same period reassuring their members that mad cow disease was a strictly animal problem and that the voices warning of risks to humans were media hypesters and vegetarian crackpots. Their sudden new advice seemed PR-driven to many farmers, who remained understandably skeptical about the need to take it seriously. As a result, sales of rendered animal protein declined briefly for a few days and then returned to their previous levels. "Rendering company Darling International Inc. of Irving, Texas, for example, saw its stock price drop briefly but said business was unaffected after cattlemen approved a voluntary ban on feed that includes processed animal byproducts," reported the Reuters news service.[18] Wisconsin's agricultural newspaper, *Agri-View,* sent an editor to survey the situation and drew similar conclusions:

> Livestock and veterinary groups don't appear to be drawing many Wisconsin volunteers to the public relations war against bovine spongiform encephalopathy (BSE).
>
> Dairy industry officials say they've seen almost no change in dairy cow rations since the British "mad cow" scare of late March and early April. Renderers report that any initial losses in ruminant protein sales due to the publicity have since been recaptured. Indeed, meat-and-bone meal sales volumes appear to have risen in recent weeks as dairy farmers cope with rising soymeal prices. . . .
>
> "The voluntary ban is not particularly realistic," says Randy Shaver, a dairy scientist at the University of Wisconsin-Madison. . . .
>
> Sales were cut in half during the first week of the hullabaloo, says Mike Langenhorst, executive vice-president for Anamax, in Green Bay [and vice-president of the National Renderers Association]. The losses were particularly great in the company's dairy business. But Langenhorst says Anamax regained half those losses the following week, and local sales of dairy feed are actually a bit higher than before the crisis.
>
> "Basically, we're sold out," adds Ken Cross, district manager for National By-Products, Inc., Berlin. "Sales don't seem to have been affected." . . .
>
> Meat-and-bone meal sales have been aided by rising soymeal prices and farmers' skepticism of the BSE issue. . . .
>
> Scott Gunderson, [University of Wisconsin] Extension dairy agent in Manitowoc County . . . says he isn't aware of anyone leaving the animal proteins because of the voluntary ban.
>
> Says Gunderson, "Until (the ban) becomes mandatory, I don't see that changing."
>
> Shaver largely agrees with that view. At the normal price relationship, he says, a dairy farmer substituting soymeal for meat-and-bone meal in a typical ration spends about a nickel more per cow per day. . . . For a 100-cow herd, the difference works out to about $1,500 a year. While Shaver notes that this won't cause the dairyman to lose his farm, it's enough to make a dairyman reluctant to abandon the animal feed—especially since he knows his neighbors are probably using it.
>
> Shaver thus does not expect any major changes in feeding practices until farmers get some sort of edict from the federal government. "A lot of people are waiting for the shoe to drop from the FDA," he notes.[19]

As an effective policy measure, the voluntary ban was a joke, a scam, a nothing. As a PR ploy, however, it worked brilliantly. No major media outlet reported that cow cannibalism was widespread and continuing full bore in the United States. The exception was Howard Lyman's appearance on the Oprah Winfrey Show, and the industry's "food disparagement" lawsuit quickly drove her into silence. Under advice from attorneys, Oprah not only stopped speaking about the issue but declined to make videotapes of her original interview available to inquiring journalists. The message to other media was clear: "Mention mad cow disease, and we'll sue you." If they could shut up Oprah, they could shut up just about anyone.

There was little evidence that the Oprah show had caused significant financial damages to the beef industry. "One of the things we keep hearing is Oprah said she was not going to eat hamburgers anymore, and all of a sudden the price drops out of futures on beef," said James Reagan, the National Cattlemen's Director of Product Safety. "No one seems to mention that also the price dropped out of coal, natural gas, crude oil. Commodities were down on that day. *All* commodities went down, nothing stayed up. It was kind of interesting that the next day everything had gone back up to about where it was."

"So you don't attribute the drop necessarily to Oprah?" asked interviewer Tom Clark, during Reagan's appearance on Wisconsin Public Radio.

"Well, if people credit her with the drop in that, they also need to credit her with the drop in futures for coal, natural gas and crude oil," Reagan replied.

During the interview, which took place three days after the Oprah show aired, Reagan served up a contradictory mixture of soothing platitudes and outright falsehoods. At first he said the industry's "voluntary ban" was working, then admitted that rendered protein was still being fed but said the amount was small—"less than one percent." Questioned further, he declined to define the meaning of his statistic and said instead that the Cattlemen didn't "have a good handle" on the amount being fed:

CLARK: I think some people are concerned about something called a voluntary ban. It seems like an oxymoron.

REAGAN: Well, it may be a voluntary ban, but I'll tell you what, you go out and you start talking to the renderers in this country. They have taken it very seriously. I was meeting with some yesterday, and they have not used it since that time. . . .

CLARK: Does that mean that none of these animal products now are being used in the feed of cattle in the United States?

REAGAN: The thing that you have to remember is that—people have talked about that a lot—the actual use of ruminant dry proteins in cattle feed is very, very low. It's probably—it's less than one percent. . . . Why do we use it? It's a source of protein, it's a source of minerals. Sometimes some people use it in starter rations, starter diets for cattle, and y'know, they may be on it for a week, two weeks at the max, so actually the use of it is very little. . . .

CLARK: I'm still not clear. We talked just before . . . about the voluntary ban, and then you mentioned when some animal products are actually being used. Is there in fact a ban that's a total ban on these rendered cattle parts getting into cattle feed in the United States, or is there not? I'm not clear on that.

REAGAN: There is not a total ban at this time. There is a voluntary ban. NCBA has taken a real firm stand on that. What we have in place is we have a beef quality assurance program. . . .

PHONE-IN CALLER: I wonder if I could get some clarification on some numbers that your guest just gave a little while ago. He said that one percent of the feed might come from rendered sheep products, something like that, and then you said that cattle are often fed just for one week or so in their life. I'm wondering, . . . if 90% of all young cattle are fed for one week, that could still just give you that one percent.

REAGAN: No, no, no, they're not. Actually very, very few cows are ever fed that. I can't give you the exact numbers because I don't think we have a good handle on it, but what we do know if we talk to the feed producers, the renderers, it's just not being used. . . .

CLARK: What's your take on the connection between BSE and the brain damage that may or may not or appears to be linked in humans in England? Where do you think the research is on that?

REAGAN: There is no link. The link they have is that both of them are diseases of the central nervous system. . . . There are some major differences there that I think a lot of people do not understand. . . . There is no scientific evidence that says there is a relationship between BSE and that if you eat meat in Great Britain that you would develop CJD or BSE or whatever.

CLARK: There are concerns, though, that there may be a link that just hasn't been proven yet. Is that fair?

REAGAN: I think we have to look at it as being a concern, but . . . we deal with science, sound scientific evidence. Somebody can make some statement that "This is what I believe," and if they make that statement, that has to be considered a concern to that individual. That does not mean that they have sound scientific evidence that that is the case. That does not say that there is a cause-and-effect relationship. They have made that statement in Great Britain, that they think there may be a link, but according to their ministry of health in that country—they come out and say that there is no link, there is no sound scientific evidence. There's a lot of work that shows that there is no link. There are differences. There are similarities, I'll grant that. Both of those are diseases of the central nervous system, but they are completely different.[20]

There was no law to stop James Reagan from claiming that England's ministry of health denied any link between BSE and CJD, even though Health Minister Stephen Dorrell had been the person who made the March 20 announcement. Reagan was free also to claim that BSE and CJD were "completely different," just as Howard Lyman was free to claim that BSE "could make AIDS look like the common cold." Neither of these statements had much backing in "sound scientific evidence," but people tend to believe what they want to believe. The difference between the Cattlemen and Lyman, however, is that James Reagan was able to make his remarks over the airwaves without fear of legal reprisal, while Lyman's remarks brought down the wrath of corporate attorneys seeking to sue him into submission and silence.

The meat industry in fact repeatedly thrust forward misleading arguments aimed at persuading the public that there was "no evidence of any link" between BSE and nvCJD. Some of that misinformation flowed through the Hill & Knowlton public relations firm, one of the funding sources behind the Animal Industry Foundation and its campaign to enact "agricultural product disparagement laws." On April 1, 1996, Hill & Knowlton executive Nancy L. Glick released the following statement on behalf of former U.S. Surgeon General Dr. C. Everett Koop:

> There is absolutely no clinical evidence that beef can transmit Creutzfeld-Jacob [sic] Disease. . . . [S]uch a link is speculative and has never been proven. Furthermore, unlike the British cattle herd, the U.S. cattle herd does not carry BSE. The U.S. government, cattle and beef industries took steps long ago to protect U.S. cattle from contracting BSE. Consumers of U.S. beef should feel completely safe.[21]

Aside from the fact that the venerable Dr. Koop did not even seem to know the correct spelling of Creutzfeldt-Jakob Disease, his statement was carefully and cleverly worded to convey a misleading impression. Of *course* there was "no clinical evidence" that beef can transmit CJD. In order to produce "clinical evidence," you would have to deliberately expose humans to the infectious agent under laboratory conditions and then monitor them systematically, observing and documenting the physiological processes by which the disease incubates, emerges and and kills them. It is not at all clear that such an experiment would even be *possible* given the current state of scientific knowledge, but even if it were possible, there are obvious ethical reasons why it should never be undertaken.

The available evidence was not "clinical proof." It was epidemiological evidence, combined with pathological examinations which revealed that "new variant CJD" showed clear differences upon autopsy from previously-seen, conventional cases of CJD. Even without "clinical evidence," this available evidence was strong and compelling to scientific researchers who, unlike Dr. Koop, had actual expertise in the TSEs.

In the absence of clear scientific answers regarding the nature and origins of mad cow disease, conspiracy theories sprang up offering alternative explanations. Harash Narang continued to keep the details of his research secret, while his supporters circulated reports that the government was attempting to suppress his results. A French farmer speculated that the epidemic was a marketing ploy by the U.S. beef industry: "I think the United States put pressure on Britain to destabilize the European beef market so that American suppliers could monopolize the market."

A personal tragedy involving Carleton Gajdusek intersected strangely with the international uproar. Three weeks after the March 20 announcement broke in England, Gajdusek returned home from an urgent BSE conference in Europe to find a dozen armed police and FBI agents waiting to arrest him. "They came from all directions," said Dr. Paul Brown of the U.S. Public Health Service, who was with Gajdusek at the time of the arrest. Brown said the arresting agents searched him and Gajdusek while holding guns to their heads and forced them to lean spread-eagled against their cars. "It was like the Unabomber," he complained.[22]

Gajdusek was charged with child abuse and unnatural perverted sex practices with one of the teenage boys he had adopted from Micronesia. His family and scientific colleagues vigorously denied the charges, describing the arrest as the culmination of a six-month "witch hunt" during which Gajdusek had endured "incredible harassment" from law-enforcement authorities. Brown called the arrest "a conspiracy to destroy" and joined famed AIDS researcher Robert Gallo in putting up the $350,000 in bail money needed to secure Gajdusek's release.

Over the years, Gajdusek had adopted 54 children from Micronesia and New Guinea. Many had long since grown to adulthood and were engaged in successful independent careers of their own—a diplomat, a doctor, a teacher, a museum curator. Most of them quickly rallied to his defense. "We feel so angry because people don't understand. There's a group of boys and one old guy, and that triggers all kinds of speculation," said one former adoptee, now a Micronesian government cabinet minister. "We had a house full of life and happiness and learning, and people now are trying to equate it with something sick and perverted."

The accuser, however, told a different story. He had been adopted at age 16 and said the abuse had begun at age 17 (incorrectly reported as 15 in press accounts) and continued for six years. Now age 23, he was currently attending college, with Gajdusek continuing to pay his tuition. In an emotional three-hour interview with the *Washington Post,* the young man expressed a mixture of both anger and admiration for Gajdusek, who had brought him to the United States and put him through school. "I think I love Carleton, and I really respect him a lot, and I'm thankful for what he's done for me, but I don't agree with the things he did," he said. "I mean, I feel like I owe Carleton, too, and I probably would never have said anything if the FBI never asked." At first, he said, he had refused to answer their questions. "I don't know why I said no. I guess I wanted to protect Carleton," he said. "And I knew the consequences. . . . I knew a lot of other people wouldn't believe it. . . . I have so much mixed feelings that sometimes I want to just deny it all."[23]

On May 7, 1996, tragedy struck another scientist, a professor of neurosciences at the University of California-San Diego. Tsunao Saitoh and his 13-year-old daughter were gunned down in front of his home by an unknown assailant. At the time of his murder, Saitoh had just published research documenting his discovery of a "new amyloid component protein" (NACP) involved in the development of Alzheimer's Disease. The functional similarities between

NACP and Stanley Prusiner's prion protein were striking enough to renew speculation that Alzheimer's might be caused by a process similar to the process which caused the transmissible spongiform encephalopathies. This in turn provided new grist for the mill of BSE conspiracy theories. "In the months since Gajdusek's arrest and weeks since Saitoh's murder, as no other explanations have come forward, I have wondered what could have been the motivation, what the intimidation could be about," argued an internet posting by Gene Schmidt, a teacher of statistics and scientific method at Scottsdale Community College in Arizona. "Certainly the murder of Saitoh and his daughter could have been a mistake. Gajdusek could simply have gone too far in his cultural relativism," Schmidt admitted. "But there are some big money issues in the mix, such as transgenic mice, growth hormone, drug development, and chemical toxin liability."[24]

Another imaginative theory came from internet essayist Ed Gehrman in an article titled "Mad Cows and Mad Scientists," which claimed on the basis of no evidence whatsoever that "more than 200,000 U.S. citizens die each year from misdiagnosed TSE-caused diseases." Gehrman blamed this imaginary epidemic on "inept, dishonest and secretive science found in our country's national laboratories and in international organizations such as the World Health Organization (WHO). These powerful networks control the direction of most medical research but never take responsibility for miscalculations and lapses in judgment. . . . WHO has been researching scrapie since at least 1965 as a possible biowarfare agent. . . . The Department of Defense also began trying to develop 'a new infective microorganism which could differ in certain important aspects from any known disease-causing organism.' . . . During the mid sixties the quest for a new 'infectious agent' centered on the 'slow virus' thought to be found in scrapie and kuru. I contend that our national labs have been clumsily contaminating their cultures with prions. . . . The slow nature of prion diseases has prolonged a misunderstanding of the problem and perhaps allowed prions' entry into vaccines, and these vaccines have been put back into cows and you and me. The prions have begun to accumulate exponentially and we're left with the situation we have today—big trouble."[25]

Dick Marsh, meanwhile, was dismayed to see his studies regarding transmissible mink encephalopathy misrepresented in a debate between opposing camps, neither of which seemed to have actually bothered to *read* his research. Marsh had suggested that the 100,000 downer cows in the United States might contain a much smaller sub-population of TSE-infected cattle. If so, he argued, indiscriminate use of the "downer cow" label could prevent early detection of TSE-infected animals, enabling the disease to multiply into a serious epidemic.

The subtleties of this reasoning were utterly lost on internet essayists like Ed Gehrman, who simplified things by claiming that *all* 100,000 downer cows were probable carriers of mad cow disease. The subtle details were also lost on the National Renderers Association, which described as "ludicrous" Marsh's "inference that the TME outbreak that occurred on a mink ranch in Stetsonville, Wisconsin was caused by the feeding of 'downer cows.' . . . This anecdotal claim should be easy to validate through proper research protocol. The mink for a proposed experiment would be readily available, and 'downer cows' in the state of Wisconsin would not be difficult to obtain to substantiate the associative link." [26] What the renderers refused to comprehend was that a "proper research protocol" capable of evaluating Marsh's hypothesis would require testing something on the order of a million cattle—not exactly "easy to validate."

Throughout these discussions, an unstated theme kept recurring—the frustrations of human beings as they grappled with a disease whose nature lay outside the boundaries of available scientific knowledge. An almost blind faith in the sureness of the scientific method led commentators from all sides to prefer almost any theory that would save them from having to think the unthinkable—that this was a case where science had simply failed to provide clear answers, and that the wisdom needed to deal with the mad cow crisis would have to come from some human source outside its cloistered walls.

RECKONING

Truth and Consequences

"Science," said English philosopher Thomas Hobbes, "is the knowledge of consequences, and dependence of one fact upon another." If only things were that simple.

Prior to the watershed British announcement of March 20, 1996, "science" did not know what the consequences would be of feeding BSE-infected beef to the human population. After March 20, it had a pretty good clue, but it still didn't know for sure. The industries which stood to suffer from those consequences continued to downplay and deny the steadily mounting evidence. The rendering industry's Frank Burnham, for example, argued that the "current BSE scare is due largely to sensationalized stories in the British press—based on speculation not fact—linking BSE in cattle to CJD in humans. There is, in fact, no scientific fact directly linking CJD to BSE or BSE to sheep scrapie."[1]

National Renderers Association scientific advisor Don Franco echoed the same theme: "Will the rendering industry be regulated on existing risks, perceived risks, public perception, political expediency or science? We, as an industry, plead for a scientific assessment based on conditions in the U.S. Leave out the anecdotes, eliminate the emotion and let proven scientific findings dictate policy changes, if any are indicated. . . . We must not indulge in premature announcements like occurred in the U.K. lest we succumb to the same catastrophe! . . . Let us not make hasty decisions that could negatively impact all the involved industries."[2]

Speaking at the Association's annual convention in October 1996, NRA Executive Director Bruce Blanton compared BSE and other safety concerns to a "boa constrictor" around the industry's neck. "A myriad of nonscientific based safety issues are threatening our exports and the way we run our businesses," he said. "For right or wrong the idea of greater safety has arrived. We must deal with it whether we like it or not." He worried, however, that "this kind of scrutiny left unchecked will inevitably lead to stricter and stifling regulations."[3]

"There is an expressed opinion that has a degree of validity that states, err on the side of safety," Franco said. "To that analogy I add, the error could be avoided if science remains the dominant consideration for instituting change."[4]

These expressions of faith in the surety of science flew in the face of the fact that "science" has been struggling, with only limited and gradual success, to unravel the mysteries associated with the transmissible spongiform encephalopathies. Its failures cannot not be laid at the feet of the researchers—individuals whose ranks included brilliant minds, relentless workaholics and heroic visionaries.

The best scientists have always understood that even brilliance and perseverance cannot unravel all of nature's mysteries. In the 20th century, however, a glorified *religion* of "science" has emerged, becoming a dogmatic faith in something imaginary and transcendent with magical, godlike powers. Don Franco is not alone in his belief that science can save us from human error and therefore from the need to err on the side of safety. The news carries constant reports of miracle cures for baldness, impotence and cancer. Amazing new discoveries promise sweetness without sugar and fat that won't fatten. Internet technology claims to transcend the limitations of space and time, instantly connecting people and information from scattered points across the globe. On popular TV shows like *Star Trek*, science fiction offers fantasies of ever-greater miracles in the future: space travel at velocities beyond the speed of light, time travel, force fields, the ability to create synthetic "life-forms" and whole new worlds, telepathic communications, instant healing with easy handheld gadgets, even immortality.

This new popular religion has elevated scientists to the status of priests tending flock over the rest of the lowly human herd. It is easy, of course, for scientists like anyone else to succumb to the flattery that comes with this status—the notion that they are somehow smarter than the rest of us, that their insights are more valuable, more "rational," more Spock-like and less subject to the vagaries of human emotion and political corruption. In the debates over BSE and other product safety, the defenders of industry found that scientists made useful symbols. The world would run much better, they argued, if "objective" science could govern unhindered by the messy, emotional politics and debates that make up democracy.

Inside corporate boardrooms and government ministries, however, the powers-that-be held a different, less sentimental regard for their scientist-employees. Like any other employees, scientists were hired to do a job, and when they failed to do that job, they ceased to be useful.

During 1996, at the zenith of the mad cow uproar in Europe, a few documents came to light that cast a revealing look backwards on the history of how the issue had been handled. The first was written by Guy Legras, the European Union's Director-General for Agriculture. In his notes during a September 1990 meeting, Legras had written simply, "BSE: Stop any meeting."[5]

Another revealing document was an internal memo written on October 12, 1990 by an official from the European Commission's Consumer Policy Department and addressed to his superiors. The memo included minutes from a meeting of the EU's Standing Veterinary Committee, which quoted committee members stating, "We must take a cold attitude towards BSE so as not to provoke unfavorable market reactions. No longer should BSE be spoken of. This point should no longer come up as an item on the agenda. . . . We are going to ask the United Kingdom, through official channels, to stop publishing any more research results. . . . *In a general context, this BSE affair must be minimized through disinformation.* Better to say that the press has a tendency to exaggerate"[6] (emphasis added).

Publication of these documents prompted the usual denials and spin control, with government ministers insisting that they had never seen the memos in question and that they certainly did not reflect official policy. A third document, however, was even more explicit and more damning. Written in 1993, it was the work once again of Guy Legras—a letter addressed to an Italian official who had requested an investigation into possible links between BSE and Creutzfeldt-Jakob Disease. "In my experience, all discussion of BSE inevitably causes problems in the meat market," Legras had replied. "We have already had an alarm last January after a program on German television, and it is only by dint of prudence and discretion that we have been able, for the moment, to avoid a panic. . . . In order to keep the public reassured, it is essential that we ourselves do not provoke a reopening of the debate. If you can help me, we need to be prudent and avoid the discussion getting into the scientific committees."[7]

On October 10, 1994, Legras sent yet another letter, this time addressed to the German minister of health, calling for Germany to muzzle its scientists who continued to argue for a ban on British beef. "I find it quite unacceptable that officials of a national government should seek to undermine community law in this way, particularly on such a sensitive subject," Legras wrote. "The persons concerned have had their opportunity in the [European Union] committees to debate their opinions. These have been rejected by the vast majority of EU experts. I would ask you therefore to ensure that this debate is not continued, particularly in an international forum."[8]

One of the scientists raising questions was Arpad Somogyi of the Berlin-based German Federal Institute for Health. Somogyi was a scientist with a ferocious resumé, including a 12-year stint as director of the government's Department of Drugs, Animal Nutrition and Residue Research. He chaired the Codex Committee on Nutrition and Foods for Special Dietary Uses with the Joint Food Standards Program of the United Nations Food and Agricultural Organization and the World Health Organization, and served on numerous other high-level advisory bodies, including the WHO's Expert Advisory Panel on Food Safety.

Since 1993, Somogyi had argued forcefully in favor of a precautionary principle with respect to BSE. Speaking at a toxicology forum, he said he had become alarmed after seeing evidence showing that the disease had been successfully transmitted to a wide range of test species. "We cannot sit back and wait until more evidence comes in," he urged his colleagues in 1994. "To do so would be callous disregard for the health of the consumer."[9]

During hearings before the European Parliament in 1996, Somogyi testified that he had complained about the commission's attempts to stifle scientific debate at a meeting of the EU's Scientific Veterinary Committee in September 1994. "If you do not let us speak out and one day it is proven that there can be transmission to man, you could find yourselves in court," he had warned. The warning went unheeded, and Germany stood alone among its European neighbors in calling for strict protective measures. "The others accused us of hysteria and panic-mongering," Somogyi recalled.[10]

In the end, it seemed, even *scientists* were as silly and emotional as the rest of the fainting rabble. The only people manly enough to resist the hysteria, "cold" enough to view the situation objectively, brave enough to ignore all hints of danger, wise enough to rise above politics—were the politicians themselves, and their appointed bureaucrats.

⊗ ⊗ ⊗

By year-end 1996, the evidence that BSE had crossed the species barrier from cows to humans remained incomplete, but it was steadily mounting. Experimental methods of "strain typing" provided one link. Researchers had known for some time that different strains of scrapie in sheep produced specific, characteristic patterns when they were injected into mice. After the mice became sick, you could cut their brains into sections and count the number of abnormal lesions in each region. A chart of the scores for each region would match the charts of other mice that had been exposed to the same strain. In France, researchers reported that they had done a similar experiment involving three macaque monkeys injected with tissue from BSE-infected cows. All three monkeys developed spongiform encephalopathies, and when researchers examined the patterns in their brain, they found striking similarities to the flower-shaped amyloid plaques found in the human victims of new variant Creutzfeldt-Jakob Disease. "This study provides evidence supporting the hypothesis that the BSE agent is responsible for the emergence of the new form of CJD in humans," the researchers wrote.[11]

One experiment in progress seemed to offer a ray of hope. British prion researcher John Collinge was still trying, unsuccessfully, to transmit BSE to mice which had been genetically engineered so that they produced a human instead of a mouse version of the prion protein. If these transgenic mice stayed healthy, it might mean that humans were also immune. The altered animals did indeed survive, long past the point at which normal mice would be expected to succumb. On the internet, British food industry consultant Ralph Blanchfield posted periodic updates on their progress, reporting that the mice "remain well at 264 days after inoculation," were "still fit after 320 days . . . it looks encouraging," "still fit and well, now past the 400-day milestone," "440 days and still counting," "still fit and well after passing the 500 days milestone." Blanchfield declared Collinge's work "the most interesting experiments to date" and said the mice offered "without doubt experimental scientific evidence" for the safety of beef.[12]

Unfortunately, Collinge himself did not find his results very reassuring. Even before the British government's March 1996 announcement, he had publicly expressed concern that BSE might be linked to the deaths of teenagers. Later, in September 1996, Collinge penned an editorial for the *New England Journal of Medicine*, stating that the nvCJD cases indicated "a new risk factor for Creutzfeldt-Jakob disease" and pointed to BSE as the likely cause.[13] In October 1996, he told reporters again that the new cases of CJD in humans "have a startlingly uniform pathology: early age of onset, psychiatric disturbances and a relatively long period before death occurs, about 14 months. This indicates a single cause—BSE—though we cannot yet say whether it will lead to 20 or 100,000 deaths a year." [14]

These remarks prompted an instant decline in Collinge's scientific status among the beef industry's defenders. "I'm increasingly disturbed by the quotations being attributed to Dr. Collinge," stated Robert LaBudde, a meat industry consultant with a Virginia company called Least Cost Formulations. In an angry internet posting, LaBudde complained that "Collinge is in effect saying to the public, 'If my mice die, there is a direct connection between BSE and v-CJD. On the other hand, if they don't die, you should trust my personal opinion that there is an unproven, direct connection and ignore my own experiments. And, by the way, the great CJD plague is coming.' . . . Are there any scientists out there amongst the ax-grinders and technicians? Aren't any of you troubled by the use of science as a cloak for opinion in this way? The lack of objectivity? . . . What do we do until the real scientists prove something conclusively? Apparently, we puff up our chests and speculate in the press, quote technical jargon, and reference pseudo-scientific tomes with reams of subjective statistics that mean and prove nothing." [15]

"I have to support Robert LaBudde on an important point," Blanchfield chimed in. "While it is legitimate for scientists to express personal opinions that go beyond what available scientific knowledge supports, they should be very careful to present them in an appropriately tentative way." [16]

Neither LaBudde nor Blanchfield realized yet that Collinge was on the brink of publishing additional findings that would virtually settle the debate. Collinge had designed a new, elegant method that used molecular "signatures" instead of mouse autopsies to identify different TSE strain types. The molecular markers made it possible to identify strains in days rather than years, and showed that the human victims of nvCJD had "a strain characteristic distinct from other types of CJD and which resembles those of BSE transmitted to mice, domestic cat and macaque, and is consistent with BSE being the source of this new disease." [17]

The new evidence forced even Blanchfield to admit that Collinge had produced "scientific backing for what was previously conjecture." [18] Backing down, Blanchfield guessed that the odds of a BSE link to new variant CJD were now greater than 90 percent.

Collinge thought the probability was even higher. "It goes off the scales if you try to put a P-value on this," he said during a presentation to a BSE conference in Washington, DC. "You have to discard the hypothesis that these are merely sporadic cases we haven't seen before."

"If BSE is not the cause of nvCJD, what are the other possibilities?" someone asked.

"I don't have any," Collinge replied. "The only plausible explanation I can think of is that it's BSE by another route. . . . It does seem to have the characteristic BSE signature. BSE is really the only plausible candidate." [19]

Study of the first ten victims of nvCJD showed that all ten shared a common genetic feature. The 129th link in their gene sequence for the prion protein coded exclusively for the amino acid methionine. In scientific terms, they were "homozygous for methionine at codon 129." Only 38 percent of the human population fit this profile, which suggested that the other 62 percent *might* prove resistant to the disease. The genetic specifics of the new strain also highlighted a possible fatal weakness in the earlier experiment that Collinge had initiated using transgenic mice. He had given them a human prion protein that was homozygous for *valine* at codon 129. His mouse test was therefore apparently useless at predicting whether BSE would kill people who were homozygous for methionine.

The mice in fact continued to show no signs of illness. "I'm pleased to say that we've now exceeded 600 days," Collinge said in December 1996. "There aren't many of them left. They're starting to get quite elderly now. That's good news as far as it goes, but it's important not to overinterpret these results. We've only inoculated 50 mice. If we've got an infection that proves fatal in only one out of 1,000 animals, the experiment might not show any result but we would still have a catastrophe in the human population." [20]

❀ ❀ ❀

As the idea that BSE had passed into humans evolved from a hypothesis into a near consensus, the British now had a more pressing question to consider: How many human bodies would fall?

In November 1996, British government scientists attempted an estimate based on the number of nvCJD cases to date, which by then had risen to 14. Researchers with the CJD Surveillance Unit in Edinburgh issued a paper predicting that the number of cases would rise gradually and reach a peak of several hundred per year in 2003, followed by a decline like the one that was already occurring in the cattle population. "It now looks as though the total number of cases over the whole course of the disease will be in the hundreds, rather than the thousands," said Dr. James Ironside, one of the authors of the study. The people most likely to be at risk were those who had eaten lots of hamburgers or other cheap beef. Attempting to put a favorable spin on things, Ironside argued that the new figures did not bear out the "doomsday scenario that some have predicted."

Others pointed out that it was still virtually impossible to make firm predictions about the future course of an epidemic based on so few confirmed cases. The same afternoon that Ironside's comments appeared, the Royal Statistical Society met in London to consider the available evidence. Its president, Professor Adrian Smith, offered an estimate of "zero to millions." The *Lancet,* which had been expected to publish Ironside's paper, instead ran an editorial agreeing with Smith. "Zero to millions is correct because it is the best estimate available with the known information," the editorial argued. "In truth, a useful prediction is impossible. Crucial parts of the equation remain unknown, in particular the incubation period in human beings and the minimum infective dose of the prion organism. The only way to estimate either is by continuing observation. There will be no quick answer. At the current rate of finding new cases, 2-3 further years of observation will be needed, unless there is a rapid increase in finding new cases. . . . What is less clear is what the public needs to know: absolute risk estimates or a range reflecting current uncertainties? When 'don't know' is the correct answer, then that is what should be printed. Anything else betrays people's trust." [21]

In January 1997, *Nature* published another stab at estimating the size of the epidemic in a study written by epidemiologists and scientists from the government's National CJD Surveillance Unit. Their projections ranged between a low of 75 deaths and a high of 80,000. "We hesitate to draw sweeping conclusions from calculations based on few data and several currently unverifiable assumptions," they cautioned. "Enormous uncertainty inevitably surrounds any modeling when only 14 cases of the disease have been confirmed and without good information about the incubation period distribution. Still, . . . two tentative conclusions may be drawn. First, it would be premature to conclude that because only 14 U.K. cases have been confirmed so far, any subsequent epidemic will necessarily be small. Second, although the number of cases over the next few years may provide a better indication of how large any epidemic might eventually be, much uncertainty may remain even in four years' time." [22]

The British elections of 1997 saw a stinging voter rebuke of John Major's Conservative Party, bringing a Labour government to power for the first time in more than a decade. The new government's responsibilities included coping with the rising toll of human casualties. July 1997 marked the second month in a row in which two new human deaths were added to the list, raising the official body count to 21—a tally which did not yet include Donna-Marie McGivern, a Scottish 15-year-old who had begun showing symptoms in January, 1997. Doctors at Glasgow's Southern General Hospital were waiting until her expected death to confirm a diagnosis, having discontinued their former practice of performing brain biopsies on suspected nvCJD patients while they were still alive. Such an extreme procedure was now acknowledged to be "pointless and severe," given the total lack of any cure. Donna-Marie's distraught family, literally praying for a miracle, announced plans to take their daughter to the Blessed Virgin's shrine in Lourdes, France, to implore for God's intervention. [23] Other British nvCJD families appealed for more earthly justice, calling on the new Labour government to initiate a formal inquiry into the entire matter. One member of parliament called it a "gross injustice" that the British beef industry was being compensated for its financial losses, but the human nvCJD victims had been left high and dry. [24]

In August, commentators pointed out that the number of cases appeared to be growing exponentially—three cases in 1995, ten in 1996, and eight more already by July 1997 (not including young Donna-Marie). [25] The number was still too small to forecast future trends, but it was entirely possible that British beef-eaters were entering the early stages of an epidemic bell-curve.

"I am now coming round to the view that doctors working in this field have to say what they think, even though this may give rise to anxieties which later turn out to be groundless," Professor Collinge said in August 1997. "We have a heavy weight of responsibility to warn, but we have to be aware that what we say may be scary and may do irremediable economic damage. But it can no longer be denied that it is possible, even likely, that we may have to face an epidemic. It is impossible to predict the size of the epidemic—it may only involve hundreds, but it could be Europe-wide and become a disaster of biblical proportions. We have to face the possibility of a disaster with tens of thousands of cases. We just don't know if this will happen, but what is certain is that we cannot afford to wait and see. We have to do something, right now. We have to find the answers, not only to the questions of the nature of the disease, but to find a way to develop an effective treatment."

In America, meanwhile, the beef industry's careful public relations activities continued to keep the issue out of the public eye. "Our issues tracking research showed us that, following the worldwide firestorm of attention to mad cow disease, consumer confidence in American beef was the highest it had been since we began tracking it in 1992," said Max Deets of the National Cattlemen's Beef Association.[26] In July 1997, NCBA launched its latest $13.5 million dollar advertising campaign around the theme of "Beef, it's what you want." The purpose of the campaign, a spokesperson said, was to exploit consumers' "strong emotional attachments to beef, unlike any other meat."[27] (The campaign proved ill-timed when, less than a month later, an outbreak of E. coli 0157:H7 prompted USDA to demand a recall of 25 million pounds of hamburger from Hudson Foods Inc.—the largest food recall ever in history.)

The huge advertising budget contrasted with a much smaller amount, $150,000, provided jointly by the American Meat Institute and the Cattlemen to fund an upcoming study by Colorado State University which would examine a surprising BSE risk factor brought to the government's attention by researchers at Texas A&M University. The researchers had discovered that pneumatic stun guns used to knock out cattle at slaughter apparently drive brain particles, the most infectious tissue in BSE-positive animals, into cattle lungs and livers, thereby creating a means by which infected tissue could be eaten by unsuspecting consumers.[28]

Other BSE related research continued, with minimal funding compared to the meat industry's massive investment in advertising and public relations. The science journal *Nature* published startling laboratory findings which indicated that the heralded "species barrier" to transmission of TSE among cattle, sheep and humans may be more like a sieve than a real barrier. Researchers were able, in test tubes, to "convert" normal human prion proteins to TSE-infected protein by exposing them to CJD. The startling part of the research was that human prions had also flipped when exposed to scrapie and BSE.

Scientists and the government attempted to put the best possible spin on the results, noting that both the BSE and scrapie infected protein were "less efficient" than CJD at converting normal human protein to the TSE-infected variety. One of the researchers, James Hope of the Institute for Animal Health, concluded that "BSE is no more transmissible to humans than is sheep scrapie," but this assurance seemed bizarre given the scientific consensus that people were already dying from eating BSE-infected meat. The results sent internal shock waves throughout the U.S. sheep industry, which feared the implications since their own herds are already populated with scrapie-infected sheep.[29]

Could the Nightmare Happen Here?

By 1996, BSE had been reported in ten countries outside England, mostly in other parts of Europe. More than two-thirds of the reports outside the U.K. came from Switzerland, which reported more than 200 cases. This statistic seemed puzzling at first because the Swiss seemed to lack most of the requisite risk factors. They had imported hardly any living cattle from Great Britain. Their sheep population was small and virtually scrapie-free, and their rendering industry used high temperatures which were considered more effective at reducing levels of TSE infectivity. Unfortunately, Switzerland had also imported significant quantities of rendered animal feed from England during the years between 1985 and 1990.

The question, then, was why the disease had *failed* to pop up more in other countries. Switzerland was certainly not the only country which had imported British meat and bone meal. In fact, British renderers had reacted to their domestic feed ban by slashing prices so they could dump their products on the export market. The cheap price attracted customers as far away as Israel and Thailand, causing British feed exports to climb from 5,000 tons a year in 1985 to 30,000 tons by 1989. Most of the cut-price feed went to France, which in fact was the source for most of Switzerland's British-origin meat and bone meal. The French had imported enough of the stuff that Professor Marc Vandervelde, Switzerland's BSE expert at Bern University, figured they ought to be seeing around 200 cases a year all by themselves. Instead, the French had only declared a cumulative total of 22 cases as of June 1996. Holland, Luxembourg and Belgium had also imported thousands of tons of contaminated feed but had declared zero cases of BSE.

Even British cattle exported to other parts of Europe seemed suspiciously resistant to the disease. Some 57,900 British breeding cattle had been exported between the years of 1985 and 1990, of which 1,668 would have been expected statistically to die from BSE. Instead, only 29 cases had been reported, sparking speculation that cases outside Switzerland were being covered up. "We are an island of BSE in Europe," Switzerland's Vandervelde said with deliberate sarcasm. "The disease stops at our border."[1]

Farmers and governments have an obvious incentive to conceal the true incidence of BSE in their countries. This in turn creates a window of opportunity through which infected animals might slip into the United States, notwith-standing U.S. policies against the importation of cattle from affected countries.

By April 1997, the USDA had inspected 5,621 brains of U.S. cattle, with-out finding any cases of the disease. "BSE is NOT in the United States," insisted an internet web page maintained by USDA's Animal and Plant Health Inspec-tion Service (emphasis in the original).[2]

Hidden behind this denial, however, were some flaws in the surveillance methodology. To begin with, its coverage of the country was uneven. A full fourth of the brains examined had come from a single state—Kentucky, which accounted for 1,406 of the brains submitted. By contrast, only 226 brains had been submitted from Wisconsin—the dairy state where most known cases of transmissible *mink* encephalopathy had occurred, including the cases which had convinced Richard Marsh to look at downer cows as a likely source. In Minnesota and Idaho, the other states where TME outbreaks had occurred, USDA had only looked at 22 and 47 brains respectively. Only *one* brain had been examined in the entire state of Florida, an important beef and dairy state.[3]

An even more fundamental problem is that even the best executed sur-veillance would only detect the disease *after* it has arrived in the United States, by which time the damage would already have been done. "If BSE does occur in the U.S., it won't have its economic impact from the number of cows it affects," Marsh had warned as early as 1993. "Even in Great Britain, there were only one or two cows per herd that were affected. It isn't a disease that has its economic effect by killing the animal. It has its economic effect by the public perception it causes, by the lack of exports—the fact that once you are a BSE-positive country, it severely limits your use of cattle products. We would only have to have one infected animal in this country to become a BSE-positive country, and no longer be able to export our cattle products, nor use our cattle tissue in biological products. In the United States, we have about 650 biolog-ical products that come from cattle that are used in humans. Of these, 380 con-tain proteins from cattle. If we ever become a BSE-positive country, we could no longer source any of these proteins from American cattle. As an example, Eli Lilly makes a great deal of the insulin used in humans in this country, and about half of it comes from pigs and cows. If we become a BSE-positive coun-try, they will not be able to source any of this cattle insulin from American cows. . . . We're not going to be able to export cattle products, either as beef or embryos. It will happen overnight. There's not a single news organization in this country that does not have a BSE file, so they will be able to get some-thing in the paper the next day as soon as the USDA announces that we're a BSE-positive country. The bottom will drop out of beef consumption. The American public will just quit eating beef."[4]

Following the June, 1993 publication of these remarks, Marsh endured harassment and threats of lawsuits from the meat industry, and was warned to stop making trouble by officials of his own university. The events of 1996 brought grim vindication. Marsh was "the man who warned us about mad cow disease" bragged the UW–Madison's alumni magazine. "Roger Wyse, dean of the College of Agricultural and Life Sciences, says that Marsh's early warning against feeding ruminant protein embodied the appropriate role for a research university—'to provide facts and expert judgment to the public policy formation process.'" Sadly, this vindication came less than a year before Marsh's death from cancer at the untimely age of 58. The obituary in his local newspaper described him as "the primary factor in alerting the world to the inherent dangers of feeding cattle byproducts back to cattle," who "accurately predicted the possibility of situations such as the mad cow disease outbreak in England several years before this happened."[5]

Marsh was not the only leading TSE expert who believed that BSE could occur in the United States. "Is BSE endemic? My answer to that is yes," said Clarence Gibbs of the National Institutes of Health. "CJD occurs at the rate of 1 per million in the population per year, wherever you look, all over the world. . . . If we accept the fact that CJD occurs at that rate all over the world, and if we confirm that all mammalian species thus far tested have the prion protein, . . . then hypothetically, every mammalian species in the world should have its own spongiform encephalopathy, which means that the disease is endemic in all species. You cannot escape it. That's what we're discussing here, not whether or not we have recognized the disease in this country *yet*. . . . If the incidence rate is 1 to 2 in a million, how many cattle brains do you have to look at before you're going to find something?"[6]

"There's no way that we can test for the one-in-a-million scenario," admitted USDA's Linda Detwiler, the official in charge of the U.S. surveillance program. "To rule it out, every year we'd have to look at 2.3 million brains in the United States. Unless some miracle happens and Congress gives us *all* its money, that's not going to happen. . . . You just have to do all the preventions. You can't stop the one-in-a-million from occurring."[7]

Neither Detwiler nor Gibbs believed that a doomsday situation was on the horizon for the United States. "The beef in this country is probably the finest in the world," Gibbs said. "I have been most impressed with the controls in this country to protect the health of the public. I have no doubt that consumers are very safe."[8] At the same time, he was becoming increasingly frustrated with the slow pace of progress toward a regulation that would ban further cannibalistic feeding practices. "The ban must be total and not partial, and as soon as possible," he said. "It's really irritating that this thing is being talked to death. We have to proceed with all due haste."[9]

The primary reason for the delay, of course, was the refusal of the meat industry to recognize that human risks existed. As the evidence of human deaths became inescapable in England, however, even the beef industry's resistance began to waver. For the U.S. cattle industry, the economic consequences alone of a potential epidemic like England's were simply too stark to ignore.

On January 3, 1997, the Food and Drug Administration finally offered a "proposed rule" which would "declare that protein derived from tissue from ruminant animals and mink is not [generally recognized as safe] by qualified experts, for use in ruminant feed and is therefore a 'food additive' under the law. As a result, . . . such tissues would be deemed adulterated." FDA had solicited comments prior to proposing the rule, and "a number of comments from scientific organizations and individual scientists strongly suggest that . . . ruminant and mink tissue is not [generally recognized as safe] when fed to ruminants. Some of these comments submitted data and information that would support such opinions. Only a few comments included statements by scientists, or scientific organizations, to the contrary."

The FDA argued that there is "no immediate threat to the public health in the United States," but added that failure to take preventive action could have serious consequences:

> The data and information raise concern that BSE could occur in cattle in the United States; and that if BSE does appear in this country, the causative agent could be transmitted and amplified through the feeding of processed ruminant protein to cattle, and could result in an epidemic. The agency believes that the high cost, in animal and human lives and economics, that could result if this scenario should occur, justifies the preventive measure reflected by the proposed regulation. . . .
>
> BSE could develop in the United States from three possible sources: Transmission of TSEs from other susceptible species, spontaneous occurrence, and importation in live animals or animal products. . . . The greatest risk factor for cattle may not be the single occurrence of a BSE case. Instead, the greatest risk may arise from the potential, given the prolonged incubation period, for unrecognized amplification of BSE in the cattle population, resulting in a potential for greater animal exposure. . . .
>
> Once developed, BSE could remain undetected for several years because of its long incubation period and because, at present, it can be diagnosed reliably only by microscopic brain examination after death. During the period between introduction and diagnosis, the disease could spread as it apparently did in the U.K. via intake of infective feed. If regulation was delayed until after discovery, the costs would be substantial. . . .
>
> Based on the relative size of the U.S. and U.K. dairy cattle populations, these projections suggest that if BSE were introduced in the United States and spread in a similar manner, the disease would destroy 299,000 U.S. cattle over 11 years. . . . (These calculations assume that a feed prohibition would be implemented very soon after the first case is diagnosed, and that the prohibition would immediately begin to affect the underlying rate of new infection. If a feed prohibition were not implemented at that time, the number of cattle deaths would be much higher.) [10]

By the time the first case *was even detected*, in other words, the United States could already be looking down the barrel of an epidemic roughly *twice* the size of Britain's.

FDA's proposed rule certainly marked a step in the right direction, but the agency still faced intense pressures from powerful sectors within the livestock industry, particularly the renderers. Moreover, there were contradictions and questions which the proposed rule did not attempt to address.

Mad Pig Disease?

To begin with, the FDA rule only contemplated banning the feeding of mink and ruminant animals back to *ruminants*. What about feeding to *non*-ruminant species, such as chicken and pigs? Those practices had existed for much longer than the practice of feeding large quantities of rendered animal protein to cattle. During that extended period, no one had documented a confirmed outbreak of a TSE in chicken or pigs, and FDA believed therefore that a future outbreak was unlikely. Still, laboratory research *had* succeeded in experimentally transmitting BSE to pigs, so an outbreak was at least theoretically possible.

"The feeding of swine protein to swine should be prohibited, at least until there is scientific evidence available on the possibility that swine are or are not able to transmit a TSE agent," stated Dr. Karl Lonberg-Holm, a retired virologist turned small-scale farmer, in his 1996 written comments to the FDA. "It would be more desirable to prohibit the feeding of all mammalian meat products to mammals which are in the human food chain," Lonberg-Holm stated. "It is, for example, possible that pigs already transmit swine (or porcine) TSE, but that we do not recognize this because the latent period before physical symptoms appear is greater than the lifetime of a pig (usually half a year, but up to several years in the case of brood sows). Thus swine might be capable of propagating a hypothetical TSE agent through 'blind passages.' "

Lonberg-Holm laid out his worst fears in what he called "an improbable scenario for disaster. . . . Although it seems unlikely that any swine agent would be able to efficiently infect humans, the slight chance that one could do so would lead to a public health disaster. Consider the following scenario: A pig spontaneously develops a TSE agent. This animal is within one of the large factory-like businesses that have more than 100,000 animals and which is vertically integrated so that the same corporation handles all operations from feed production to marketing pork. The offal of the pig, when rendered to protein meal, might infect many other animals within a month or so. Within a year there may be 100,000 infected animals that have already been sent to the market and consumed by the public. . . . If the latent period for the disease is long enough in swine, no overt symptoms would have been detected among pigs at the same time that much of the human population of North America had already become infected." Lonberg-Holm considered the probability of such a scenario to be "very low," but "probably much higher than the probability that our civilization will be destroyed by the impact of an asteroid."[11]

There is a chance, unfortunately, that the asteroid may already have hit. In early 1997, a federal veterinarian named Matsuo Doi contacted the Government Accountability Project (GAP), a Washington, DC-based nonprofit organization which exists to protect government whistleblowers from harassment, intimidation and firing. In 1979, Doi had conducted a study for USDA of 106 pigs with a mysterious central nervous system disorder at a packing plant in upstate New York. The pigs in question showed symptoms that were strikingly similar to the characteristics of scrapie or transmissible mink encephalopathy: "Excitable or nervous temperament to external stimuli such as touch to the skin, handling and menacing approach to the animals is a common characteristic sign among swine affected with the disease. . . . Many animals have been found to be 'downers' at first observation; if the hindquarters of these downers are raised they may be able to walk one or two steps and then fall to the ground." Dr. Karl Langheinrich, a USDA pathologist, examined the brains of 60 affected animals. In one, he noted "degeneration of neurons, the reactivity of the glia . . . Scrapie of sheep, and encephalopathy of mink, according to the literature, all produce focal vacuolation of the neurons similar to the kind as described for this pig." [12]

Neither Doi nor Langheinrich were experts in the transmissible spongiform encephalopathies, and their study occurred in 1979, seven years before BSE was even detected in British cattle. Their information was never brought to the attention of people who *were* experts. After 15 months, the pig study was discontinued for lack of funding, but the symptoms that Doi and Langheinrich had observed were so striking that they continued to mention them over the years to students and scientific colleagues. When the British BSE announcement hit the headlines in 1996, Doi was stunned to see video footage on the evening news that showed cows staggering just the way his pigs had. Fearful that U.S. pigs might already be carrying a spongiform disease, he spent the subsequent year pleading with USDA officials to conduct an investigation. Finally, in frustration, he contacted GAP in order to turn whistleblower.

"Although USDA has been aware of the dormant study and its role for nearly a year, it has not acted on it," said GAP Food Safety Director Felicia Nestor, who charged that USDA officials were not only dragging their feet but actively misinforming public interest groups, the media, and even the national association of federal veterinarians. On repeated occasions, officials had said that slides of pig brains from the 1979 study were unavailable because they had been sent to scientists in England who were studying mad cow disease. In reality, the USDA never sent any slides to England. "Agency officials repeatedly misrepresented scientists' investigations and conclusions to consumer groups and government employees and neglected to keep other agencies also working on TSE issues informed," Nestor said. "The USDA had to be pushed to investigate scientific evidence which only they had." [13]

Michael Hansen, the Consumers Union scientist who began warning about the practice of cow cannibalism back in 1993, also questioned USDA's handling of the Doi study. In addition, he pointed to two separate epidemiological studies—both with Carleton Gajdusek among the authors—that link consumption of pork to Creutzfeldt-Jakob Disease in humans. One study, published in 1973, surveyed past eating habits of CJD patients and found that over a third were reported to have eaten brains. "Clearly, far fewer than one-third of the general population consumes brains, so there is an overabundance of brain eaters among the CJD patients," Hansen said. "Sources at USDA tell us that approximately one million animal brains are removed for human consumption every year. If each brain eater consumed only one brain a year, this would mean that less than 1% of the population consumes brains." [14] Even more disturbing was the fact that some 71% of the CJD patients who ate brains were reported to have a "preference for hog brains." [15]

The second study, published in 1985, looked for correlations between CJD and consumption of 45 different food items which ranged from raw oysters to hot dogs. Nine items showed a statistical correlation, six of which came from pigs: roast pork, ham, hot dogs, pork chops, smoked pork, and scrapple. "The present study indicated that consumption of pork as well as its processed products (e.g., ham, scrapple) may be considered as risk factors in the development of Creutzfeldt-Jakob Disease," the authors concluded. "While scrapie has not been reported in pigs, a subclinical form of the disease or a pig reservoir for the scrapie agent might conceivably be present."[16]

"The fact that evidence from a pig study and human studies both point to an unrecognized TSE in pigs is very disturbing," Hansen said. "That's why the FDA's rule prohibiting feeding of meat and bone meal is inadequate. The language of the rule states that you can't use protein from any mammalian tissue in ruminant feeds, but they've created a taxonomic loophole for pigs by excluding them from the category of 'mammals.' Not only is this arbitrary and contrary to fact, it sends a dangerous message by suggesting that pigs are safer than other mammals—even though the 1979 Doi study tells us that pigs may *already* be infected with a TSE-like disease."[17]

Hansen admitted that the Doi study is hardly definitive, nor are the human epidemiological studies. At a very minimum, however, the possibility of TSEs occurring in pigs, chickens or even fish demands further study. Stanley Prusiner's prion theory suggests that the TSEs are caused by a totally new type of disease agent—something that hovers somewhere on the border between living organisms and toxic chemicals, with properties that violate long-held axioms of biology. Industry representatives and their scientists like to characterize the risk from this rogue infectious agent as "miniscule" or "vanishingly small," but there is no real scientific content to these adjectives. The truth is that no one knows.

Finally, the FDA Acts

Although Britain began banning animal cannibalism in 1988, the U.S. failed to follow suit for almost a decade, during which time billions of pounds of U.S. cattle were fed back to other cattle. The FDA bureaucracy finally moved beyond "proposed" rules and took its first real regulatory action on June 4, 1997—four years after activist Jeremy Rifkin had petitioned for action, and more than a year after England conceded the link between mad cow disease and human deaths.[18] The news media reported on the new regulations in keeping with its traditionally low standards for accuracy when dealing with mad cow disease.

On June 3, 1997, the Associated Press circulated an outrageously inaccurate story which stated that the FDA had "banned the use of virtually all slaughtered-animal parts in U.S. livestock feed." In fact, the FDA was not banning the feeding of rendered animal by-products, but primarily attempting to halt the feeding of ruminant animals such as cattle, sheep and goats back to other ruminants. The rendering industry could, however, continue processing "slaughtered-animal parts" into feed supplements for pigs, chickens, fish, pets and other animals, and those animals could in turn be converted into protein supplements for feeding back to cows—as well as to their own species.

The new regulations prompted a separate news release from the Consumers Union, which managed to elbow its way into some of the coverage of FDA's announcement. The Associated Press story noted that CU's Jean Halloran called the ban "totally inadequate to protect the public health" because it exempted pork. The following day, however, the Associated Press dropped Halloran's criticisms and in a very brief story simply repeated the false assurance that "the government has banned the use of virtually all slaughtered-animal parts in U.S. livestock feed."[19]

Consumers Union is best known as the publisher of *Consumer Reports* magazine. Unlike many so-called public interest groups, CU has a strict policy of accepting no industry funding or advertising. It does not typically wade into controversial cutting-edge issues and aggressively challenge FDA food policies, but the threat of food-borne spongiform encephalopathy had aroused the scientific concerns of its research staff, especially Halloran and CU food safety researcher Michael Hansen. Their national news release of June 3, 1997 minced few words in ripping the FDA's long-overdue regulations, pointing out that "TSEs are known to occur in sheep and in wild deer and elk in the U.S. Remains of these animals can be used to make feed for pigs, and pig remains can be fed to any food animal."

"By failing to include swine in the rule, FDA has left the door open for a mad cow-like disease to circulate in the United States," Hansen charged. "FDA claims we are safe because we have never seen swine infected under natural conditions. But it could just mean we have not looked hard enough. Most commercial pigs are slaughtered at the age of six months, long before they would be expected to exhibit any signs of the disease." Hansen pointed out that swine protein constitutes 16 percent of all rendered mammal protein. "We are still feeding mammal protein to food animals," he said bluntly. "If any of that protein is contaminated, the disease will spread. . . . The epidemic in the United Kingdom involved ten years of bureaucrats ignoring the warnings of scientists and underestimating the seriousness of the risks. The FDA seems bent on repeating those mistakes," Hansen concluded.[20]

While the U.S. media's coverage of the new FDA regulations continued its dismal trend of parroting official assurances, the CU news release did catch the attention of the editors of *Genetic Engineering News*, an expensive trade publication serving the pharmaceutical industry. *GE News* invited Hansen to expound on CU's concerns in a column titled "The Reasons Why FDA's Feed Rule Won't Protect Us from BSE." Hansen repeated the above concerns, and noted that the U.S. regulations were out of step with measures that had already been taken in Europe: "The U.K. has prohibited feeding meat and bone meal (MBM) from any mammal to all feed animals. The European Union . . . has banned use of all mammalian MBM in any ruminant feed."

Hansen also discovered a bizarre regulatory bombshell buried 18 pages into the dull bureaucratic prose of the 44-page FDA regulations. "Perhaps the most egregious problem with the FDA rules is that they would permit known TSE-positive materials to be used in pet food, pig, chicken and fish feed—FDA only requires that it be labeled 'Do not feed to cattle and other ruminants.'

Thus, carcasses of scrapie-infected sheep and TSE-infected deer could legally be sent to the renderer and converted into pet and pig rations. We frankly are astounded that the FDA would permit TSE-positive materials to be used for any purpose. The decision flies in the face of recommendations from the World Health Organization International Consultation on TSEs and Public Health Issues held last year. WHO urged that 'no part of any animal which has shown signs of a TSE should enter any food chain (human or animal).'" Hansen pointed out that under the FDA regulations "the U.K. could apparently ship BSE-contaminated [meat and bone meal] to the U.S." for animal feed, and that European Union countries "could decide to ban importations of U.S. meat because our [animal] feed laws are not as protective as theirs."

FDA's rule also exempted blood and blood products, but Hansen pointed out that "Dr. Paul Brown of the National Institutes of Health announced that his lab had injected blood from mice infected with CJD into the brains of healthy mice, and the latter subsequently developed a TSE. This work conclusively demonstrates that blood and blood products do carry the TSE-causing agent. If this is true for CJD, we must assume that it would be true for other TSEs. The rule also exempts gelatin, which comes primarily from the hide of pigs and cows. Yet . . . FDA's own TSE Advisory Committee concluded that not enough scientific evidence exists to state that gelatin does not contain the TSE-causing agent . . ."[21]

Hansen and other Consumers Union staff personally discussed their concerns with top FDA officials including Dr. Steve Sundlof, head of the FDA's Center for Veterinary Medicine, but to no avail.[22]

Despite knowing the dangers of animal cannibalism since 1988, the U.S. Food and Drug Administration had waited almost a decade to begin banning such practices, and its regulations contained gaping loopholes clearly designed to protect the interests of industry, not consumers. The U.S. Department of Agriculture, charged with the contradictory challenge of both regulating meat and simultaneously promoting increased sales, had turned a blind eye to the evidence of its own investigators that a TSE agent could already be spreading in U.S. pigs, which under the new regulations can still be fed back to other pigs, cows, chickens and pets.

This pattern of bureaucratic bungling and meat-industry bias raises the obvious question of whether government agencies possess the resolve necessary to effectively implement and enforce even these inadequate guidelines. During the many months of comments that went into drafting the new regulations, industry groups deluged FDA with their formal written criticisms regarding restrictions on feeding rendered by-products. The renderers' comments frequently argued that bans would be impossible to enforce, because once animals have been rendered, the resulting meat and bone meal cannot be easily tested to determine what species it came from. To even the trained eye, as an old Blues song says, "it's all meat from the same bone." Monitoring compliance has already been a problem for the European Community, according to a 1997 *Nature* report which found that bone meal often contained as much as five percent mammalian protein, even though such protein has theoretically been banned in Europe. The U.S. rendering industry annually produced a total of 6.2 *billion* pounds of meat and bone meal alone.[23] Another indication of the difficulties inherent in enforcement appeared in the summer of 1997 when a European scandal revealed that enterprising exporters had carried on a large black market that sold banned British beef to unsuspecting consumers in other parts of Europe.

The Precautionary Petard

In *Deadly Feasts,* author Richard Rhodes recounts an "apocalyptic" phone conversation he had with Carleton Gajdusek a few months after the British government's announcement of March 20, 1996. "They don't have the least idea what caused the human cases," Gajdusek said. "It's kuru and nothing but kuru, and any species could be carrying it—dairy cows, beef cattle, pigs, chickens. They need to assess the risks and deal with it realistically. All the pigs in England fed on this meat-and-bone meal. The disease hasn't turned up in pigs only because you don't keep pigs alive for seven or eight years; they're killed after two or three years at most. When we kept pigs we'd inoculated in our laboratory for eight years, they came down with scrapie. Probably all the pigs in England are inoculated. And that means not only pork. It means your pigskin wallet. It means catgut surgical suture, because that's made of pig tissue. All the chickens fed on meat-and-bone meal; they're probably infected. You put that stuff in a chicken and it goes right through. A vegetarian could get it from chicken-shit that they put on the vegetables. It could be in the tallow, in butter—how the hell am I supposed to measure infectivity in butter? No one on earth knows how to do that. These people who've come down with CJD have given blood. It's undoubtedly in the blood supply. . . . And by the way, it could be in the milk. That hasn't been excluded either."[24]

Another unexpected avenue of CJD risk hit the headlines in the U.S. in August 1997, when researchers studied five unrelated patients who had been seen with CJD at a clinic in western Kentucky and found that all five had a history of eating squirrel brains. Although squirrel brains are eaten by some people in rural areas, it was hardly a popular food item. No cases of TSE had ever been documented in a squirrel, but the link was suggestive enough that researchers urged "caution . . . in the ingestion of this arboreal rodent."[25]

The number of hypothetical risks from these novel disease agents seems endless. They could pop up in medicines, in organ transplants, in gelatin (which is used in everything from dessert mixes to medicine gel-caps), or in garden fertilizer made from rendered bone meal. The experts tend to argue that each of these hypothetical avenues, taken individually, poses little danger. Government and industry officials worry that public discussion of hypothetical risks could trigger unnecessary panic. The truth is that the risks come from so many directions and are so unpredictable that consumers can't and shouldn't be expected to cope with those risks by selectively boycotting products suspected of harboring an unseen infection. There are too many bullets to dodge, and the shots may be blanks anyway. What we need is good data, and in the meantime we need serious implementation of measures to prevent the disease from spreading—*not* just surveillance that will only alert us to tragedy after it has already arrived. We need the precautionary principle.

When evidence of the dangers from BSE first began to appear, sensible policymakers should have been expected to practice a precautionary principle, basing their policies on worst-case assumptions about the disease and its dangers. Instead, they placated industry and relied on blind faith in "science," using the limited range of what they did understand as the basis for predictions that later turned out to be terribly flawed. The problem was not simply that they lacked knowledge. The problem was that they had a *little* knowledge, which in this case turned out to be a dangerous thing indeed. In the memorable words of British epidemiologist Sheila Gore, they discovered that they had been playing "Russian roulette with no information on the odds." [26]

Human ignorance is as inescapable a part of the human experience as life and death themselves. That is why people throughout history have planned their lives and their societies in order to allow for unknown as well as known dangers. In times of war, generals plot strategic retreats to be taken in case they suffer unexpected defeats in battle. Businesses set aside reserve funds that they can draw upon in case of unanticipated losses. Individuals buy insurance as a precaution against the possibility of unforeseen accidents or illness.

There are many things that we cannot ever hope to know, and some tragedies are truly unavoidable. As individuals, we don't know when or how death will come from a myriad of unseen causes. We cannot predict the weather beyond short periods. We have no way of knowing which children born this year will rise to become great artists and humanitarians, and which will become murderers and thieves. When the Fore began consuming their relatives in ritual acts of cannibalism, they had no way of knowing that they would cause an epidemic. At the time that the feed industries first began to use rendered meat and bone meal, they also had no way of knowing that they were setting in motion a chain of events with deadly consequences.

What the precautionary principle requires, is that *when risks become known*—even hypothetical, unproven risks—*action should be taken to avoid them.* This is especially true in a high-tech society characterized by systems of global mass production, where even a single mistake carries potentially disastrous consequences. By failing to follow the precautionary principle sooner, England dealt its beef industry a blow from which it may never recover, and it has left millions of people fearful that they may already be doomed to a horrible death from an illness which takes decades to manifest.

"BSE is the Chernobyl of food safety," says author Nicols Fox, in her 1997 book, *Spoiled: The Dangerous Truth About a Food Chain Gone Haywire.* "Just as the world's worst nuclear accident transformed public thinking about the wisdom of producing electricity by a means with the potential to be so damaging for so long a time, BSE is the warning shot across the bow of intensive farming practices, the worldwide distribution of agricultural products, and the demand for cheap food. It underscores the dangers inherent in creating a division between animal and human medical science and making the erroneous assumption that they are not directly related. It also underlines the inherent flaw in entrusting the safety of food to a government agency that is at the same time mandated to protect the agricultural industry."[27]

Actually, the practice of feeding rendered animal protein back to cattle is a fairly low-tech innovation by modern standards. It does not begin to compare with the complexity and scope of changes being considered and introduced as a result of advances in biochemistry and genetic engineering. The history of BSE offers a chilling warning of the unpredictable dangers inherent in these efforts to tamper with biology.

According to developmental biologist Stuart Newman, the dangers are even greater and harder to foresee as innovations become more technologically sophisticated. "The basis for the early criticism of recombinant DNA technology was that by transferring genes from one type of organism (e.g., mice, humans) into another (E. coli) it would be possible to inadvertently create new pathogens," Newman observed. "The perspective was that biological boundaries are real, and that DNA wasn't simply 'information' that could be freely passed from one type to another with impunity. Although there have been no documented cases of new diseases arising from recombinant DNA manipulations, the major point has turned out to be valid. It seems that emergent diseases—Ebola virus, hantavirus, possibly AIDS, and new versions of old diseases like flu—come about by interaction between previously separated species, and transfer of pathogens into new hosts. This can be brought about by ecological disruption, like clearing the rainforests. In the case of mad cow disease, it happened when, for economic reasons, herbivores were fed offals derived from other species, something they would never eat in nature. . . . Basically, commercial interests forced the crossing of biological boundaries, leading to a new disease."

We need science to help us deal with these issues, just as we need farmers to produce the food we eat and governments to set and enforce the rules of the game. But we also need the warning voices—the Richard Laceys, Dick Marshes, Howard Lymans and Michael Hansens of the world—the so-called "fearmongers" who worry about hypothetical dangers before others think they matter. We need to protect their right to speak freely, because otherwise decisions that affect us will be made without our full knowledge and consent, without debate, without the messy but necessary politics that makes up democracy.

Industry has enormous powers to make its voices heard in these debates, yet it never seems to feel that it has enough power. It would be convenient, from its perspective, to shield itself from "hysteria, panic and instability" if it could limit the debate to "experts," through censorship measures such as "food disparagement laws," and through public relations strategies that drive out candor and distance officials from the public that they are supposed to serve.

If we let industry set the rules, however, there will literally be no limit to what we'll swallow, and the nightmare of mad cow disease—or something just as bad, or worse—not only *can* happen here, but almost certainly *will*.

Glossary of Terms

Alzheimer's Disease—a progressive brain disease causing dementia and eventual death.

Amyloid plaque—a microscopic mass of accumulated proteins found in brain tissue.

Animal and Plant Health Inspection Service (APHIS)—a branch of the U.S. Department of Agriculture which deals directly with animal disease issues, including scrapie and bovine spongiform encephalopathy.

Bovine spongiform encephalopathy (BSE)—a form of transmissible spongiform encephalopathy seen in cattle and commonly known in Britain as mad cow disease. BSE was first observed in England in 1986 and has since been seen in smaller numbers in other countries, mostly in Europe.

Creutzfeldt-Jakob Disease (pronounced KROYTZfelt-YAHKohb, abbreviated CJD)—a form of transmissible spongiform encephalopathy found in humans. CJD is mostly observed in people age 50 or older. Most cases have no known cause, but approximately 15 percent are associated with genetic predisposition to the disease. See also *Gerstmann-Straussler Syndrome* and *Fatal Familial Insomnia,* and *nvCJD.*

Encephalopathy (en-seff-uh-LOP-uh-thee)—disease of the brain

Fatal Familial Insomnia (FFI)—a rare human form of transmissible spongiform encephalopathy. FFI is a genetically-caused disease, but can be transmitted infectiously in experiments with laboratory animals.

Fore (FOR-ae)—one of the indigenous groups inhabiting Papua New Guinea. Their practice of ritual cannibalism was linked to an epidemic of kuru disease.

Gajdusek (GUY-du-shek), *D. Carleton*—American pediatrician and virologist, awarded the Nobel Prize for his studies of kuru disease in Papua New Guinea.

Gerstmann-Straussler-Scheinker Syndrome (GSS)—a rare human form of transmissible spongiform encephalopathy. GSS is a genetically-caused disease, but can be transmitted infectiously to experimental laboratory animals.

Horizontal transmission—contagious spread of an infectious disease between unrelated members of a herd or flock of animals.

Kuru—a form of transmissible spongiform encephalopathy observed in the 1950s among natives of Papua New Guinea who practiced ritual cannibalism.

Mad cow disease—see *bovine spongiform encephalopathy.*

Ministry of Agriculture, Fisheries and Food (MAFF)—the British equivalent of the United States Department of Agriculture (USDA).

National Cattlemen's Beef Association (NCBA)—the main trade and lobby association of the beef industry in the United States, established in 1994 through a merger between the National Cattlemen's Association (NCA) and the National Live Stock and Meat Board.

National Institutes of Health—a network of U.S. federally funded research institutes which support and conduct biomedical research into the causes and prevention of diseases.

National Renderers Association—the main trade and lobby association of the rendering industry in the United States.

nvCJD—a new, variant form of Creutzfeldt-Jakob Disease which has claimed unusually young victims in England and one victim in France. In 1996, British scientists found evidence indicating that nvCJD was the result of human exposure to BSE-contaminated beef.

Ovine—of or related to sheep.

Prion (pronounced PREE-on)—a deformed protein identified by biologist Stanley Prusiner as the likely infectious agent responsible for causing and transmitting transmissible spongiform encephalopathies. The word "prion" is a hybrid of "protein" and "infectious."

PrP—Scientific terminology for the "prion protein" believed to be responsible for causing transmissible spongiform encephalopathies. PrP^{nor} is used to designate the normal, noninfectious form of the protein, which is believed to occur naturally in all mammalian species. PrP^{sc} designates the abnormally folded form of the protein associated with scrapie and other animal TSEs.

Recombinant bovine growth hormone (rBGH)—a genetically-engineered drug designed to increase a cow's milk production. Some scientists have expressed concern that use of the drug could encourage feeding practices that facilitate the spread of bovine spongiform encephalopathy.

Ruminant—a cud-chewing animal with a four-chambered stomach. The first chamber is called a rumen. Ruminant animals including cattle, sheep, goats and deer have shown susceptibility to transmissible spongiform encephalopathies, as have a number of non-ruminant species.

Scrapie—the form of transmissible spongiform encephalopathy (TSE) found in sheep and goats. Scrapie was the first-observed TSE, and scientists sometimes use the word as a generic term referring to TSEs in general.

Slow viruses—diseases such as Acquired Immunodeficiency Syndrome (AIDS), characterized by unusually long incubation periods (measured in years rather than in days or weeks) between the time of exposure and the emergence of symptoms. Transmissible spongiform encephalopathies such as kuru, scrapie and Creutzfeldt-Jakob Disease were once thought to be slow virus infections.

Specified bovine offals (SBO)—cattle organs deemed unfit for human consumption under British law on the theory that they were more likely than other tissues to carry the infectious agent which causes BSE. The SBOs included brain and spinal tissues, along with spleen, tonsils and thymus.

Species barrier—a characteristic of most transmissible spongiform encephalopathies that makes them easier to transmit between animals of the same species than from one species to another.

Spongiform Encephalopathy Advisory Committee (SEAC)—The official committee of scientists appointed to advise the British government during its handling of the BSE crisis.

Transmissible mink encephalopathy (TME)—the mink form of transmissible spongiform encephalopathy.

Transmissible spongiform encephalopathy (TSE)—the generic name for a class of central nervous system illnesses seen in various animal species including humans, sheep, cows, mink, deer and cats. TSEs are invariably fatal, and autopsies of the brain usually show microscopic, spongelike lesions. An abnormally folded protein, known as a *prion,* is believed to be capable of transmitting the disease.

Vertical transmission—spread of disease from parent to child, which can imply that the disease is either infectious or genetically inherited.

Notes

Foreword

1. Robert LaBudde, "Re: CJD on ABC TV evening news 5.12.97," internet posting on the BSE-L mailing list, May 13, 1997.
2. John Stauber and Sheldon Rampton, *Toxic Sludge Is Good for You* (Monroe, ME: Common Courage Press, 1995), p. 56.

The Girl Who Wouldn't Go Away

1. Cummings, Jeffrey L., *Dementia: A Clinical Approach* (Butterworths, 1983).
2. Peter Silverton, "The Girl Who Cooked Her Own Meals," *Mail on Sunday / Night & Day Magazine,* May 12, 1996.
3. Alison Little, "Government Defends BSE Response," *PA News,* Jan. Oct. 96.
4. Statement by the Secretary of State for Health on BSE/CJD, British House of Commons, Mar. 20, 1996.
5. Philip Webster and Jeremy Laurence, "New Infection Linked to Mad Cow Disease," *Times* (London), Mar. 21, 1996.
6. Michael Hornsby, "EU Postpones Decision on Beef Byproducts," *Times* (London), Apr. 11, 1996.
7. Chris Court, "Suicide Tragedy of Beef Farmer," *PA News,* June 19, 1996.
8. Tim Moynihan, "Farming Hit by High Suicide Rate," *PA News,* June 30, 1996.
9. Brian Farmer, "Counseling Service for Farmers in BSE Despair," *PA News,* June 30, 1996.
10. Court, op. cit.
11. Giles Elgood, "Mad Cow Fears Worry Nervous World," Reuters, June 11, 1996.
12. Robin Young, "Germans Lay Low After Beef Gaffe," *Times* (London), June 6, 1996.
13. Nick Robinson, "Cow Cull Could Cost £700M," *PA News,* Mar. 26, 1996.
14. Katherine Butler, "Ban Worsens U.K. Relations with Brussels," *Independent* (London), Mar. 26, 1996.
15. Peter Blackburn, "EU Shuns Scientific Advice, Keeps British Beef Ban," Reuters, Apr. 10, 1996.
16. Irene Malbin, "CTFA: Cosmetic Ingredients Not from BSE Countries," *PR Newswire,* Apr. 3, 1996.
17. USDA, FDA, CDC, "USDA, U.S. Public Health Service Announces Support for Industry" (news release), Mar. 29, 1996.
18. Richard Lacey, *Unfit for Human Consumption* (Souvenir Press: 1991). Quoted in Peter Cox, *The New Why You Don't Need Meat* (London, U.K.: Blooomsbury, 1992), p. 46.
19. Geoffrey Cannon et al., "British Beef: Mad Cows and Englishmen," *Independent* (London), May 20, 1990, p. 19.

Food Fight

1. The Oprah Winfrey Show, Apr. 16, 1996.
2. Howard Lyman, interview by John Stauber, Jan. 15, 1997.

3. Jim Barr to General Managers and Communicators, National Milk Producers Federation (memorandum), Apr. 4, 1996, p. 1.
4. "Oprah Moves World Markets," AP, Apr. 17, 1996.
5. "Cattlemen Condemn Oprah Show," UPI, Apr. 18, 1996.
6. Ibid.
7. "Oprah Says Did Not Intend CME Cattle 'Oprah Crash,' " Reuters, Apr. 23, 1996.
8. "Oprah Causes Beef Industry Flap," *Meat Processing* (Watt Publishing Co., Mount Morris, IL), June 96, p. 8.
9. Thomas Goetz, "After the Oprah Crash," *Village Voice,* Apr. 29, 1997, p. 39.
10. Petition by Paul F. Engler and Cactus Feeders, Inc. against Oprah Winfrey, Harpo Production, Howard Lyman and Cannon Communications, U.S. District Court, Texas Northern District, May 28, 1996.
11. Goetz, op. cit.
12. Ibid.
13. James Grossberg, Seth Berlin and Thomas Newton, "Food Disparagement Bills Defeated in California, Enacted in Oklahoma and Texas," *Libelletter* (New York, NY: Libel Defense Resource Center), June 1995, p. 1.
14. Gary Taubes, "The Game of the Name Is Fame. But Is It Science?" *Discover,* Dec. 1986, p. 28.
15. Peter Spencer, "Origins of Spongiform Encephalopathies," presented at the International Symposium on Spongiform Encephalopathies, Georgetown University, Feb. 12-13, 1996.

First Tremors

1. David Zizzo, "Scrapie: Perplexing Disease Fatal for Sheep, Linked to Human," UPI, June 3, 1982.
2. G.D. Hunter, *Scrapie and Mad Cow Disease* (New York: Vantage Press, 1993), pp. 25-26.
3. Ibid., p. 14.
4. Ibid., pp. 17-18.
5. Ibid., pp. 16-17.
6. Ibid., pp. 22-23.
7. Ibid., pp. 27-28.
8. Ibid., pp. 94-95.
9. H.B. Parry, *Scrapie Disease in Sheep,* ed. D.R. Oppenheimer (New York: Academic Press, 1983), pp. 76-77.
10. Ibid., pp. 32, 74-76.
11. Hunter, op. cit., p. 93.
12. I.H. Pattison, M.N. Hoare and J.N. Jebbett, "Spread of Scrapie to Sheep and Goats by Oral Dosing with Foetal Membranes from Scrapie-affected Sheep," *Veterinary Record,* no. 90 (1972), pp. 465-468. See also T. Onodera et al., "Isolation of Scrapie Agent from the Placenta of Sheep with Natural Scrapie in Japan," *Microbiology and Immunology,* no. 37 (1993), pp.. 311-316.
13. Hunter, pp. 32-33.
14. Ibid., pp. 63-68.
15. Stanley B. Prusiner, "The Prion Diseases," *Scientific American,* v. 272, no. 1 (Jan. 95), pp. 48-57.
16. Hunter, p. 98.
17. Ibid., pp. 103-104.
18. Ibid., p. 83.

Kuru

1. Vincent Zigas, *Laughing Death: The Untold Story of Kuru* (Clifton, NJ: The Humana Press, 1990), pp. 119-120.
2. Ibid., p. 58.
3. Ibid., p. 57.
4. Ibid., p. 46.
5. Ibid., p. 115.
6. Ibid., p. 122.
7. Ibid., pp. 132-134.
8. Ibid., pp. 142-151.
9. Ibid., p. 154.
10. Ibid., p. 171.
11. Judith Farquhar and D. Carleton Gajdusek, eds., *Kuru: Early Letters and Field-Notes from the Collection of D. Carleton Gajdusek* (New York: Raven Press, 1981), p. 2.
12. Hunter, p. 226-228.
13. Farquhar, p. 41.

14. D.C. Gajdusek, ed., *Correspondence on the History and Original Investigations on Kuru: Smadel-Gajdusek Correspondence, 1955–1958* (U.S. Department of Health, Education and Welfare, 1976), p. 50.
15. Zigas, p. 242.
16. Farquhar, pp. 36-37.
17. Gajdusek, p. 66-67.
18. Ibid.
19. Farquhar, p. 28.
20. Ibid.
21. Farquhar, pp. 39-40.
22. Zigas, pp. 237-238.
23. Roger Bingham, "Outrageous Ardor," in *A Passion to Know,* ed. Allen L. Hammond (Charles Scribner's Sons, 1985), p. 19.
24. Farquhar, p. 32, and Bingham, p. 13.
25. June Goodfield, *Quest for the Killers* (Boston, MA: Birkhäuser Boston, 1985), pp. 32-33.
26. Gajdusek, p. 173.
27. Farquhar, p. 259.
28. Goodfield, p. 21.
29. Ibid., p. 26.
30. Zigas, p. 276.
31. Ibid., pp. 280-281.
32. Goodfield, p. 33.
33. R.M. Glasse & Shirley Lindenbaum, "The Highlands of New Guinea: A Review of the Ethnographic and Related Problems," in *Essays on Kuru,* ed. R.W. Hornabrook (Papua New Guinea: E.W. Classey, 1976), p. 13.
34. Goodfield, p. 35.

The Virus that Wasn't There

1. Zigas, p. 305.
2. Bingham, p. 18.
3. Ibid., p. 21.
4. Goodfield, p. 17.
5. Hunter, pp. 100-101.
6. Bingham, pp. 19-20.
7. Hunter, p. 101.
8. Joseph Carey, "New Look at an Old Enemy: the Study of Viruses Offers Challenges and Hope," *U.S. News & World Report,* May 12, 1986, p. 65.
9. Jon Cohen, "Flying Dutchman: Jaap Goudsmit, AIDS Virologist," *Science,* v. 260, no. 5112 (May 28, 1993), p. 1263.
10. Tracy L. Glisson, "A Comic Stew with Bite," *St. Petersburg Times,* June 21, 1991, p. 27.
11. Peter Duesberg, "The Enigma of Slow Viruses: Facts and Artefacts" (book review), *Lancet,* v. 342, no. 8873 (Sept. 18, 1993), p. 729.
12. Bingham, pp. 15-16.
13. Paul Brown et al., "'Friendly Fire' in Medicine: Hormones, Homografts, and Creutzfeldt-Jakob Disease," *Lancet,* v. 340 (July 4, 1992), p. 24.

Cannibal Meat

1. Frank Burnham, *Rendering: The Invisible Industry* (Fallbrook, CA: Aero Publishers, 1978), p. 5.
2. Van Smith, "What's Cookin'?" *City Paper* (Baltimore, MD), Sept. 27, 1995.
3. Dennis Mullane, preface to *The Original Recyclers,* eds. Don A. Franco and Winfield Swanson (National Renderers Association, 1996).
4. Ibid., p. 1.
5. Fred Bisplinghoff, "Current Commercial Processing of Animal Proteins in the U.S.," presentation during a two-day symposium on Tissue Distribution, Inactivation and Transmission of Transmissible Spongiform Encephalopathies (TSEs) of Animals, Riverdale, MD, May 13-14, 1996.
6. Burnham, pp. 17-18, 25.
7. Bisplinghoff, op. cit.
8. Burnham, p. 41.
9. Franco, pp. 120-121.
10. Burnham, p. 105.
11. Ibid., p. 107.
12. Franco, pp. 229, 231-232.
13. Burnham, p. 41.
14. Beatrice Trum Hunter, "What Is Fed to Our Food Animals?" *Consumers' Research,* Dec. 1996, pp. 13-14.

15. Frank Burnham, "Rendered Products Gain Ground in Animal Nutrition," *Render Magazine,* v. 8, no. 4 (1979), p. 10.
16. "Can We Keep Our Livestock Healthy?" *Farm Journal,* March 1978, p. 21.
17. Burnham, "Rendered Products Gain Round," p. 11.
18. "Bovine Spongiform Encephalopathy: Rendering Policy," USDA Animal and Plant Health Inspection Service, 1991.
19. Bisplinghoff, op. cit.
20. Burnham, *Rendering: The Invisible Industry,* pp. 19, 125.
21. "Rendering Plants—Good Practices for Employees" (pamphlet), U.S. Department of Health, Education and Welfare, HEW Publication No. (NIOSH) 76–150 (Apr. 96), pp. 7, 17.
22. Burnham, *Rendering: The Invisible Industry,* pp. 127-128.
23. Ibid., p. 129.
24. Ric Grummer interview by John Stauber, Feb. 17, 1997.
25. Fred Bisplinghoff, "Salmonella No Hazard to Dairymen," *Render Magazine,* v. 22, no. 4, pp. 9, 20.
26. Paul Brown, Michael A. Preece and Robert G. Will, "'Friendly Fire in Medicine: Hormones, Homografts, and Creutzfeldt-Jakob Disease," *Lancet,* v. 340 (July 4, 1992), p. 25.

Acceptable Risks

1. Ian Stewart, "Playing with Numbers," *Guardian* (London), Mar. 28, 1996.
2. Art Harris, "'I'm Alive'; Bystander Hit in Police Chase Relies on His Inner Strength," *Washington Post,* Oct. 20, 1979, p. A1; and Sandra G. Boodman and Judith Valente, "Arlington's 'Hot Pursuit' Policy was Factor in $5 Million Judgment," *Washington Post,* Mar. June 83, p. B4.
3. Robert Meyers, "Police Chases Kill 500 Yearly," *Washington Post,* Apr. 27, 1980, p. B1.
4. Peter Perl, "The High-Speed Chase Dilemma," *Washington Post,* Nov. 5, 1981, p. DC-1; and Nancy Lewis and Judith Valente, "$5 Million Awarded for Crash Injury," *Washington Post,* Mar. 2, 1983, p. C1.
5. "MBD: A Brief Description," company internal document, undated.
6. Andrew Chetley, *The Politics of Baby Foods* (New York: St. Martin's Press, 1986), p. 29.
7. Ibid., p. 53.
8. Ibid., p. 129..
9. MBD Update and Analysis, Confidential for Chlorine Chemistry Council; Activist Update: Chlorine, May 18, 1994.
10. Ibid.
11. Jack Mongoven to Clyde Greenert and Brad Lienhart, "Re: MBD Activist Report" (memorandum), Sept. 7, 1994.
12. Ronald Duchin, "Take an Activist Apart and What Do You Have?" *CALF News Cattle Feeder,* June 91, pp. 9, 14.
13. Mongoven to Greenert and Lienhart.
14. Jack Mongoven, "The Precautionary Principle," *Eco-logic,* Mar. 95, pp. 14-15.
15. Ibid., p. 16.
16. Patricia Hausman, *Jack Sprat's Legacy* (New York: Richard Marek Publishers, 1981, pp. 28, 96-101.
17. Wayne Swanson and George Schultz, *Prime Rip* (Englewood Cliffs, NJ: Prentice-Hall, 1982), pp. 145-146.
18. Robert E. Taylor, *Beef Production and the Beef Industry* (Minneapolis, MN: Burgess Publishing, 1984), pp. 42, 45.
19. Ibid., pp. 40-42.
20. Hausman, pp. 182-183.
21. Anita Manning, "A Beefed-up Attack on Meat Eaters," *USA Today,* Sept. 10, 1990, p. 1D.

22. Dan Looker, "Cattlemen Using Scientists to Combat Diet Assertions," Gannett News Service, May 17, 1990.
23. Dottie Enrico, "Fur's Flying," *Newsday,* Jan. 15, 1990, p. 1.
24. Steve Kopperud, "Animal Rights Statements Clarified" (letter to the editor), *Journal of Commerce,* July 22, 1988, p. 8A.

Outbreak in America's Dairyland

1. R.F. Marsh and R.A. Bessen, "Epidemiological and Experimental Studies on Transmissible Mink Encephalopathy," *Transmissible Spongiform Encephalopathies: Impact on Animal and Human Health,* ed. Fred Brown, Heidelberg, Karger-Verlag, Developments in Biological Standardization, Heidelberg, June 23-24, 1992.
2. R.F. Marsh and W.J. Hadlow, "Transmissible Mink Encephalopathy," *Rev. Sci. Tech. Off. Int. Epiz.,* 1992, 11 (2), pp. 544-545.
3. Marsh and Bessen, op. cit.
4. Marsh and Hadlow, op. cit.
5. Richard Marsh interview by authors, Sept. 26, 1996.
6. R.F. Marsh, "Transmissible Mink Encephalopathy," *Prion Diseases of Humans and Animals,* ed. Stanley B. Prusiner (Chichester, England: Ellis Horwood), p. 301.
7. Hunter, pp. 29-32.
8. Marsh and Bessen, p. 4.
9. D. Burger and G.R. Hartsough, "Transmissible Encephalopathy of Mink," Monograph No. 2, Workshop and Symposium on Slow, Latent, and Temperate Virus Infections, National Institutes of Health, Bethesda, MD, Dec. 7–9, 1964, p. 305.
10. R.F. Marsh et al., "Epidemiological and Experimental Studies on a New Incident of Transmissible Mink Encephalopathy," *Journal of General Virology* (1991), 72, p. 592.
11. Marsh interview, Sept. 26, 1996.
12. Joel McNair, "BSE: A Ticking Time Bomb for Downer Cows?" *Agri-View* (Iola, WI), June 17, 1993, p. 1.
13. Ibid.

Mad Cows and Englishmen

1. Michael Hornsby, "Farmer Describes Horror at Seeing the Birth of BSE," *Times* (London), June 24, 1996.
2. "It's Dog Eat Dog on Swedish Farms," *Guardian* (London), Dec. 13, 1985.
3. Mike Harrison, "Three Treated for Suspected CJD," *PA News,* Apr. 25, 1996.
4. Hornsby.
5. Peter Martin, "The Mad Cow Deceit," *Mail on Sunday / Night & Day Magazine,* May 12, 1996.
6. Richard Kimberlin, "Current Science on the Tissue Distribution of TSE," presentation during a two-day symposium on Tissue Distribution, Inactivation and Transmission of Transmissible Spongiform Encephalopathies (TSEs) of Animals, Riverdale, MD, May 13-14, 1996.
7. Hunter, pp. 81-83, 106.
8. Kimberlin, op. cit.
9. G.A.H. Wells et al., "A Novel Progressive Spongiform Encephalopathy in Cattle," *Veterinary Record,* Oct. 31, 1987, p. 419.
10. John Young, "Attack Over Sale of Diseased Meat," *Times* (London), Jan. 30, 1989.
11. John Young, "Mystery Disease Strikes at Cattle," *Times* (London), Dec. 29, 1987.
12. David Brown, "Madness Sets Bovine Brainteaser," *Sunday Telegraph,* Apr. 24, 1988.
13. T.A. Holt and J. Phillips, "Bovine Spongiform Encephalopathy," *British Medical Journal,* 1988, no. 296, pp. 1581-82.

14. Richard Kimberlin, "Current Science on Transmission of TSE," presentation during a two-day symposium on Tissue Distribution, Inactivation and Transmission of Transmissible Spongiform Encephalopathies (TSEs) of Animals, Riverdale, MD, May 13-14, 1996.

15. Brown, op. cit.

16. "Disease Update: Bovine Spongiform Encephalopathy," *Veterinary Record*, v. 122, no. 20 (May 14, 1988), pp. 477–78.

17. John MacGregor (British Minister for Agriculture), news release, July 7, 1988.

18. *Scottish Farmer,* Nov. 6, 1988, quoted in "New Brain Disease—Could It Spread to Humans?" *Agscene,* Aug./Sept. 1988.

19. Richard Southwood et al., *Report of the Working Party on Bovine Spongiform Encephalopathy,* London HMSO, 1989.

20. Ibid.

21. Ibid.

22. Ibid.

23. "Appearance of Cattle Disease Usually Associated with Sheep Prompts Israel and Australia to Ban British Cows," AP, Feb. 9, 1988.

24. David Jackson to John Stauber (letter), Aug. 22, 1996.

Scrapie, American-Style

1. Memo from A.B. Thierman to Robert R. Oltjen, "Review of Potential Research on Bovine Spongiform Encephalopathy, Meeting of ARS Task Force, April 24, 1989, Washington, DC" (meeting minutes), May 11, 1989, p. 1.

2. Ibid., p. 2.

3. Ibid., p. 3.

4. "Proceedings of an International Roundtable on Bovine Spongiform Encephalopathy," *Journal of the American Veterinary Medical Association,* v. 196, no. 10 (May 15, 1990), p. 1687.

5. Ibid., p. 1689.

6. Ibid., p. 1687.

7. Ibid., p. 1676.

8. "Farmer Accused of Deliberately Infecting Sheep," UPI, Mar. 13, 1988.

9. Jack Parnell (U.S. Deputy Secretary of Agriculture, USDA) to Maynard L. Potter (letter), Feb. 26, 1990.

10. Delmar R. Cassidy et al., response to letter by Vincent Marshall, *Journal of the American Veterinary Medical Association,* v. 198, no. 11 (June 1, 1991), p. 1851.

11. Maynard L. Potter to Jack Parnell (letter), Jan. 16, 1990.

12. Maynard L. Potter to Jack Parnell (letter), Jan. 23, 1991.

13. Jack Parnell to Maynard L. Potter (letter), Feb. 15, 1991.

14. Warren C. Foote, "Partioning of Time and Route of Vertical Transmission of Scrapie in Sheep and Goats," project progress report, Oct.-Dec., 1991, pp. 4-5.

15. J.C. McConnell and W.C. Dees to Senator Strom Thurmond (letter), Feb. 14, 1991.

16. "Report of USDA's Scrapie Meeting, May 10-11, 1988," notes taken by Grover W. Roberts.

17. Dale Cochran to Clayton Yeutter (letter), June Aug. 89.

18. American Sheep Industry Association, *ASI Issue Brief: Scrapie,* Oct. 1989.

19. Marsh interview, Sept. 26, 1996.

20. James Lein to APHIS (letter), Sept. 10, 1991.

21. Fred Dailey to Edward Madigan (letter), Jan. 31, 1992.

22. George Scott to APHIS (letter), Apr. 89.

23. Tom Harkin to Clayton Yeutter (letter), Mar. 10, 1989, p. 2.

24. Sandra Cox to APHIS (letter), Mar. 20, 1989.

25. Vincent Marshall, letter to the *Journal of the American Veterinary Medical Association,* v. 198, no. 11 (June 1, 1991), p. 1850.

26. Cassidy et al., op. cit.

27. USDA Animal and Plant Health Inspection Service, "APHIS History," timeline prepared for dedication of APHIS headquarters building, Sept. 13, 1995.

28. USDA Animal and Plant Health Inspection Service, "Scrapie Flock Status Definitions and Enrollment Information," Aug. 22, 1996.

29. USDA/APHIS, *Qualitative Analysis of BSE Risk Factors in the United States,* Jan. 1991, pp. 1, 15.

30. USDA/APHIS, *Quantitative Risk Assessment of BSE in the United States,* Jan. 1991, p. 1.

31. *Qualitative Analysis,* p. 19.

32. *Quantitative Risk Assessment,* p. 14.

33. *Qualitative Analysis,* p. 15.

34. USDA/APHIS, *Bovine Spongiform Encephalopathy: Rendering Research Priorities,* 1, 1991, pp. 2-3.

35. Ibid., pp. 3, 8.

36. Gary S. Colgrove, USDA Agricultural Research Service, "Scrapie/BSE File Update" (memo), July 2, 1990.

37. Bisplinghoff, op. cit.

38. Ibid.

Bent Proteins

1. Paul Brown and Carleton Gajdusek, "Survival of Scrapie Virus After Three Years' Interment," *Lancet,* Feb. 2, 1991, pp. 269-70.

2. Paul Brown, Pawel P. Liberski, Axel Wolff and D. Carleton Gajdusek, "Resistance of Scrapie Infectivity to Steam Autoclaving after Formaldehyde Fixation and Limited Survival after Ashing at 360°C: Practical and Theoretical Implications," *Journal of Infectious Diseases,* no. 161 (Mar. 1989), p. 470.

3. Hunter, pp. 55-56.

4. Paul Brown, Michael A. Preece and Robert G. Will, "'Friendly Fire in Medicine: Hormones, Homografts, and Creutzfeldt-Jakob Disease,'" *Lancet,* v. 340 (July 4, 1992), p. 24.

5. Stanley B. Prusiner, "The Prion Diseases," *Scientific American,* v. 272, no. 1, (Jan. 1995), pp. 48-57.

6. Gary Taubes, "The Game of the Name Is Fame. But Is It Science?" *Discover,* Dec. 1986, p. 28.

7. Hunter, p. 85.

8. Prusiner, op. cit.

9. Taubes, op. cit.

10. Ibid.

11. Ibid.

12. Prusiner, op. cit.

Worst-Case Scenario

1. David A.J. Tyrell, *Consultative Committee on Research into Spongiform Encephalopathies: Interim Report* (British Ministry of Agriculture, Fisheries and Food, 1989).

2. Richard W. Lacey, *Mad Cow Disease: The History of BSE in Britain* (England: Gypsela Publications, 1994), p. 85.

3. Richard Lacey, "Mad Cows Put Me Off Meat for Life," *The Vegetarian,* Feb. 1993.

4. Lacey, *Mad Cow Disease,* p. 56.

5. David Fletcher, "Professor Claims Poison Outbreak is Worst Ever," *Daily Telegraph,* Dec. 17, 1988, p. 2.

6. David Fletcher, "Test All Chickens for Salmonella, Urges Professor," *Daily Telegraph,* Dec. 21, 1988, p. 2.

7. Lacey, "Mad Cows Put Me Off Meat for Life."

8. Virginia Matthews, "Food Hygiene Leaflet 'a Crafty Diversion,' " *Daily Telegraph,* May 23, 1989, p. 4.

9. Ibid

10. David Brown, " 'Don't Panic' Plea on Bug," *Sunday Telegraph,* Jan. 15, 1989, p. 2.

11. Virginia Matthews, "Salmonella Poisoning Tally 'May Reach 1m," *Daily Telegraph,* Apr. 11, 1996, p. 6.

12. Peter Pallot, "Egg Salmonella is 'Rampant' in Chicken Flocks," *Daily Telegraph,* Aug. 18, 1989, p. 2.

13. "WHO Calls for Urgent Actions Against Salmonella," Xinhua News Service, Apr. 28, 1989.

14. Peter Pallot, "Food Poisoning 'Out of Control,' " *Daily Telegraph,* Apr. 13, 1989, p. 1.

15. David Simpson, "Dramatic Increase in Salmonella Cases," Press Association Newsfile, July 26, 1989.

16. Virginia Matthews, "Food Industry Urged to Go on Offensive Over 'Left Smears,' " *Daily Telegraph,* May 31, 1989, p. 6.

17. Lacey, *Mad Cow Disease,* p. 83.

18. Ibid., p. 56.

19. Ibid., p. 57.

20. Ibid., p. 91.

21. Ibid.

22. Ibid., p. 92.

23. Michael Hornsby, "Antelopes in British Zoos Are Dying of Brain Disease," *Times* (London), Mar. 12, 1990.

24. Nicholas Schoon, "Cat Had Illness Similar to 'Mad Cow' Disease, Vets Say," *Independent* (London), May 11, 1990, p. 3.

25. Lacey, *Mad Cow Disease,* pp. 94-95.

26. Richard Palmer and Ian Birrell, "Leading Food Scientist Calls for Slaughter of 6M Cows," *Times* (London), May 13, 1990.

27. Geoffrey Cannon, Steve Connor, Helen Hague and David Nicholson-Lord, "Mad Cows and Englishmen," *Independent* (London), May 20, 1990, p. 19.

28. Ibid.

29. "A Bareback Gummer in the Mad Cow Rodeo," *Guardian* (London), May 16, 1990.

30. "BSE Dispute Fueled by £1m Meat Promotion," *Times* (London), May 15, 1990.

31. Schoon, op. cit.

32. Lacey, *Mad Cow Disease,* p. 105.

33. Ibid., p. 108-109.

34. Ibid., p. 109-117.

35. Ibid., p. 118.

36. Ibid., p. 122.

One Bad Apple

1. Peter Montague, "How They Lie, Pt. 3: The Alar Story," *Rachel's Environment & Health Weekly,* nos. 530-534, Jan. 23-Feb. 20, 1997.

2. Frank E. Young, John Moore and John Bode, joint statement, *PR Newswire,* Mar. 16, 1989.

3. Janet Key, "Seeds of Debate Over Food Safety," *Chicago Tribune,* Mar. 19, 1989.

4. Montague, op. cit.

5. George W. Pring and Penelope Canan, *SLAPPs: Getting Sued for Speaking Out* (Philadelphia, Temple University Press, 1996), p. xi.

6. Gordon v. Marrone, NY Supreme Court decision, 1992.

7. Pring, pp. x, 2.

8. Jerry Walker, "Conservatives Seek Journalism Recruits," *Jack O'Dwyer's Newsletter,* v. 26, no. 48, Dec. 1988, p. 3.

9. "Moore Rejects Claim Tobacco Suit Victory Would Cost Mississippi," *The Commercial Appeal,* July 16, 1994, p. 1B.

10. Capital Research Center website advertisement for *The Rise of the Nanny State.*

11. Tom Holt, "Could Lawsuits Be the Cure for Junk Science?" *Priorities,* v. 7, no. 2 (1995).

12. Flyer circulated by Ohio Farm Bureau during 1996 lobbying for Ohio's agricultural product disparagement law.

13. Holt, op. cit.

14. Anthony Collings, "Food Producers Push for Laws Protecting Their Crops from Rumors," CNN, May 13, 1996.

15. Connie Koenenn, "Mind How You Disparage Asparagus or Berate Broccoli," *Los Angeles Times,* Jan. 18, 1996.

16. Eric T. Freyfogle, comments on SB 234 before Illinois State Senate Agriculture Committee, Apr. 8, 1995.

17. David J. Bederman, interview by John Stauber, Feb. 15, 1997.

18. Lee Levin, James E. Grossberg and Seth D. Berlin (attorneys with Ross, Dixon & Masback), Brief Amici Curiae of ABC, National Association of Broadcasters, Dow Jones & Company, Knight-Ridder, Los Angeles Times, New York Times Company, Magazine Publishers of America, NBC, Magazine Publishers of America, Public Broadcasting Service, Washington Post Company, Reuters America, Cable News Network, filed in Washington, DC, March, 1994.

19. Animal Industry Foundation newsletter, v. 7, no. 3 (May/June 1994).

20. Ibid.

21. Committee on Evaluation of USDA Streamlined Inspection System for Cattle, *Cattle Inspection* (Washington, DC: National Academy Press, 1990), p. 14.

22. J.O. Reagan, "E. coli O157:H4: Issues and Answers: Foodborne Pathogens," *Reciprocal Meat Conference Proceedings*, v. 46 (1993), p. 119.

23. U.S. General Accounting Office, "Food Safety: Reducing the Threat of Foodborne Illnesses," report number T-RCED-96-185, May 23, 1996.

24. Ibid.

25. Ronald Duchin, "Take an Activist Apart and What Do You Have?" *CALF News Cattle Feeder,* June 1991, p. 9.

We See Nothing

1. Gary S. Colgrove, report of April 30, 1990 meeting of the Scrapie/BSE Consultants Group, May 15, 1990.

2. Joel McNair, "Bypass Protein Still Safe," *Agri-View* (Iola, WI), Aug. 9, 1990.

3. USDA/APHIS, "Bovine Spongiform Encephalopathy: Public Relations," 1991.

4. Ibid.

5. USDA/APHIS, "Bovine Spongiform Encephalopathy: Rendering Policy," 1991, p. 4.

6. Ibid., pp. 6-10.

7. Ibid.

8. Center for Veterinary Medicine, Food and Drug Administration, "Report of Findings of Directed Inspections of Sheep Rendering Facilities," Jan. 1993, p. 1.

9. Fred R. Shank (Center for Food Safety and Applied Nutrition) to manufacturers of dietary supplements (letter), Nov. 9, 1992.

10. Linda A. Suydam (FDA) to manufacturers and importers of dietary supplements and cosmetics (letter), Aug. 17, 1994.

11. "Proceedings of an International Roundtable on Bovine Spongiform Encephalopathy," *Journal of the American Veterinary Medical Association,* v. 196, no. 10 (May 15, 1990), p. 1677.

12. Marsh interview, Sept. 26, 1996.

13. Richard F. Marsh, "Comments on Bovine Spongiform Encephalopathy," *Journal of the American Veterinary Medical Association,* v. 197, no. 4 (Aug. 15, 1990), p. 441.

14. Nicholas Schoon, "Type of 'Mad Cow Disease' May Exist in U.S. Cattle," *Independent* (London), May 14, 1990, p. 3.

15. Robert Wright, "Scientist Casts Doubt on Effectiveness of Mass Cull," *The Scotsman,* 3/28/96, p. 2.

16. R.F. Marsh and R.A. Bessen, "Epidemiological and Experimental Studies on Transmissible Mink Encephalopathy," *Transmissible Spongiform Encephalopathies: Impact on Animal and Human Health,* Karger-Verlag, Developments in Biological Standardization, ed. Fred Brown, Heidelberg, June 23-24, 1992.

17. Marsh interview, Sept. 26, 1996.

18. R.F. Marsh et al., "Epidemiological and Experimental Studies on a New Incident of Transmissible Mink

Encephalopathy," *Journal of General Virology* (1991), 72, p. 592.
19. McNair, op. cit.
20. Marsh et al., p. 591.
21. McNair, op. cit.
22. Ibid.
23. Marsh et al., p. 592.
24. Ibid., p. 593.
25. Michael Hornsby, "Of Mice, Men, Sheep and Mad Cows," *Times* (London), Dec. 19, 1991.

Counting Sheep

1. Michael Hornsby, "Mad Cow Disease Kills 500 Dairy Cattle Every Week," *Times* (London), Jan. 7, 1992.
2. Testimony by Michael Hansen, Consumer Policy Institute, to FDA's Veterinary Medicine Advisory Committee, Mar. 31, 1993.
3. Andrew Kimbrell and Joseph Mendelson, III, Foundation on Economic Trends, Petition Requesting the Food and Drug Administration to Halt the Feeding of Ruminant Animal Protein to Ruminants, June 16, 1993.
4. "Citing 'Mad-Cow' Fears, Rifkin Group Petitions FDA to Halt 'Cow Cannibalism,' " *Nutrition Week,* Community Nutrition Institute, v. 23, no. 24 (June 25, 1993), p. 2.
5. *Food Chemical News,* July 5, 1993.
6. Letter from USDA/APHIS to Andrew Kimbrell, Dec. 17, 1993.
7. Richard Teske (Center for Veterinary Medicine/FDA) to Andrew Kimbrell (letter), Dec. 15, 1993.
8. "Substances Prohibited from Use in Animal Food or Feed; Specified Offal from Adult Sheep and Goats Prohibited in Ruminant Feed; Scrapie" (proposed rule), Food and Drug Administration, Aug. 29, 1994, pp. 6-7.
9. Ibid., p. 24.
10. Pierce Miller (American Sheep Industry Association) to FDA (letter), Oct. 20, 1994, p. 4.
11. Ibid., p. 2.

12. Don A. Franco (Animal Protein Producers' Industry) to FDA (letter), Oct. 31, 1994, p. 3.
13. Richard Sellers (American Feed Industry Association) to FDA (letter), Nov. 7, 1994, p. 4.
14. A. Roland Dommert (American Veterinary Medical Association) to FDA (letter), Nov. 11, 1994.
15. Donald Luchsinger (USDA/APHIS) to FDA (letter), Nov. 14, 1994.
16. Kenneth L. Thomazin (California Department of Food and Agriculture) to FDA (letter), Nov. 22, 1994.
17. Jerome J. Breiter (American Meat Institute) to FDA (letter), Nov. 10, 1994.
18. David H. Schubert (AutoImmune Inc.) to FDA (letter), Oct. 5, 1994.
19. Gerald L. Reuter to FDA (letter), Oct. 25, 1994.
20. Doris Olander, R.F. Marsh, Debbie McKenzie and Judd Aiken to FDA (letter), Nov. 7, 1994.

Apocalypse Cow

1. Peter Martin, "Fourth Teenager is Killed by CJD," *Daily Express,* Feb. 18, 1996.
2. Emily Green, "Man with a Mission—Is Harash Narang Milking the Mad Cow Crisis?" *Guardian* (London), Aug. 20, 1996.
3. Sean Poulter, "The Scare that has Simmered for Years," *Daily Mail,* Mar. 21, 1996, p. 7.
4. Patrick Mulchrone, "Mad Cow Bug Killed My Wife," *Scottish Daily Record,* Mar. 21, 1996, p. 1.
5. Patrick Mulchrone, "Tragic Dad's Agony," *Daily Mirror,* Mar. 21, 1996, p. 4.
6. Ibid.
7. Peter Silverton, "The Woman Who Did Not Go Peacefully," *Mail on Sunday / Night & Day Magazine,* May 12, 1996.
8. Peter Martin, "Take One Last Look," *London Mail on Sunday,* Dec. 17, 1995.

9. Rachel Reynolds (personal secretary to John Majors) to Nora Greenhalgh (letter), Oct. 30, 1995.

10. Peter Silverton, "The Mother Who Bought Cheap Mince," *Mail on Sunday / Night & Day Magazine,* May 12, 1996.

11. "Questions Remain Over Victims of CJD," *Daily Telegraph,* Mar. 21, 1996, p. 5.

12. Martin, "Fourth Teenager is Killed by CJD."

13. Mike Harrison, "Three Treated for Suspected CJD," *PA News,* Apr. 25, 1996.

14. Mark Thomas, "CJD Blamed for Housewife's 'Horrible Death,' " *PA News,* Jan. 9, 1996.

15. Andrew Woodcock, "Victims of CJD," *PA News,* Mar. 20, 1996; and "CJD—The Deaths and Illnesses," *PA News,* Mar. 20, 1996.

16. Nigel Hawkes, "Fourth Farmer Examined for Rare Brain Disease," *Times* (London), Oct. 28, 1995.

17. Peter Martin, "The Mad Cow Deceit," *Mail on Sunday / Night & Day Magazine,* May 12, 1996.

18. Martin, "Fourth Teenager is Killed by CJD."

19. Peter Silverton, "The Handsome Student Who Fell Apart," *Mail on Sunday / Night & Day Magazine,* May 12, 1996.

20. Poulter, op. cit.

21. Jojo Moyes, "Victims Face Insanity and Certain Death," *Independent* (London), Mar. 21, 1996, p. 1.

22. Martin, "Fourth Teenager is Killed by CJD."

23. Ibid.

24. Philip Thornton, "CJD Blamed for Death of Man, 20," *Press Association Newsfile,* Feb. 14, 1996.

Who Will Tell the People?

1. Peter Martin, "The Mad Cow Deceit," *Mail on Sunday / Night & Day Magazine,* May 12, 1996.

2. Gillian Bowditch, "The Riddle of Mad Cow Disease," *Times* (London), Nov. 9, 1995.

3. Brian Unwin, "Suspected CJD Victim Worked in Abattoir," *PA News,* Dec. 23, 1995.

4. Martin, op. cit.

5. Finlay Marshall, "The War of Words Over Mad Cow Safety," *PA News,* Mar. 20, 1996.

6. Peter Martin, "Take One Last Look," *London Mail on Sunday,* Dec. 17, 1995.

7. Sheila Gore, "More than Happenstance: CJD in Farmers and Young Adults," *British Medical Journal,* Nov. 25, 1995, pp. 1416-18.

8. Sue Leeman, "Britain—Mad Cow Disease," AP, Jan. 9, 1996.

9. Institute of Food Science and Technology, Position Statement on BSE, Dec. 7, 1995.

10. Stephen Alderman, "Hogg Denies BSE Research Cut," *PA News,* Dec. 14, 1995.

11. Alison Little, "Government Defense BSE Response," *PA News,* Jan. 10, 1996.

12. Brian Farmer, "Beef Ban Spreads—Despite Government Reassurances," *PA News,* Dec. 14, 1995.

13. Ibid.

14. John von Radowitz, "BSE Beef 'Probably Safe' Say Scientists," Dec. 18, 1995, *PA News,* Dec. 18, 1995.

15. Nigel Hawkes, "Fourth Farmer Examined for Rare Brain Disease," *Times* (London), Oct. 28, 1995.

16. Peter Martin, "Take One Last Look."

17. Steve Connor and Michael Prescott, "BSE: A Scandal of Dither and Delay," *Times* (London), Mar. 24, 1996.

18. Ibid.

19. Ibid.

20. Ibid.

21. Finlay Marshall, "Scientists Say People Can Catch 'Mad Cow,' " *PA News,* Mar. 20, 1996.

22. Ibid., and "Britain to Admit People Get Mad Cow Disease," *Reuters,* Mar. 20, 1996.

23. James Hardy and John von Rad-
owitz, "New Mad Cow Scare Over
'Humans Can Catch It' Rumour," *PA
News,* Mar. 20, 1996.

24. John von Radowitz and Linda Jackson, "New Alarm Over Evidence
of Mad Cow Link to Humans," Mar.
20, 1996.

25. Hardy and von Radowitz, op. cit.

26. von Radowitz and Jackson, op. cit.

27. Ibid.

28. Stephen Dorrell, BSE Statement to
British House of Commons, Mar. 20,
1996.

29. Douglas Hogg, BSE Statement to
British House of Commons, Mar. 20,
1996.

Feeding Frenzy

1. Peter Silverton, "The Handsome Stu-
dent Who Fell Apart," *Mail on
Sunday / Night & Day Magazine,*
May 12, 1996.

2. Tony Delamonte, "Meltdown: The
Media and Mad Cows," *British Medical Journal,* Mar. 30, 1996.

3. Steve Connor and Michael Prescott,
"BSE: A Scandal of Dither and
Delay," *Times* (London), Mar. 24,
1996.

4. "Government Kept Us in the Dark,
Says CJD Victim's Husband," *PA
News,* Mar. 21, 1996.

5. Peter Beal, "Mother's Anger and
Heartache over Teenage Victim," *PA
News,* Mar. 21, 1996.

6. Delamonte, op. cit.

7. Peter Allen and Frank Corless, "Dorrell's Such a Swine," *Daily Mirror,*
Mar. 27, 1996, pp. 4-5.

8. Paul Brown, "Bovine Spongiform
Encephalopathy and Creutzfeldt-
Jakob Disease," *British Medical
Journal,* Mar. 30, 1996.

9. Emily Green, "The Nasty Taste of
Hysteria," *Daily Telegraph,* Apr. 24,
1996.

10. J. Ralph Blanchfield, "Re: BSE/CJD
Link," email posting to BSE-L listserv, Mar. 23, 1996.

11. Institute of Food Science and Technology, "Position Statement on
BSE," May 23, 1996.

12. J. Ralph Blanchfield, "Re: Of Mice
and Monkeys," email postings to
BSE-L listserv, May Aug. 96 and May
10, 1996.

13. Dave Harlan, "Re: Post Hoc, Propter
Hoc," email posting to BSE-L listserv, May 1, 1996.

14. "Meeting the PC Litmus Test,"
Phoenix Gazette, Apr. 2, 1996, p. B4.

15. Joint Statement by National Live-
stock and Professional Animal
Health Organizations Regarding a
Voluntary Ban on Ruminant Derived
Feed in Ruminant Feed, Mar. 29,
1996.

16. Dave Harlan, "Re: Recent FDA
Announcement," email posting to
BSE-L listserv, May 14, 1996.

17. L. Joan Spiczka, "Background,"
email posting to BSE-L listserv, Apr.
June 96.

18. "Texans Still Mad About Their Beef,"
Reuters, Apr. 4, 1996.

19. Joel McNair, "BSE Voluntary Ban
Having Little Effect on Producers,"
Agri-View (Iola, WI), May 23, 1996.

20. Interview on the Tom Clark Show,
Wisconsin Public Radio, Apr. 19,
1996.

21. "Dr. C. Everett Koop Says BSE Not
a Concern for U.S. Consumers"
(news release), Apr. 1, 1996.

22. Peter Maass, "Colleague Defends
Accused NIH Scientist," *Washington
Post,* Apr. 14, 1996, p. B3.

23. Philip P. Pan and Jackie Spinner, "A
Magical or Miserable Childhood?"
Washington Post, Apr. 27, 1996,
p. A1.

24. Gene Schmidt, "Re: Downers–U.S.,
was Welcome!" email posting to
BSE-L listserv, July 20, 1996.

25. Ed Gehrman, "Mad Cows & Mad
Scientists," posted on the Sperling
Foundation Mad Cow homepage.

26. Bruce Blanton and Don A. Franco, Comments to the FDA from APPI/NRA Regarding Docket 96N-0135, June 13, 1996.

Truth and Consequences

1. Frank Burnham, "BSE—Another Perspective," *Render Magazine,* June 1996.
2. Ibid.
3. Notes by reporter Daniel Zoll from the National Renderers' Association 63rd convention, San Francisco, Oct. 30, 1996.
4. Don A. Franco, "Science, Politics and Policy," *Render Magazine,* June 1996.
5. Patrick Smyth, "MacSharry Criticized in BSE Report," *Irish Times,* Jan. 14, 1997, p. 5.
6. "Declarations to the Standing Veterinary Committee meeting of October 9-10, 1990," Memorandum of the Department for Consumer Policy, Commission of the European Communities, Oct. 12, 1990, published in *Le Journal du Dimanche,* June 30, 1996.
7. Tony Barber, "Charges of BSE-Cover-up Investigated by Europe," *Independent* (London), Sept. 4, 1996, p. 4; and Caroline Southey, "Brussels Faces Fresh Charges of BSE Cover-up," *Financial Times,* Sept. 3, 1996, p. 1.
8. Angus MacKinnon, "Commission Tried to Gag German Warnings on 'Mad Cow' Disease," *Agence France Presse,* Oct. 9, 1996.
9. "BSE Threat to Humans Cannot Be Ignored: European Researcher," *Food Chemical News,* v. 25, no. 36 (Aug. 15, 1994).
10. "British Measures on BSE Not Strict Enough, Say German Scientists," *Deutsche Presse-Agentur,* Mar. 26, 1996.
11. Corinne Lasmezas et al., "BSE Transmission to Macaques," *Nature,* no. 381 (June 27, 1996), pp. 743-744.

12. J. Ralph Blanchfield, email postings to the BSE-L listserv, Jan. 2, May 10, May 25, June 12, July 15, and Sept. 27, 1996.
13. John Collinge, "New Diagnostic Tests for Prion Diseases," *New England Journal of Medicine,* v. 335, no. 13 (Sept. 26, 1996).
14. Robin McKie, "Collinge and Progressive CJD," *London Observer,* Oct. 12, 1996.
15. Robert LaBudde, "Re: Collinge and Progressive CJD," email posting to the BSE-L listserv, Oct. 14, 1996.
16. J. Ralph Blanchfield, "Re: Probability and the Flat Earth Society," email posting to the BSE-L listserv, Oct. 17, 1996.
17. John Collinge et al., "Molecular Analysis of Prion Strain Variation and the Aetiology of 'New Variant' CJD," *Nature,* no. 383 (Oct. 24, 1996), p. 685.
18. IFST Position Statement on BSE: Update of Oct. 29, 1996.
19. John Collinge, "The Bottom Line: Can BSE Infect Humans?" at the International Symposium on Spongiform Encephalopathies, Georgetown University, Feb. 12-13, 1996.
20. Ibid.
21. "Betraying the Public Over nvCJD Risk" (editorial), *Lancet,* v. 348, no. 9041 (Dec. 7, 1996), p. 1529.
22. S.N. Cousens et al, "Predicting the CJD Epidemic in Humans," *Nature,* no. 385 (Jan. 16, 1997), p. 198.
23. "Schoolgirl May Be Latest CJD Victim," PA News, Aug. 3, 1997.
24. John Deane, "MPs Back Inquiry Into BSE-CJD Link," PA News, July 15, 1997.
25. "Human 'Mad Cow' Case Number 21 in Britain," Reuters, London, August 4, 1997.
26. Quoted in *Render* magazine, April 1997, p. 55.
27. Leila Corcoran, "U.S. Beef Industry Rolls Out New Ad Campaign," Reuters, July 29, 1997.

28. Sarah McBride, "Worry Over 'Mad Cow' Risk Prompts Slaughtering Method," *Wall Street Journal,* July 24, 1997.

29. Maggie Fox, "Study Proves Mad Cow Disease is Catching," Reuters. London, July 16, 1997.

Could the Nightmare Happen Here?

1. Charles Clover, "EU Countries Fail to Report BSE," *Electronic Telegraph,* June 24, 1996.

2. APHIS Web page—Bovine Spongiform Encephalopathy.

3. "BSE Surveillance: Total U.S. Brain Submissions by State Through April 30, 1997" (chart available on APHIS web site).

4. Joel McNair, "BSE: A Ticking Time Bomb for Downer Cows?" *Agri-View* (Iola, WI), June 17, 1993, p. 1.

5. Obituaries, *Wisconsin State Journal,* Mar. 25, 1997.

6. "Debate: Is BSE Endemic?" at the International Symposium on Spongiform Encephalopathies, Georgetown University, Feb. 12-13, 1996.

7. Ibid.

8. Ibid.

9. Clifford Rothman and Anita Manning, "FDA Takes Aim at Mad Cow Disease," *USA Today,* Sept. 12, 1996, p. 9D.

10. Food and Drug Administration, "Substances Prohibited From Use in Animal Food or Feed; Animal Proteins Prohibited in Ruminant Feed," Proposed Rule, 21 CFR Part 589, Docket No. 96N-0135, Jan. 3, 1997.

11. Karl Lonberg-Holm to FDA (letter), May 23, 1996.

12. Masuo Doi, N. Davit Matzner and Charles Rothaug, "Observation of CNS Disease in Market Hogs at Est. 893—Tobin Packing Co., Inc., Albany, New York," USDA, Food Quality and Inspection Service, Meat and Poultry Inspection Service, 1979.

13. Joel Bleifuss, "This Mad Pig Went to Market," *In These Times,* May 26, 1997, pp. 12-13.

14. Michael Hansen, interview by authors, June 16, 1997.

15. A.R. Bobowick et al, "Creutzfeldt-Jakob Disease: A Case-Control Study," *American Journal of Epidemiology,* 98 (1979): pp. 381-394.

16. Z. Davanipour et al, "A Case-Control Study of Creutzfeldt-Jakob Disease," *American Journal of Epidemiology,* 122 (1989), pp. 433-451.

17. Hansen interview.

18. Department of Health and Human Services Food and Drug Administration 21 CFR part 589, "Substances Prohibited From Use in Animal Food or Feed; Animal Proteins Prohibited in Ruminant Feed; Final Rule," *Federal Register,* June 5, 1997, pp. 30935-30978.

19. "Animal Parts Banned In Cattle Feed," Associated Press Online, July 3, 1997.

20. "Consumers Union Criticizes FDA Decision on Mad-Cow-Disease Rule," PR Newswire, June 3, 1997.

21. Michael Hansen, "The Reasons Why FDA's Feed Rule Won't Protect Us from BSE," *Genetic Engineering News,* July, 1997.

22. Hansen interview.

23. *Render* magazine, April, 1997, p. 40.

24. Richard Rhodes, *Deadly Feasts: Tracking the Secrets of a Terrifying New Plague* (New York: Simon & Schuster, 1997), pp. 220-221.

25. Joseph Berger, et al, "Creutzfeldt-Jakob Disease and Eating Squirrel Brains," *Lancet* v. 350, no. 9078, Aug. 30, 1997.

26. Sheila Gore, "Bovine Creutzfeldt-Jakob Disease? Failures of Epidemiology Must be Remedied," *British Medical Journal,* Mar. 30, 1996.

27. Nicols Fox, *Spoiled: The Dangerous Truth About a Food Chain Gone Haywire* (NY: HarperCollins, 1997), p. 331.

Index

The Center for Media & Democracy

This book is a project of the non-profit Center for Media & Democracy, a public interest organization dedicated to investigative reporting on the hidden PR campaigns of corporations and governments.

The Center publishes a quarterly newsmagazine, *PR Watch*, and serves as an information clearinghouse for citizens, journalists and researchers. Funding is from individuals and other non-profits; no business or government grants are accepted.

John Stauber and Sheldon Rampton edit *PR Watch*, and also co-authored the acclaimed book, *Toxic Sludge Is Good For You: Lies, Damn Lies and the Public Relations Industry* (Common Courage Press), a "blistering, often hilarious exposé that blows the lid off today's multi-billion-dollar propaganda-for-hire industry."

Toxic Sludge Is Good For You reveals how public relations wizards concoct and spin the news, organize phony "grassroots" front groups, spy on citizens, and conspire with lobbyists and politicians to thwart democracy. Ralph Nader calls it "revealing and motivating." Molly Ivins says it's "terrific, don't miss it," and William Greider finds it "unmasks how corporations manipulate our democracy."

For information contact:
The Center for Media & Democracy
3318 Gregory Street
Madison, WI 53711
(608) 233-3346
http://www.prwatch.org